Wristwatches

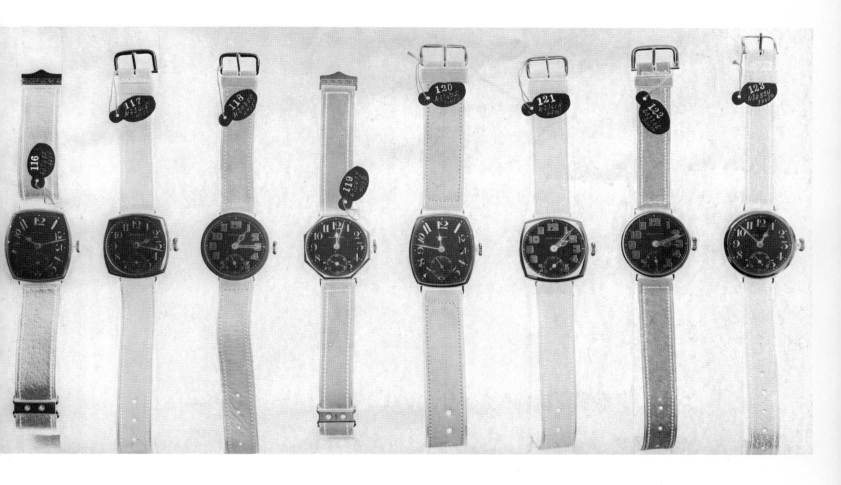

Wristwatches

History of a century's development

Helmut Kahlert
Richard Mühe
Gisbert L. Brunner

Schiffer Publishing Ltd

Lady's Art Deco Wristwatch created by Boucheron, Paris Case of onyx, with jewels; unusual miniature on blue dial, gilded 17-jewel anchor movement:

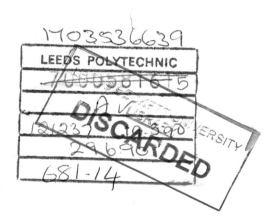
This work was originally published in German as *Armbanduhren: 100 Jahre Entwicklungsgeschichte* by Verlag Georg D.W. Callway, Munich, 1983.

Third edition
First English edition
Copyright © 1986 by Helmut Kahlert, Richard Mühe, and Gisbert L. Brunner.
Library of Congress Catalog Number: 86-61198.

Printed in the United States of America.
ISBN: 0-88740-070-1
Published by Schiffer Publishing, Ltd.
1469 Morstein Road, West Chester, Pennsylvania 19380

This book may be purchased from the publisher.
Please include $1.50 postage.
Try your bookstore first.

Concept and conception:
Christian Pfeiffer-Belli
Translated from German by Dr. Edward Force

Translator's Note

I have tried to use standard English-language watch terminology whenever I could find it; when I could not find the English term equivalent to the German one, I have translated the German term literally. I hope the reader will understand what is meant.

Glossary for the English edition:

European terminology	English terminology
anchor	lever
balance stopping mechanism	hack features
chronograph	watch with stop-watch
eternal	perpetual
hook	pin
indirect central second	sweep or center second
ligne (''')	line
rattrapante	split second
Savonette	hunting

Photographic credits

The text illustrations come for the most part from the works listed in the Bibliography and from the collections of the authors. The watches in the illustrations section were furnished by private collectors and were photographed by Günter von Voithenberg and Mathias Mühe, the firms and auction houses (see the Forword) which provided their own photographs, and by museums (Jewelery Museum in Pforzheim, German Clock Museum in Furtwangen, and the Clock Museum of Le Locle).

For the loan of the color photographs 119-125, 130-137, 271 through 278, 325-332, 333-348 we thank Sotheby's, London/New York. For the loan of the color photograph 129 we thank Mondo Publishing, Vevey, Photography by F. Rausser. The following firms kindly furnished color photographs: The Breguet Co., Paris (illustration 459), Christie's, Geneva (illustrations 460, 461), Andreas Huber Co., Munich (illustrations 462, 563-572, 574), Corum Co., La Chaux-de-Fonds (illustration 463) and Ulysse Nardin Co., Le Locle (illustration 562).

Contents

Foreword

In the history of time measurement, even in the history of mechanical clocks, the wristwatch is very modern. If we omit its predecessors, it is only a hundred years old; thus the subtitle of this book—history of a century's development—seems justified. About fifty years have passed since the wristwatch pushed the pocket watch out of popularity so intensively that the latter soon became a bit of nostalgia. Wristwatches are found throughout the world and accepted as a natural part of modern life. In 1950 some forty million wristwatches were produced in the world, and the present world production amounts to about 300 million, with a production capacity of 400 million. What for G. F. Roskopf (1813-1889) was the project of making a portable clock for everyone was achieved for great masses of the world's population in the era of the wristwatch. The process of "democratizing the clock" over the centuries seems to be completed; the transition from luxury article to utility object is finished.

But the wristwatch also documents and represents a second definite segment of clock history. Its rise inspired inventors, manufacturers and technicians to new heights of achievement in the Twentieth Century and led simultaneously to the goal of fine mechanical technology. While some made ever-higher demands on the potentialities of mechanical systems for both complex and consumer clocks, others worked on electromechanical watches, tuning-fork watches and, somewhat later, electronic watches without mechanical parts. A new technology developed so tempestuously thereby, that today even the early electromechanical wristwatches of the Sixties can be regarded as museum pieces of technical history. Surely this speedy development of technological things and processes has influenced the concept of what is worth keeping and collecting. The resulting view, which even tax laws follow, labels an object an antique only when it is a hundred years old. By such standards the wristwatch would be much too young to be an "old" clock. But if one follows the logic of technological development, then the automatic Harwood-system wristwatch, produced since 1926, must be regarded as a "classic".

There are many indications that interest in wristwatches is increasing among clock collectors and technical historians. Is it the small size that, as opposed to the collecting of large clocks, knows no spatial limits? Is one attracted by the wide variety of collectibles or by the possibility of meaningful specializing? What impact do financial considerations have, and how important is the fact that mechanical wristwatches can be repaired by watchmakers and not by just a few antique clock specialists?

Dynamic technical development has obviously shortened the length of time that a clock needs to change from a new to a collectible "old" clock. But particularly with wristwatches there is a second strong point, based less on age than on pleasure in a perfect mechanical system. The demands of electronics forced the manufacturers, especially those of complex wristwatches, to high achievements in micromechanics which rightfully attract our admiration.

Although the history of mechanical wristwatches occurs in a time rich in publication, the choice of objects and the preparation of printed materials still raises difficulties. The choice of watches was and is very wide, and many technologically interesting varieties were produced only for relatively short times or in small numbers. Catalogs of clock factories, probably the most inclusive sources of information, were rarely collected systematically. Then too, the German watchmakers' journals, representing and at the same time strengthening the standpoint of most of their readers, have scarcely documented the development of the wristwatch before 1930. Besides, many wristwatch manufacturers are reluctant to contribute information about historical development. The authors and publishers have nevertheless received much support, without which this book could not have been published.

Our thanks go to the following ladies and gentlemen: J. Abeler, Wuppertal; A. Banbery, Geneva; O, Bantele, Munich; Th. Beyer, Zurich; O. Dagge, Munich; S. Dering, Munich; F. Falk, Pforzheim; O. Habinger, Munich; F. Hemmerle, Munich; D. Herrmann, Spaichingen; H. Holze, Hannover; M. Huber, Munich; P. Ineichen, Zurich; H. Jendritzki, Hamburg; M. Klink, Munich; N. Kriegel, Bremen; G. Lang, Munich; R. Meis, Konstanz; F. Mercier, Le Locle; D. Merkel, Furtwangen; C. Pfeiffer-Belli, Munich; H. Sinn, Frankfurt; G. Schulz, Munich; E. Schuster,

Munich; P. Tauchner, Munich; S. de Villalaz, Zurich; H. Vogel, Düsseldorf, G. von Voitheberg, Munich.

And the following firms: Audemars Piguet, Le Brassus; Chopard, Geneva; Eterna, Grenchen; Flume, Essen; Berlin; Genta, Geneva; Girard-Perregaux, La Chaux-de-Fonds; IWC, Schaffhausen; Jaeger-Le Coultre, Le Sentier; Longines, Saint Imier; Omega-Tissot, Biel; Parechoc, Le Sentier; Patek Philippe, Geneva; Portescap, La Chaux-de-Fonds; Rolex, Geneva; Vacheron & Constantin, Geneva; Zenith-Movado, La Chaux-de-Fonds; Cartier, Paris.
Auction houses: Antiquorum, Geneva; UTO, Zürich; Ineichen, Zürich; Mohr, Münster, Sotheby, London/New York; Christie's, London/New York.
Clock museums: Furtwangen, Geneva, La Chaux-de-Fonds, Le Locle, Pforzheim, Stuttgart, Wuppertal, Zürich.

Writing a book about mechanical wristwatches becomes a challenge, not only because of the shortage of data and the limited opportunities to refer to organized collections and museums, but also because the history of this type of clock extends into and beyond the present day. Thus the number of critical readers is much greater than those of a book on classic old clocks. Many watchmakers and dealers can, on the basis of their profession, regard themselves as authorities on the subject.

Swiss watches form the focal point of this book. German production has been taken into appropriate consideration, French, American and Japanese watches, on the other hand, were only documented chronologically, mainly because of the difficulty of obtaining sufficient quantities of objects and materials. This book was written for as broad a spectrum of wristwatch collectors as possible. The expert may regret that more complex relationships and many details were not mentioned, but clarity and readability had priority. Technical points of interest were, though, noted on some of the illustrations.

The illustrated wristwatches are the lifeblood of the book. The text was intended to be subsidiary to the illustrations. Watch technology is stressed; thus the authors particularly value photos of clockwork. The mechanical wristwatch has developed in its lifetime into a very exact and reliable timepiece, but at the same time it has always been a very personal possession of man, his indispensible daily companion. Clock history includes not only technical history but also cultural and sociological elements. Indeed, it is not by chance that the wristwatch became the most representative type of clock of this century of ours.

Helmut Kahlert
Richard Mühe
Gisbert L. Brunner

Introduction to the Third Edition

It is just three years since the first edition of this book appeared, and yet much has changed in the interval, especially as concerns the collecting of wristwatches. There are five particular developments that mark the past three years since the appearance of the first edition of "Wristwatches".

1. The numbers of those who love "old" wristwatches have grown by leaps and bounds; it has become modern, fashionable, to own one or more old mechanical wristwatches, and naturally to wear them too. Glancing at the left wrist, and evaluating a person according to his wristwatch, can be noticed more and more often.

2. The wristwatch has become more and more of a collector's item, in which serious watch collectors are increasingly interested. The spectrum extends from those who collect only automatic wristwatches to those who collect only electric and electronic wristwatches from post-1950 years.

3. Many wristwatches have become investment objects, being sold at auctions for exorbitant prices never before paid for wristwatches of the same brands or equal quality.

4. The mechanical wristwatch, especially with automatic winding and complications, has also had an unexpected renaissance among manufacturers. This is especially true of wristwatches with "eternal" calendars, but also of those with tourbillon or repetition striking. Whoever finds that the prices of antique wristwatches have risen beyond his reach can, for the time being, content himself with highly interesting wristwatches in current production. The illustrations in this book show a variety of wristwatches that are currently produced but can be of interest to the collector even now.

5. Wristwatches are now among the regular offerings of all the noteworthy auction houses, and make up a goodly share of their business. Sales of 80 to 90% of the wristwatches offered for sale are no longer rare. The leading antique clock dealers also are now willing to offer as wide a variety of wristwatches as possible among their wares.

To be sure, and this may particularly trouble the collectors at first, as a result of this in and of itself pleasant development it is almost impossible to find interesting leftovers in the shops, or even to make good buys at flea markets and antique shows. In addition, the number of publications on the subject has increased considerably in the interim, so that the wristwatch can be said to have been covered thoroughly in literary terms as well.

For the sake of completeness, but also because the information on the technology, conservation and restoration of old wristwatches is as valid now as before, pages 123 and 124 on the collecting of wristwatches are included in this third edition unchanged from the first two editions.

ment. This provided the place to attach a woman's small round pocket watch, whereas in the previous era rectangularly formed movements were more popular. Round watches of this type often had a decorated cover, at which one must look closely to tell whether it is the housing of a watch or just a decoration.

In the first half of the Nineteenth Century the band was often formed so that a complete decorative watch or a small pocket watch could be set into it. Such attempts to change the means of carrying a woman's watch also appear later.

A decorative watch of the post-1840 period, presumably made for the court of Naples, is described in the following words: "The artistically fashioned armband is made of massive gold. Pearls and enamelwork in blue and white heighten the decorative effect. The watch, a small pocket watch with lepine movement and winding key, is concealed under a hinged lid and can be removed

T7 Around 1850, very wide, ponderous bracelets were popular among the ladies. Small round cylinder watches were built into the decorative capsules more often than was formerly thought.

T8 Silver wristwatch on a stiff ornamental band, circa 1900. Watches of this type were removed from the wrist to be set, as the hand-setting lever to its side had to be used simultaneously with the stem.

without difficulty . . ." Wristwatches of this type were generally no longer unique, but compared to the openly worn woman's pocket watch, the bracelet watch, as it was called in the 1854 Munich Industrial Exposition catalog, was a rarity. The first decorative watch on an armband made by the house of Patek Philippe dates from 1868.

The Wristwatch—a latecomer

"The idiotic fashion of carrying one's clock on the most restless part of the body, exposed to the most extreme temperature variations, on a bracelet, will, one hopes, soon disappear." Professor H. Bock of Hamburg wrote in 1917, expressing the opinion of almost everyone in the business. This hope has not been fulfilled. Two questions arise: why could the wristwatch prevail after all, and why only in the Twentieth Century and not before?

The watchmakers' answer appears plausible at first glance. The technology of the small watch was oriented to the nature of the pocket watch, not that of the wristwatch. The movements were not constructed to meet the particular pressures that necessarily result from being worn on the wrist. The developmental stages of the mechanical wristwatch seem to defend this assertion: the gradual compacting of the movement by the Swiss anchor escapement, the shock-absorbing wristwatch, the automatic watches, the ever-smaller and flatter calibers.

But one who knows the history of watches could become obdurate at this point, for many conceptions that were improved or even perfected in the wristwatch era were known long before. Perrelet (from 1770 on) and Breguet (1787) achieved significant preparations for the automatic watch. Breguet also conceptualized a shock-absorbing "Parachute System" for automatic watches, which he often improved and later built into other pocket watches. The problem of setting the hands by means of the winding stem was solved by Adrien Philippe between 1840 and 1860. Miniature clocks already appeared in the Renaissance and became a successful trade article, available in a multitude of variations, after 1800. In the first half of the Nineteenth Century, when tight-fitting men's trousers were in vogue, thin, unobtrusive pocket watches came onto the market. Why were these many tendencies not taken up earlier? In terms of technology, the wristwatch could have become reality in the Nineteenth Century. The transition from the pocket watch to the wristwatch obviously was retarded, remaining behind the technical and economic possibilities.

One must remember that the aforementioned experts of the period just after 1900 usually argued from the standpoint of the precise gentleman's

times it was not customary for men to wear bracelets; this changed only with the appearance of the modern wristwatch in the Twentieth Century. Women's bracelets, on the other hand, remained popular, though the degree varied according to varying fashions. Bracelets were especially popular in the Renaissance and the Nineteenth Century.

The theory that combining watch and bracelet first occurred in the Renaissance is supported by the history of clocks themselves. That era's characteristic joy of experimenting resulted in a wealth of clock forms. At that time efforts were also made to determine the potentialities of mechanical systems.

T4 Renaissance ring watch. Such small watches could also be worn on a bracelet.

Related to that was a trend toward miniaturisation, which made the production of the wristwatch possible.

Examples of small Renaissance watches are found in museums: in La Chaux-de-Fonds a watch made in 1648 by Johann Ulrich Schmidt of Augsburg, with works four lines in diameter, in Furtwangen a five and three-quarter line miniature watch made in 1620 by Martin Hyllius of Dresden.

There were watches in rings and sword-hilts then, so why not in bracelets?

It is said in various publications that the Earl of Leicester, favorite of Queen Elizabeth I, gave his queen in 1571 a small round jewel-studded watch fastened to an armlet. Presumably is was not fastened firmly to the bracelet but rather hung from it like a charm. It is recorded that the French philosopher and mathematician Blaise Pascal (1623-1662) wore his pocket watch on his wrist.

Another episode in the evolution of the wrist-watch is recorded in Jaquet and Chapuis. Freely translated, the text runs: A young woman sat on a park bench and lulled her child. She had fastened her pocket watch to her wrist by its chain. A passerby was amazed at this splendid idea. He went home, attached a band and two eyelets to a small pocket watch—and thus "invented" the wrist-watch.

This often-repeated story may go back to a newspaper report that first appeared in a Belgian watchmakers' journal, and that was reprinted in 1912 in the Swiss "Revue Internationale de l'Horlogerie". The editor remarks that he cannot say when or by whom the wristwatch was invented, but certainly for what purpose.

Here too there are references to young mothers and teachers who wanted to keep their watches safe from the grasping hands of children and so attached them to their wrists with leather straps, a practice that was more practical than fashionable. It seems plausible that the openly worn woman's watch was always exposed to the danger of being regarded as a toy by small children.

The first exact reference to the wristwatch, or more precisely to the decorative watch worn on the wrist, occurs in a 1790 account book of the Geneva house of Jaquet-Droz and Leschot. It is also recorded that in 1806 the Parisian jeweler Nitot created two expensive bracelets set with pearls, to be worn on both arms according to the fashion of the time. One bracelet included a small clock as an extravagant decoration, the other a small mechanically changeable calendar. They were a wedding present from Empress Josephine to her daughter-in-law Amalie Auguste, a daughter of King Maximilian I of Bavaria, the later Princess of Leuchtenberg.

This (new?) appearance of the decorative clock worn on the arm also fits into the style of the time. Bracelets gained popularity and, as in the Renaissance, the imaginative form of the clock attained a new high point, especially in the hands of masters from Geneva and Paris. Bassermann, in the 1917 catalog of a privately owned South German clock collection, describes a clock of this era with the following words: "Bracelet, with a watch at the clasp. Gold. The bracelet woven of a wide system of rings. The clasp is octagonal, enameled dark blue, and set with a double row of jewels. Above the balance set with jewels, below the face. Probably Geneva work, about 1790."

Typical of these early predecessors of the wrist-watch is their octagonal, oval or pointed-oval form and the layout of their front, with the visible usually jeweled balance wheel above and the small enameled face with steel hands below. Similar forms were also used for pendant watches or ring watches. These watches were worn on bands of varying form: chain-link band, bracelet, hair or satin band. The position of the clock-face shows them to be decorative clocks on armbands rather than wristwatches in a functional sense.

In the following decades other watches were made individually to be worn on the arm, for example, by the Breguet firm between 1831 and 1838. The size of the movement was noted as eight lines (18.5 mm). About the middle of the Nineteenth Century wide, heavy-looking bands were in fashion, often having on their exterior a capsular attach-

T6 Empress Josephine's wedding present, two costly bracelets with watch and calendar. Work of Nitot, Paris, 1806.

T5 Typical early type of watch worn on the arm. Probably a post-1800 Geneva creation. Below is the small enameled face, above it the visible balance set with diamonds.

Origin of a new type of clock

What is a wristwatch?

It would not seem to take many words to explain what a wristwatch is: a small clock worn on the wrist, a combination of bracelet and clock. The German word "Armbanduhr" (arm-band clock) expresses the type of attachment, which can range from a heavy ring to a light chain. The concept of the wristwatch appears clear and simple compared to the word "pocket watch", which gives a highly incomplete idea of how this type has been worn in its history, for in a strict sense, pocket watches were exclusively men's watches since 1820. Still it might be well to distinguish between the wristwatch and the older decorative watch worn on a bracelet, which cannot, in terms of its function, be regarded fully as a wristwatch.

Not only the fact of being worn on the arm, but also the manner of reading the time, is definitive for the wristwatch: quick and simple, with the movement of bending the arm. Even those who preferred the pocket watch could see a definite advantage in this. Only the wristwatch makes it possible to read the time at a glance without any other motions. Practical and useful, quick and simple, the wristwatch always has these advantages.

The earliest known forms of watches worn on the arm, though, do not fulfill these conditions, for the axis of their dials, from the 6 to the 12, is not parallel to the band but perpendicular to it, parallel to the arm. Whoever wants to read their time must make a movement resembling a Fascist salute, said Alfred Helwig in 1930. The fact that the small dials and tiny hands of these women's watches are barely visible at arm's length makes for more difficulty.

Therefore these types are better called bracelets with watches than wristwatches, "bracelet-montre" and not "montre-bracelet", as originally happened when jewelers and watchmakers could not agree on what to call the new type of watch. Arm-band watches with the clock-face position familiar to us, wristwatches in a functional sense, began to appear around 1850.

If we nevertheless place the boundary between predecessors and early types around 1880, this is done for two main reasons. From this time on the decorative wristwatch existed as a genre, its popularity depending on changes of style, particularly clothing styles, but without any further actual interruptions. Then too, slowly but surely, more and more men and women came to the

T1-3 Bracelets with watches. The arrangement of the face makes reading the time difficult. The watch hung from the bracelet is a curiosity of the time. From the advertisement of a Viennese clock dealer, 1891.

The early predecessors

In the literature one finds few definite dates for the wristwatch's early history. So one is compelled to spread out a great array of individual items and use assumptions in place of facts. The watch and the band have their individual histories. Unlike the ancient days, in the Middle Ages and modern

conclusion that the wristwatch was useful and practical in their work.

T9 *Case and movement of a 1907 Swiss Eterna lady's watch, a typical watch of the time.*

T10 *Turn the face 90 degrees and the pocket watch becomes externally a wristwatch. The advertisement dates from 1913. Eight-day wristwatches were later completely replaced by automatic watches.*

pocket watch, which was safely housed in the vest pocket and handled with care. One look at the women's watches of the time changes the perspective. Although called "pocket watches" in the terminology of the trade, these were worn openly, as before, on a short necklace or a brooch, on a long chain, or fastened in various ways to a belt.

In the one case it was rather difficult to read the time; in the other a mortal blow to the movement was possible every time one sat down if the free-swinging watch hit the edge of the furniture. Even if the customary built-in cylinder movement did not live up to any high standards of precision, in terms of functional security the position on the arm was definitely preferable to the previous one. In later decades similar cylinder movements were built into wristwatch cases by the millions and so seem to have met certain practical requirements of life. This too shows that technical factors could not have been decisive for the late appearance of the wristwatch.

Therefore we shall try to regard the origin of the wristwatch in relation to the historical development of clocks and the formation of a specific awareness of time as an expression of European cultural development. Clocks and other time-measuring devices of the most varying kinds have served, with varying intensity, to sensitize people to the passing of time and make them aware of time periods. They set the limits that are necessary to be able to plan and use time sensibly. On the other hand, a certain stage of development of time awareness requires an appropriate kind of time measurement. The two processes influence each other; clocks make us aware of time, while changed requirements and procedures demand new types of clocks. The wristwatch too, as the outstanding clock genre of our century, owes its general popularity to such influences.

A look into history shows that clocks keep coming closer to us. They thus strengthen our tendency to be aware of time. Thus the public striking clocks of the Middle Ages contributed significantly to changing our concepts of time from one of days that differed in length according

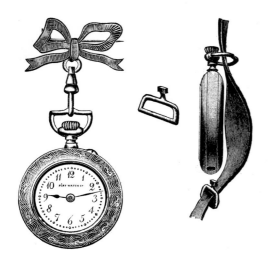

T11 *With a few attachments this pendant watch could be turned into a wristwatch. The model came onto the market in 1912 and is indicative of the transition time from the pocket watch to the wristwatch.*

T12 *Advertisement from Omega related to the 1932 Olympic Games, in which Omega participated in timing.*

to the season to our customary one in which every day or night hour is the same length. The next step was reached when indoor clocks became common. Public measurement of time was made more complete by the use of household clocks.

Last came portable clocks, at first ornamental as well as functional and therefore only at times worn visibly on one's clothing. In the latter half of the Nineteenth Century the tendency grew to have one's clock in one's vest pocket all day, and now it has "become part of us". The wristwatch can be regarded, apart from the specialized medical use of the pacemaker, as the last stage of this development, at least for the time being. It is as near as our skin and always in sight, even at night.

But the wristwatch could only come to dominance when a specific need for it existed. This need is rooted in the requirements of modern-day commercial and social life, where in many situations it is necessary to read the time quickly, at one glance. And yet, do arguments of utility and purpose suffice to explain the mass acceptance of the wristwatch? Perhaps there is another component, which is involved with modern man's inner disposition and his standpoint toward time. Sigmund von Radecki addresses this subject when he very critically determines that we have become slaves to measured time and so must be held by chains—"the wristwatch is the handcuff of our time".

But enough of philosophy. The wristwatch is the appropriate timepiece for an age typified by big business and bureaucracy, rationalization and striving to achieve, working hours and planned free time. Punctuality is a social virtue, not only

because it simplifies organizational duties, but also because it takes into consideration the limited time budgeting of others. What was once the privilege of kings has become a general way of life.

In a "Guide to Success and Harmony in Life" published in 1920, when the wristwatch had just become an alternative, are the following lines: "On the path that time travels year-in, year-out, stands man. He has signed a contract with it, a good contract. Time has placed itself at his disposal . . . Success is based on time."

The wristwatch is now more than just a practical timepiece; it has become a representative of our way of life. In the present we are experiencing the last stage of this development: the perplexity with which many wearers of quartz wristwatches react when their chronometer does not agree to the second with the time announcements on television.

Perhaps the fact that men formerly hesitated to accept the new way of wearing the watch is better explained by sociological and psychological arguments than technical ones. For centuries the bracelet was typically feminine. On the other hand, at least in the latter half of the Nineteenth Century, the vest-pocket watch and chain were a masculine symbol. In a time in which sexual roles grew strongly farther from each other, a man who wore a wristwatch had to reckon with being regarded by his peers as "soft", if not downright effeminate. Only "real men" were not exposed to this criticism: cavalry officers, sportsmen, aviators and such. Perhaps the watchmakers who expressed themselves so vehemently for the pocket watch and against the wristwatch were unconsciously defending a symbol of masculinity.

OMEGA

MONTRE DE HAUTE PRECISION

sur BRACELETS extensibles ou BRACELETS cuir

I

T13 *Wristwatches of 1913. Various Swiss firms advertised in German trade journals at that time, using large-scale advertisements to promote wristwatches.*

Armband-Uhren

Nummer	Linie			Qualität B Kronen
506	12	Lentille,	**Metall**, Metall-Cuv., **Leder-Armband**	31.—
507	13	"	" " " "	27.—
508	15	"	" " " "	24.—
509	12	Lentille,	**Stahl**, Stahl-Cuvette, "	32.50
510	13	"	" " "	28.50
511	10	Lentille,	**Silber**, ohne Cuvette, "	50.—
512	10	Tonneau,	" " "	56.—
513	10	Lentille,	" **Silberzug-**, "	63.—
514	11	Lentille,	" ohne Cuvette, Leder-Armband	42.—
515	12	"	" Silber-Cuvette, "	36.—
516	13	"	" " "	32.—
517	15	"	" " "	29.—
518	10	Lentille,	**Tula**, ohne Cuvette, Leder-Armband	53.—
519	10	Tonneau,	" " "	60.—
520	10	Lentille,	" " **Tulazug-Armband**	65.—
521	11	"	" " Leder-Armband	45.—
522	10	Lentille,	**Gold 14 karat**, ohne Cuvette, Leder-Armband	102.—
523	10	Tonneau,	" " ohne Cuvette, Leder-Armband	145.—
524	10	Lentille,	" " **Goldzug-Armband** ohne Cuvette	145.—
525	10	Lentille,	" " **Goldzug·Armband mit Email**, ohne Cuvette	180.—
526	11	Lentille,	" " ohne Cuvette, **Leder-Armband**	96.—
527	12	Lentille,	" " Gold-Cuvette, "	94.—
528	13	"	" " "	94.—
529	10	Calotte,	" " ohne Cuvette	78.—

Preiserhöhung für Zifferblatt Fondant 1.20
" " " Metall, versilbert oder vergoldet . . . 2.—
Preiserhöhung für Radium-Zifferblatt, 12 und 13''' . . 7.—

Wichtige Bemerkungen!

DIESES PREIS-VERZEICHNIS (1914) ANNUL
LIERT ALLE FRÜHEREN.

BEI GLEICHZEITIGER ABNAHME VON
6 STÜCK UND MEHR WIRD EIN RABATT VON
5% BEWILLIGT.

BEI BARZAHLUNG WIRD EIN KASSA-SKONTO
VON 5% BEWILLIGT.

Sämtliche Verkaufsstellen der Omega-Uhren in Österreich
Ungarn haben sich bindend verpflichtet, keine weiteren Bonifika
tionen auf die hiermit angegebenen Preise zu bewilligen un
würden solche Bonifikationen ein hohes Pönale mit sich bringer

Alle Omega-Uhren sind mit nachstehenden Schutzmarke
versehen:

Oᴍᴇɢᴀ auf dem Werke

im Gehäuse (mit einigen Ausnahmen)

Ω
OMEGA auf dem Zifferblatt

Alle Teile der Omega-Uhren sind auswechselbar. Ma
verlange die Spezial-Preise für die Furnituren.

Die in diesem Preis-Verzeichnisse angegebenen Gehäuse
gewichte der Golduhren sind Rohgewichte. Der Goldabfall be
der Dekoration und Politur der Gehäuse stellt die Differenz de
wirklichen Gewichtes dar. Die Gehäusefedern in den Savonnette
sind im Gewichte nicht mit inbegriffen.

T14 *Catalogs of Omega wristwatches from 1926 (above) and*
1914 (below).

Wristwatch versus pocket watch

The first decades

Napoleon I used to say that the difference between him and his opponents was that they did not know how much five minutes were worth. Therefore he recommended that his officers work for Master Breguet. Military needs were also an important developmental factor in the history of the wristwatch. About 1880 C. Girard-Perregaux of La Chaux-de-Fonds, among other Swiss firms, provided wristwatches for the German Navy, as Jaquet and Chapuis report in their standard work on Swiss watches. They were round watches, ten to twelve lines in diameter, in gold—later matt gold—cases, which were worn on a metal chain band. They were presumably the first wristwatches in series production.

The wristwatch probably first proved itself as a practical military implement in the Boer War (1899-1902), and this experience later had a positive effect on the civilian market in England. In a large advertisement in the Leipzig Watchmakers' Journal of 1904 the Swiss "Omega Watch Syndicate" published a British artillery officer's report: "Knowing the importance of exact timing in an active army corps, before I left Canada I bought a dozen Omega wristwatches ... Steady use during many months of service in a mounted corps is surely a stringent test, especially when one considers the extremes of heat and cold, the heavy rain and the constant sandstorms." The lieutenant colonel comes to the final conclusion that the wristwatch is an "indispensible part of field equipment".

The wristwatch gained worldwide use in World War I (1914-1918). Soldiers on both sides quickly realized that the conditions of modern warfare no longer allowed one to unbutton overcoat and uniform jacket whenever it was necessary to look at one's watch. In the very first months of the war it was reported that "not only officers, but troops in general customarily wore their watch on their left wrist". The number of new watchbands coming onto the market increased from day to day, according to a German journal. Names like "Army" (Geneva), "Poilu" (as French soldiers in the war were called, Paris), and "Mars" (Cologne) for special watchband clasps point in the same direction. For the U. S. Army Cartier developed a wristwatch called "Tank".

There could not have been better conditions for spreading the use of the wristwatch than this war, as was stated in an anniversary publication of the Swiss watch industry. If the Swiss had feared export deficits at the beginning of the war, they soon found the situation had changed as the belligerent powers recognized the value of the wristwatch that met the soldiers' needs so well. Especially popular at that time was the round caliber 13 watch, that often was fitted with a luminous dial.

But the first significant success of the wristwatch was not gained among men, but among women, first as an ornament whereby until 1900 the dial, as with its predecessors around 1800, was set so that its 6-12 axis ran at a right angle to the band. Thereafter women's wristwatches developed more and more as combinations of utility and decoration.

T15 *World War I (1914-18) made a necessary, useful implement of the wristwatch. A robust case, protective glass and strongly luminous numbers characterize the soldiers' watches of these years.*

T16 *"Imperial Crown luminous-dial watch for field use" with two-year guarantee, by Huber, Munich.*

T17 *The soldier's watches of World War I influenced the appearance of the robust sportsman's watch in the following years. Luminous dial and hands, second dial. Swiss escapement. West End Watch Co. (above) and Longines (below).*

In the years after 1880 the woman's wristwatch was, to be sure, not a commercial success, but neither was it a rarity. The products of Swiss manufacturers found varying acceptance in different countries. While samples from a watchmaking firm were returned from the U.S.A. and Chile, orders followed from Peru. For a short time styles of dress also had an influence. Before 1900, when longsleeved dresses were in style, the wristwatch, according to contemporaries, suffered a setback. On the other hand, since 1890 the advertisement pages of watchmakers' trade papers repeatedly show pictures of wristwatches.

The further spread of wristwatches is not attributable to society ladies, though, but to feminine employees, whose numbers increased in Germany from 93,000 to 452,000 between 1882 and 1907. "More and more women are stepping into public life," it was stated in the first report on wristwatches, which appeared in a German watchmakers' trade paper (South German Watchmakers' Journal) in 1902. Women working as cashiers and store clerks, in post offices, schools and health services, brought the wristwatch into common use even before World War I.

The traditional, openly worn lady's watch did not meet the requirements of working life. Wearing the watch on the wrist decreased the danger of damage, theft and loss, allowed quick reading of the time, and still allowed its use as an ornament. Sociologically seen, the wristwatch seems at the time even to have been a kind of status symbol of the gradually emancipated woman. Briefly stated, the idea is that not the fashion, but the office smoothed the way for the wristwatch.

In the 1880-1920 era yet another realm must be mentioned for its positive effect on the popularity of the wristwatch: the world of spare time, sport and modern means of transportation. An example is the announcement of a Munich wholesaler, who offered 14-line, 15-jewel wristwatches in 1909 and appealed particularly to "horsemen, officers and motorists". In a business report of the Dingeldein firm of Hanau in 1902 are the following lines: "Distribution is mainly in Switzerland and France, but also in the better areas of Germany. Women are wearing wristwatches most often for travel or sport. One also sees many men wearing them, though of course in more massive form." Even if it was only a small part of the population that could afford an additional watch for travel and sport, the later image of the wristwatch as a "modern" type of watch was taking shape here. The wristwatch was indispensible for aviation, which was gaining popularity then. Cartier made a special model for the Brazilian air pioneer Santos-Dumont in 1904, and if we can jump rather far ahead in time, Lindbergh relied on a wrist chronograph by Longines in his 1927 trans-Atlantic flight.

Another means of transport had an even greater effect in promoting the wristwatch: the bicycle. Even before 1900 protective cases were offered that allowed one to attach the watch to the handlebars and so have it in view. When one imagines the prevailing road conditions of the time, cobblestone paving in the cities, untarred roads in the country, and in addition higher and less secure bicycles than today, one must admit that it was a very adventurous undertaking to take out a pocket watch while riding a bicycle. The bicycle also helped to make the advantages of the wristwatch apparent to a wide spectrum of the populace.

T18 *Two gold women's pocket watches with Swiss cylinder movements, made around 1895 (left) and 1905 (right). Like countless other women's watches, these were converted to wristwatches. Because of the second dial the axis of the watch on the right could not be turned. The decorated reverse side is no longer visible when the watch is worn on the wrist.*

The effect of these trends to the benefit of the wristwatch can be seen in the new production of watches, but also in the extent to which pocket watches were already being worn on the arm. Certain types of bands, such as belts with leather capsules or metal bands with special attachments, allowed the option of using a watch as either a pocket watch or a wristwatch. After 1910 ornamental accessories for women appeared, which allowed the watch to be worn on a chain, a brooch, a chatelaine or on the arm, according to one's preference or social situation.

Women's pocket watches often were converted to wristwatches as well. Basically, four work processes had to be carried out: shortening the bow knob and stem, fitting a new winding knob, turning the dial by 90 degrees, and adding the attachment for the band. Pocket watches converted as an afterthought are usually easy to recognize, by the traces of soldering the attachments or the newly attached dial. Generally a look at the back of the case is sufficient, for real wristwatches have no decoration there.

After 1910 the wristwatch, as opposed to the ornamental watches made before then, was an important part of the production programs of many Swiss manufacturers. This was shown impressively at the Swiss National Exposition of 1914. The same year also brought an important technical success. A round Rolex watch, with 25 mm diameter movement, was given a class A certificate by the Kew Observatory in England. This showed that a wristwatch could also be a chronometer.

With research at its present state, the question must remain open as to which part of the population first made use of the wristwatch not as an ornament but as a functional, practical timepiece. Was it the officers of the Imperial German Navy or the Swiss governesses, the streetcar drivers of Paris (as another source states) or another group unknown to us who first decided to wear their pocket watches on a leather armband? But the following time-frame seems to be established:

(text continues on page 45)

T19 *Rolex wristwatch, which in 1914 received a class A rating from the Kew Observatory, England.*

Reinigen, Zusammensetzen, Ölen, Regulieren

Die Armbanduhr muß, wie früher hervorgehoben wurde, fast jedes Jahr ganz gereinigt werden. Mit einer Halbreinigung kommt man selten gut aus, denn wenn man nur die kleinen Räder oder die Gangpartie reinigt, dann sitzt im Minuten- und Federhausrade noch Schmutz genug, der sich schnellstens wieder auf die übrigen Teile verbreitet. Manchmal kommen Uhren zur Reparatur, die einen schlechten Gang machen und scheinbar noch nicht unsauber sind, so daß man verleitet wird, an Gangstörungen zu denken. Aber in der Regel macht die Unruh erst dann wieder einen flotten Gang, wenn die Uhr ganz gereinigt worden ist. Sofern auch nur die Zapfen der Gangteile in etwas verdicktem Öl laufen, schwingt bereits die Unruh träge, was schließlich bei der Kleinheit der Teile nicht besonders verwunderlich ist. Diese Beobachtung kann man sehr oft schon in einem halben oder gar einem Vierteljahr nach der Reparatur machen. Das wird sich ganz nach der Behandlung richten, die der Uhr durch den Träger zuteil wird. Man unterlasse daher auch nie, beim Reinigen das untere Decksteinplättchen und die Rückerpartie abzunehmen, damit die Decksteine und die Unruhlochsteine ordentlich gereinigt werden können. Der Reparateur, der da glaubt, sich diese Mühe und Umstände ersparen zu können, wird bald durch Nackenschläge eines Besseren belehrt werden.

Beim Reinigen entferne man auch den Grat, der sich bei neuen Uhren zahlreich an den Rändern der Brücken, Ausdrehungen und Löcher in der Werkplatte befindet, da er vielfach lose sitzt, sich nach und nach ganz löst, dann an eine unrechte Stelle gelangt und die Uhr zum Stehenbleiben bringt.

Man verwende zum Reinigen nur reines Benzin bester Sorte, das man nach dem Gebrauch nicht wegschüttet, sondern in einer besonderen Flasche aufhebt, damit es für weniger feine Werke noch verwendet werden kann. Gutes reines Benzin, ein sauberes, feines und faserfreies Stück Leinwand zum Abtrocknen und eine reine Bürste machen die halbe Arbeit. Die ganz feinen Spiralfedern tauche man in allerfeinstes Benzin, das nur in Apotheken erhältlich ist; man riskiert dabei wenigstens nicht, daß die Umgänge nach dem Benzinbade noch zusammenkleben, wie es bei der Verwendung gewöhnlichen oder unreinen Benzins gewöhnlich der Fall ist. Dieses feine Benzin, das zu Medizinalzwecken angewandt wird, ist zwar teuer, doch wird immer nur sehr wenig davon gebraucht.

Über das Reinigen des Gehäuses haben wir schon an anderer Stelle gesprochen, so daß wir darauf nicht mehr einzugehen brauchen.

Braun gewordene Metallzifferblätter reinigt man durch Eintauchen in eine stark verdünnte Zyankalilösung (starkes Gift, daher mit Vorsicht zu gebrauchen!) und sofortiges Nachspülen in Wasser. Hierbei werden aber leicht die Zahlen, wenn sie nicht mit Lack, sondern nur in Tusche aufgetragen sind, undeutlich. Bessere Ergebnisse erzielt man mit pulverisiertem Weinstein, den man mit Wasser zu einem Brei anrührt; diesen Brei trägt man mit Wasser auf das Blatt auf, und mit trockener Watte reibt man dann nach. Leuchtzahlen erleiden bei beiden Verfahren keinen Schaden.

Während man sonst gewohnt ist, das Zusammensetzen einer Taschenuhr in der Weise vorzunehmen, daß man erst die kleinen Räder, dann die Gangteile einsetzt und zuletzt die Federhauspartie und den Aufzug hinzufügt, muß man bei Armbanduhrwerken, wie in so vielem, auch hierin vom Alltäglichen abweichen.

Man fängt am besten mit der Federhauspartie und dem Aufzugmechanismus an, da man gerade beim Einsetzen des letzteren nicht immer glatt wegkommt, und dann ist es besser, fest zupacken zu können und nicht auf die eingesetzte Unruh Rücksicht nehmen zu müssen. Es kommt allerdings vor, daß Federhaus und Minutenrad eine gemeinsame Brücke haben und auch einige der folgenden Räder, selbst bis zum Ankerrade, vor dem Minutenrade eingesetzt werden müssen; da muß man sich eben dreinschicken. Sind dann Aufzug und Räderwerk eingesetzt und die Aufziehwelle an Ort und Stelle, dann kann man durch langsames Aufziehen und Laufenlassen der Räder ausprobieren, ob alles freiläuft. Dann wird der Anker eingesetzt und der Gang nochmals nachgeprüft, insbesondere daraufhin, ob die Zähne ausreichend auf Ruhe fallen und genügend verlorener Weg vorhanden ist. Hierauf folgt das Einstellen der Unruh. Zum Ölen der Gangpartie und der dünneren Zapfen der Räder nehme man dünnflüssiges Öl und sei hierbei ja recht sparsam, denn ein Zuviel schadet immer, während ein Zuwenig kaum von Übel sein kann. Ich habe beispielsweise noch keinen angerosteten Zapfen in Armbanduhrwerken angetroffen, was wohl schon mit dem Umstande erklärt werden kann, daß sie gar nicht so lange

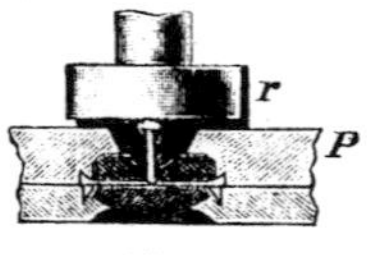

Abb. 54

Abb. 55

gehen können, ohne im allgemeinen reparaturbedürftig zu werden. Ankergabel und Ellipse brauchen deshalb überhaupt kein Öl, selbst ein sogenannter Ölhauch ist überflüssig. Ganz anders gestaltet sich die Sache bei zu reichlichem Ölgeben. Da ist zum Beispiel der obere Ankerzapfen mit dem ganz kurzen Ansatz. Das hier überschüssige Öl verbreitet sich zwischen Brücke und Anker (siehe auch Abb. 53) und hemmt des letzteren freie Bewegung; schließlich läuft es durch das Hin- und Hergehen des Ankers bis zu den Anschlagstiften, und die Gabel fängt an zu kleben, was sehr bald am trägen Gang zum Ausdruck kommt.

Der untere Zapfen der Unruhwelle (vergl. Abb. 54) steht manchmal fast ohne Ansatz an der Sicherheitsrolle *r*, und diese geht dann ganz knapp über der Ausdrehung in der Werkplatte *P*, so daß sich dieser enge Raum bei zu reichlichem Ölgeben sofort mit Öl füllt, wie dies in der Abbildung dargestellt ist. Dadurch wird nicht nur die freie Schwingung der Unruh gehemmt, sondern das Öl kann auch den Umfang der Sicherheitsrolle erreichen, wodurch das Sicherheitsmesser bei Erschütterungen zum Ankleben kommt. Ähnlich geht es beim Lochstein im Unruhkloben (s. Abb. 55) zu, wenn dieser an der Aufdeckung keine erweiterte Senkung hat und die Spiralrolle sich ziemlich knapp am Kloben *B* dreht; dann füllt das reichlich gegebene Öl diesen Raum aus und kann nun über die Spiralrolle *S* seinen Spaziergang bis zur Spiralfeder und zum Unruhschenkel ausdehnen. Diese Angaben mögen manchem als Phantastereien erscheinen; sie sind jedoch weiter nichts als Tatsachen aus den Vorkommnissen der Praxis. Natürlich mußten hier in den Abbildungen die Verhältnisse in übertriebenem Maßstabe gegeben werden, um überhaupt eine Vorstellung von den verhängnisvollen Wirkungen zu reichlichen Ölens liefern zu können.

Das richtige Ölen der Gangpartie erfordert auch einen richtigen Ölgeber, den man sich durch Ausprobieren passend herrichten muß.

In den Lochstein im Unruhkloben gibt man am besten erst dann Öl, wenn Unruh und Spiralfeder so weit am Kloben geordnet sind, daß sie eingesetzt werden können. Hat nämlich der Lochstein schon vorher Öl, so kann es sehr leicht vorkommen, daß der obere Zapfen bereits Öl angenommen hat und dann beim Einsetzen der Unruhpartie leicht mit den Umgängen der Spiralfeder in Berührung kommt, was zur Folge hätte, daß letztere zusammenkleben. Den Aufzugsrädern gebe man dickflüssiges Öl und auch nur gerade so viel, daß es nicht auseinanderfließen kann.

Wenn nun das Werk so weit zusammengesetzt und geölt ist, so wird man es ganz aufziehen und nun seine Freude an den lebhaften Unruhschwingungen haben oder — auch nicht. Wenn die Schwingungen in der senkrechten Lage ein wenig nachlassen, so muß man sich dreinschicken, denn das ist bei den im Verhältnis zu dicken Unruhzapfen und auch minderwertigen Lochsteinen nicht anders zu erwarten. Lassen die Schwingungen aber bedenklich nach, besonders dann, wenn die Unruh über der Gabel steht, dann wird das Sicherheitsmesser auf einer Seite noch zu wenig Luft an der Sicherheitsrolle haben oder die Ellipse an der inneren Rundung der Gabelhörner streifen. Auch in diesem Falle wird man sich mit den zu weiten Zapfenlöchern abfinden und durch geeignetes Abbiegen der Begrenzungsstifte noch etwas mehr Luft zu schaffen suchen müssen.

Lassen die Schwingungen in einer bestimmten horizontalen Lage des Werkes (Zifferblatt oben oder unten) auffällig nach, so liegen irgendwie noch Streifungen vor, die verschiedener Natur sein können: der Anker kann an der Brücke, die Spiralfeder an den Unruhschenkeln, am Minutenrade oder am Unruhkloben, auch am Spiralklötzchen streifen, die Unruh am Minutenrade oder an der Ankerbrücke, die Gabelhörner an der Hebelscheibe, die Ellipse am Sicherheitsmesser; möglicherweise reicht auch ein Unruhzapfen nicht genügend weit durch den Lochstein, so daß er also nicht auf dem Decksteine läuft. Über das Vorhandensein der Mehrzahl dieser Fehler muß man übrigens schon beim Beginn einer Reparatur Feststellungen machen. Kommt man überhaupt zu keinem Erfolg, d. h. schwingt die Uhr in allen Lagen schlecht, dann findet man gewöhnlich, daß die Feder zu schwach ist. In so manchen Fällen ist es jedoch unmöglich, eine stärkere Feder einzusetzen, da sie nicht die genügende Anzahl von Entwicklungsumgängen ergibt. Die Uhr ist also im wahren Sinne des Wortes verbaut.

Das Aufsetzen des Zifferblattes geschieht am besten, wenn das Werk im Gehäuse ist, denn oft muß man beim Einsetzen der Aufziehwelle feststellen, daß das Zeigerstelltrieb sich schiefgestellt hat und ein Einstecken der Welle unmöglich ist. Wenn dann das Zifferblatt mit seitlich im Werkplattenrande angeordneten Schrauben befestigt ist, dann sieht man sich genötigt, das Werk wieder aus dem Gehäuse zu nehmen. Zweckmäßig ist es, wenn das Gehäuse derart eingerichtet ist, daß die Aufziehwelle schon vor dem Einsetzen des Werkes in das Gehäuse eingesteckt und befestigt werden kann.

Ist das Zifferblatt mit den sogenannten Zuckerhutschrauben zu befestigen, die manchmal knapp zwischen zwei Brücken eingeklemmt sitzen, dann achte man beim Hochschrauben wohl darauf, daß man die nahestehende Brücke nicht mit hochhebt und womöglich einem Triebe auf diese ungewöhnliche Weise die „Luft abschneidet". Besser ist es dann, wenn man die Schraube nach unten dreht, denn das leichte Metallblatt — um ein solches handelt es sich meistens — wird auch von e i n e r Schraube genügend gehalten, und obendrein sorgt der Glasrand schon dafür, daß es nicht schlottert.

Beim Zeigeraufsetzen achte man darauf, daß der Stundenzeiger nicht auf dem Blatte streift; es gibt nichts Fataleres als die blanken oder dunklen Ringe auf den Metallblättern, die von der Nachlässigkeit irgendeines Arbeiters Zeugnis ablegen. Zum Aufdrücken des Minutenzeigers haben wir ein großartiges Hilfsmittel in unseren Bürstenstielen: sie sind handlich, beschädigen das Zeigerauge nicht und rutschen auch nicht ab. **Klopfen mit dem Hammer ist streng verboten! Haben sich inzwischen in dem Werke Staubfasern angesetzt, wie sie immer in jedem Arbeitsraum in der Luft** herumfliegen, dann blase man nicht mit dem Munde, denn der Hauch ist feucht und es kann auch Speichel dabei sein und in den feinen Teilchen Rost erzeugen. Man bediene sich vielmehr zum Staubausblasen eines Gummiballes mit Rohr, der aber nie zu anderen Zwecken verwendet werden darf und stets unter Verschluß gehalten werden muß, damit er nicht selbst Fasern annimmt. Sehr gute Dienste leistet übrigens beim Reinigen der kleinen Uhren ein gewöhnlicher H a a r p i n s e l, ein sogenannter Tuschpinsel mit einem Federkiel. Da dessen zugespitzte Form nichts nützt, stutzt man ihn kurzerhand mit einer scharfen Scheere fast bis zur Hälfte zurück. Mit diesem so hergestellten Bürstchen kann man in die verborgensten Winkel gelangen, was mit unsern gewöhnlichen Bürsten nicht möglich ist.

Ist nun die Uhr fertig, dann wird man sie regulieren, und hat man sie schön reguliert, dann geht sie beim Kunden, der sie seiner eigenen Behandlung unterwirft, doch nicht richtig. Hat man die Unruh gut abgewogen, sei es nun eine Zylinder- oder eine Ankerunruh, hat man die Zapfen gut poliert, die Spiralfeder richtig gelegt, dann lege man sich selber mit gutem Gewissen auf sein sanftes Ruhekissen und überlasse das Weitere dem lieben Herrgott, denn selbst der wird nicht einmal verlangen, daß man aus einer gewöhnlichen Armbanduhr eine Präzisionsuhr machen soll, wenigstens nicht von dem, der um sein tägliches Brot zu kämpfen hat. Man muß bei einer Armbanduhr immer vorsichtig und fürsorglich sein, um mit ihr nicht noch mehr Arbeit zu bekommen, als man schon hat. Darum gehe man mit der Spiralfeder recht vorsichtig um, und beim Reinigen der Unruh achte man darauf, daß man die Schrauben nicht lockert und den Reifen nicht verbiegt, was bei den aufgeschnittenen und obendrein noch weichen Unruhen nur mit größter Mühe zu vermeiden ist. Darum prüfe man auch jede Unruh vor dem Aufsetzen der Spiralfeder nochmals nach, ob sie nicht wieder einen Schwerpunkt bekommen hat, damit man im Notfalle noch rechtzeitig wieder nachhelfen kann.

Beim Schwerpunktausgleichen vermeide man überhaupt ein voreiliges Abfeilen oder Beschweren, denn gewöhnlich ist die Unruh nur verbogen, was man ja durch Nachprüfung im Rundlaufzirkel sofort entdecken kann.

Wie oft kann man sehen, daß bei der Spiralfeder ein viertel oder halber Umgang durchgesteckt ist. Wozu dient eigentlich das überflüssige Schwänzlein? Mir kommt es vor wie der Blinddarm, von dem man auch nicht weiß, wozu er dient, und nach dessen Beseitigung der Mensch ruhig weiter lebt; darum einfach weg mit diesem Spiralfeder-Anhängsel bis auf ein kurzes Stümpfchen, denn sonst schlägt nur der äußere Spiralfederumgang dagegen, und die Uhr reguliert nicht, oder, wenn es in respektvoller Entfernung abgebogen ist, steht es den Unruhschraubenspitzen im Weg.

T20 *Excerpt from B. Hillmann, The Wristwatch...Berlin 1925, concerning watch maintenance.*

The watches shown on the next 20 pages come from the archives of Vacheron & Constatin, Movado, Patek Philippe & Co., Jaeger LeCoultre and Omega. This archive material was taken unretouched from photo albums. Generally no notes exist about the survival of the watches. The pictures are meant to show the diversity of production and complement the following picture section. I would like to thank the firms again for providing this material. I hoped to obtain comparable materials from other firms, but unfortunately this did not happen.

Christian Pfeiffer-Belli

Movado

In 1881 Achille Ditesheim, then 19 years old, opened a clock factory in La Chaux-de-Fonds, with a work force of six watchmakers. Soon his brothers Leopold and Isidor joined him, and the firm was renamed L.A.I. Ditesheim (after the first initials of the three brothers).

By 1890 the firm already employed 30 workers. Their production concentrated on pendant-, pocket- and women's wristwatches. The wristwatches of L.A.I. Ditesheim used cylindrical movements exclusively until appropriately small, reliable and exact escapement movements were developed.

Early in the Twentieth Century Isaac Ditesheim, Leopold's twin brother, joined the firm. Seeking an appropriate and impressive name for the firm, the Ditesheim Brothers settled on the name "Movado" in 1905. Movado comes from the then newly-invented international language, Esperanto, and means "always in movement".

In 1924 Movado opened its first agency in the United States, in New York.

Toward the end of the Sixties a relationship with Zenith of Le Locle was established, and in 1971 the firm's headquarters was moved to Le Locle.

Jaeger-LeCoultre

The firm of LeCoultre was founded in 1833 in Le Sentier, in the Vallée de Joux.

Jacques LeCoultre and his son Antoine had concentrated on the improvement of steel for watch parts. Antoine LeCoultre subsequently became known for his production of high-quality drives, the development of the "LeCoultre Stichel" and, in 1844, the invention of the "Milliometer", which allowed exact measurements to 1/1000 of a millimeter.

In 1930 his grandson Jacques-David LeCoultre merged with Edmond Jaeger, an Alsatian industrialist, watchmaker to the French Navy and supplier of Cartier, and the firm was called Jaeger-LeCoultre.

In 1929 Jacques-David LeCoultre had tried unsuccessfully to take over a majority of Patek Philippe stock, with which he had been associated since 1905 as their main supplier of components.

Omega

In 1848 the 23-year-old Louis Brandt began to make clock components in La Chaux-de-Fonds. After his sons Louis and César joined the firm, it was renamed Louis Brandt & Fils. A year after its founder's death, in 1880, it was moved to Biel, where a watch factory was established using industrial manufacturing methods.

By 1894 a caliber of watch had been developed that was given the name of Omega. The use of the last letter of the Greek alphabet was meant to symbolize the achievement of the ultimate in watch technology.

After the death of the brothers Louis and César in 1903 the third generation came to power and gave the firm the name of "S.A. Louis Brandt & Frere, Omega Watch Co." The first catalog under the Omega name appeared in 1904, in a printing of 10,000 copies.

From 1925 on an important association was developed with the watchmaking firm of Charles Tissot & Fils in Le Locle, which formerly had concentrated on the production of luxury clocks for the Russian market, and had lost this market through the October Revolution.

In 1930 the S.S.I.H. Holding Company (Societe Suisse pour l'Industrie Horlogere) was founded, under whose roof Omega and Tissot were joined by the firms of Lemania, Rayville, Lanco, Cortébert, Marc Favre, Hamilton, and in 1971 the Economic Swiss Time Holding (ESTH) with its low-price Agon, Buler, Continental and Ferex watches.

T21 *Productions of the Movado factories around 1921.*

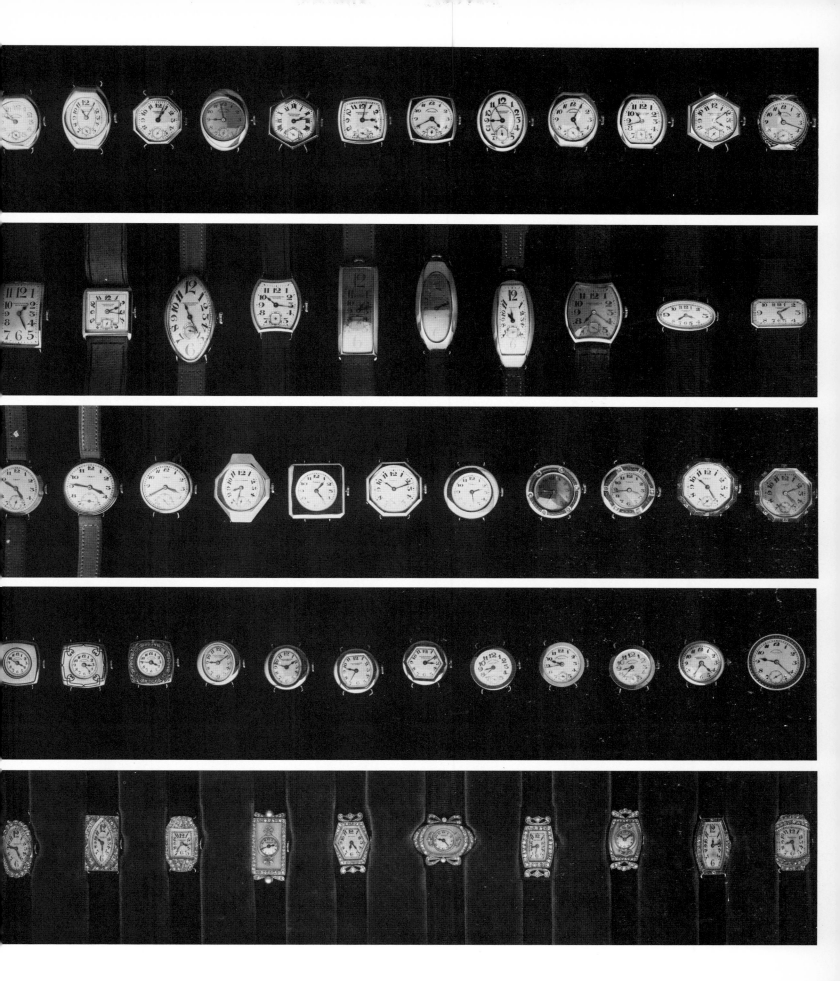

T22 *Productions of the Movado factories around 1921.*

1918 △   1923 ▽   1918 △   1923 ▽   1919 △   1929 ▽   1924 △   1922 ▽   1923 △   1922 ▽

T23 *Specimens of Vacheron & Constantin production.*

Vacheron & Constantin

In 1755 Jean-Marc Vacheron, age 24, founded a clock factory. He had one apprentice working with him. In 1785 Abraham Vacheron, son of Jean-Marc Vacheron, succeeded him. He succeeded in gaining a number of French aristocrats as customers. At the outbreak of the French Revolution Abraham Vacheron lost these customers from one day to the next. In 1794 a revolutionary regime took over in Geneva, in 1798 Geneva became a part of France.

1922 △   1930 ▽   1923 △   1930 ▽   1925 △   1937 ▽   1929 △   1937? ▽   1930 △   1940? ▽

T24 *Specimens of Vacheron & Constantin production.*

In 1810 Abraham Vacheron turned the factory over to his son Jacques-Barthélémy. He and FranÇois Constantin founded the new firm of Vacheron & Constantin in 1819 (in 1815 Geneva became the 22nd canton of Switzerland).

Quite early, in 1839, Vacheron & Constantin began the manufacture of first-class watches.

As of December 18, 1880 the firm added the Maltese cross trademark to its name, as is still seen on the firm's watches today.

△ 1912   △ 1913   △ 1912   ▽ 1915   △ 1912   ▽ 1915   △ 1913   ▽ 1917   △ 1913   ▽ 1917

T25 *Specimens of Vacheron & Constantin production.*

Patek Philippe & Co.

On May 1, 1839 the watchmaking firm of Patek, Czapek & Co. was founded in Geneva by Antoine Norbert de Patek and François Czapek. The firm was dissolved when its contract expired in 1845, as a result of disagreements between Patek and Czapek. Before that, Patek had already come to know and respect Jean Adrien Philippe, who had developed modern winding apparatus for pocket watches from 1842 on.

On May 15, 1845 the firm of Patek & Co. was founded by Antoine Patek, Adrien Philippe and Vincent Gostkowski. François Czapek continued alone under the name of Czapek & Co., but in 1869

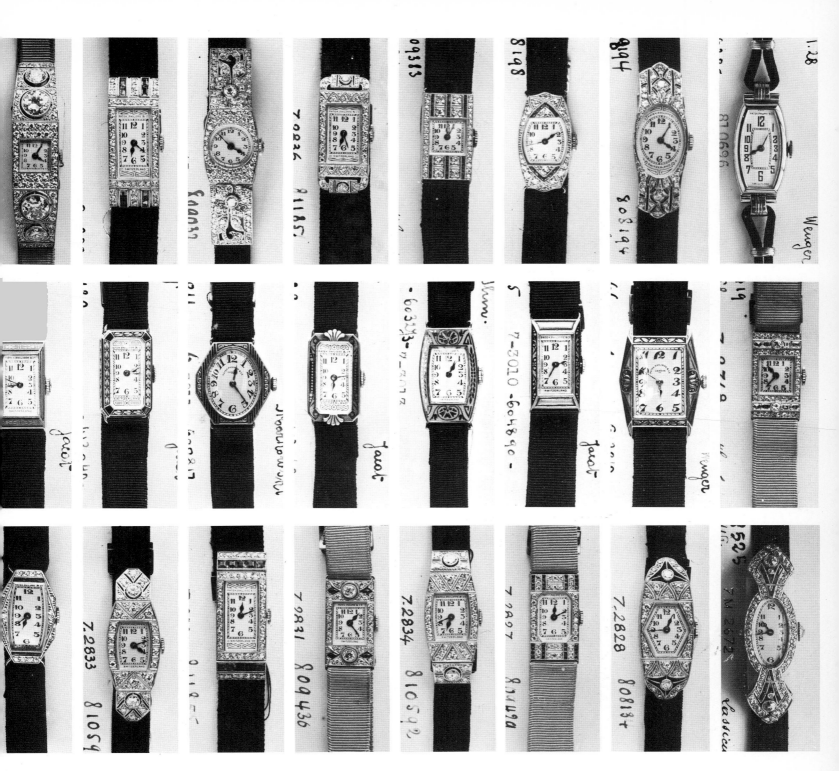

T26 *Specimens of Patek, Philippe & Cie. production, circa 1920 to 1925.*

this firm was completely dissolved. The name "Patek Philippe & Co." was established on January 1, 1851.

An important economic change took place on February 1, 1901. With a capital of 1.6 million Swiss francs, the "Ancienne Manufacture d'Horlogerie Patek & Co. S.A." came into being.

On account of the worldwide depression that began in 1929 a buyer for the greater part of the firm's shares of stock had to be found. This turned out to be the owners of the clock-face number factory "Fabrique de Cadrans Stern Frères", Charles and Jean Stern. This firm had been Patek Philippe's only supplier of numerals.

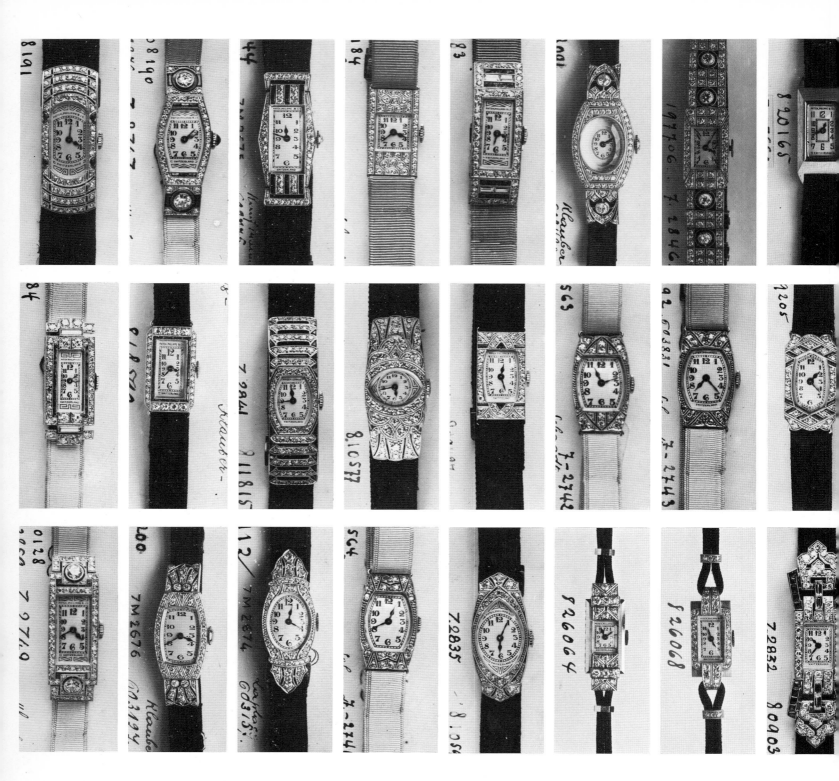

T27 *Specimens of Patek, Philippe & Cie. production, 1920 to 1930.*

On June 14, 1932 the partnership of Adrien Philippe ended. He was the grandson of Jean Adrien Philippe.

In 1933, under the direction of Jean Pfister, the firm again set up its own component factory.

Today the Patek Philippe firm is still owned by the Stern family.

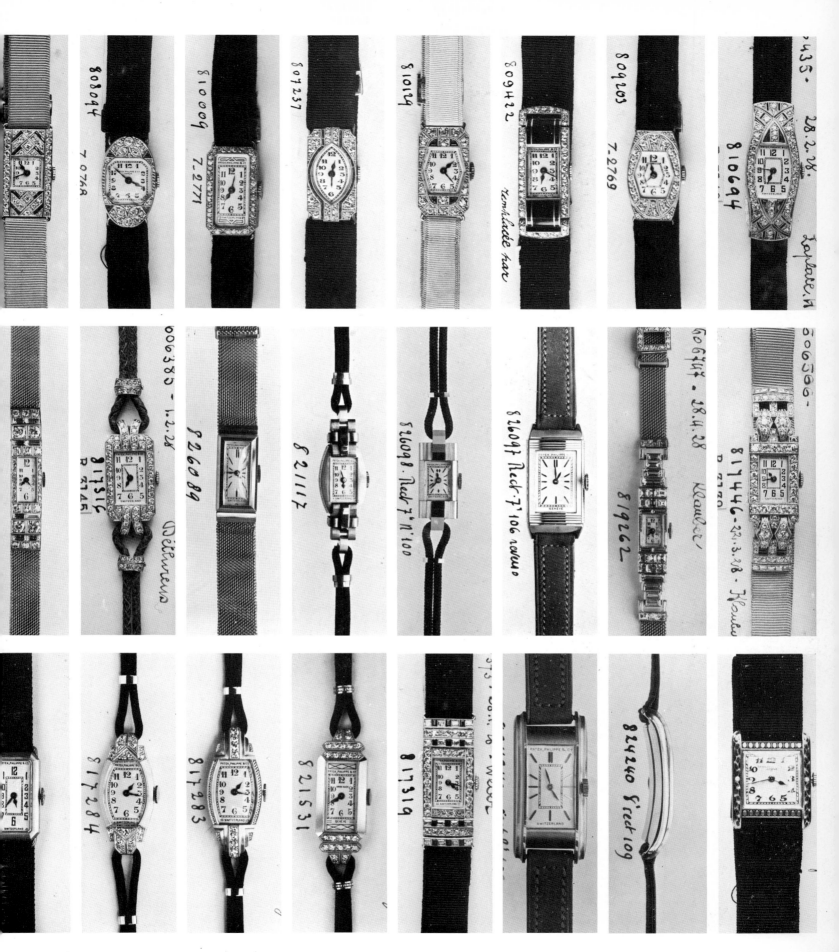

T28 *Specimens of Patek, Philippe & Cie. production, 1925 to 1938.*

29

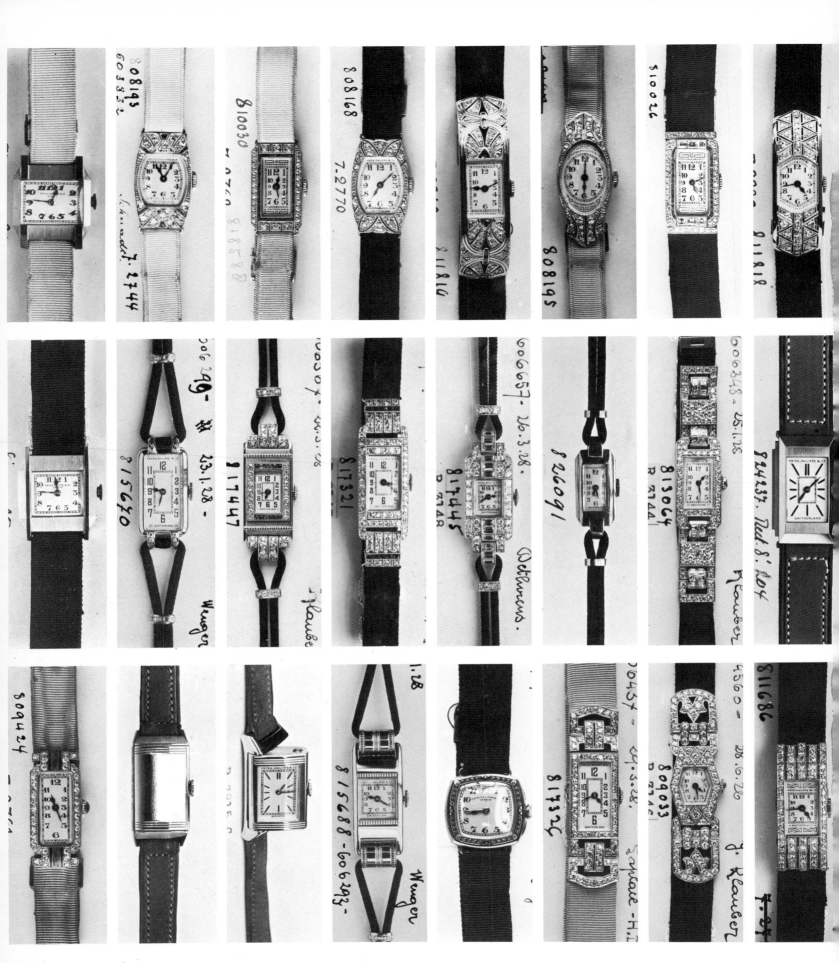

T29 *Specimens of Patek, Philippe & Cie. production, 1925 to 1938.*

30

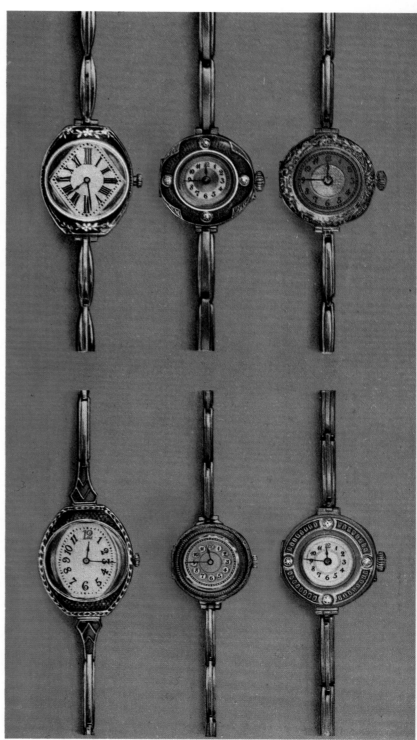

T30 *From the catalog of a Swiss wholesaler, 1914/15. Note the preference for the red number 12.*

T31/32 *Following double page: see illustration 518a-c on page 314.*

T33 *Designs of decorative watchbands from the production of ESZEHA (Chopard), Geneva, circa 1920.*

T34 *Specimens of Omega production, 1924.*

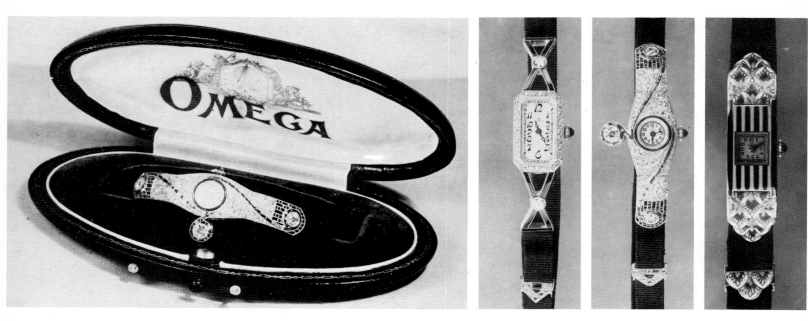

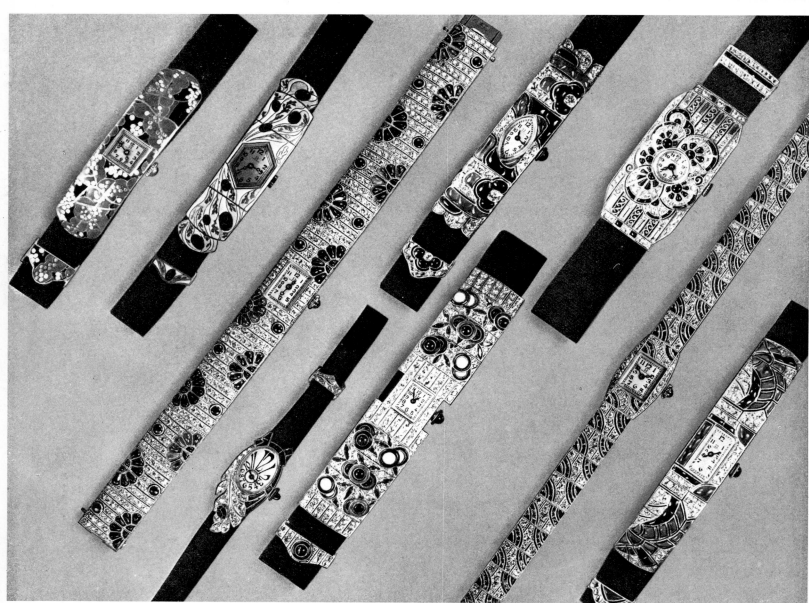

T35 *Specimens of Omega production, 1925.*

T36 *Specimens of Omega production, circa 1925-1930.*

T37 *Specimens of Patek, Philippe & Cie. production, 1910 to 1935.*

T38 *Specimens of Patek, Philippe & Co. production, 1910 to 1935.*

T39 *Specimens of Omega and Tissot production, 1933-1935.*

T40 *Specimens of Omega and Tissot production, 1934-1936.*

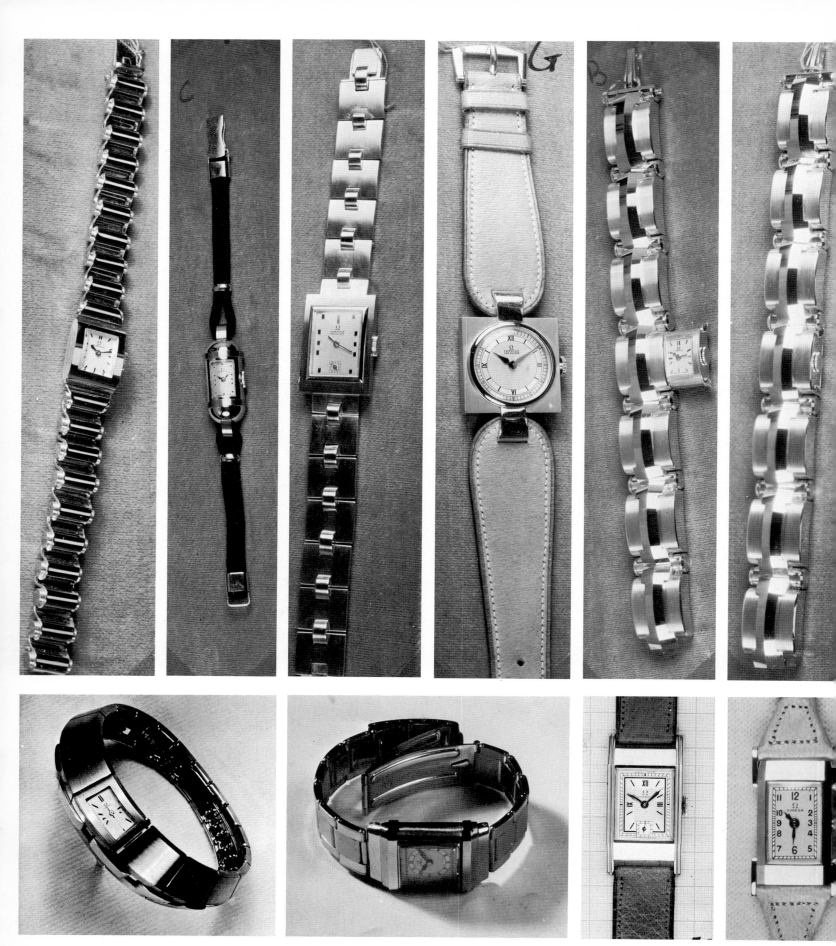

T41 *Specimens of Omega production, 1937.*

T42 *Specimens of Omega and Tissot production, 1937 to 1953.*

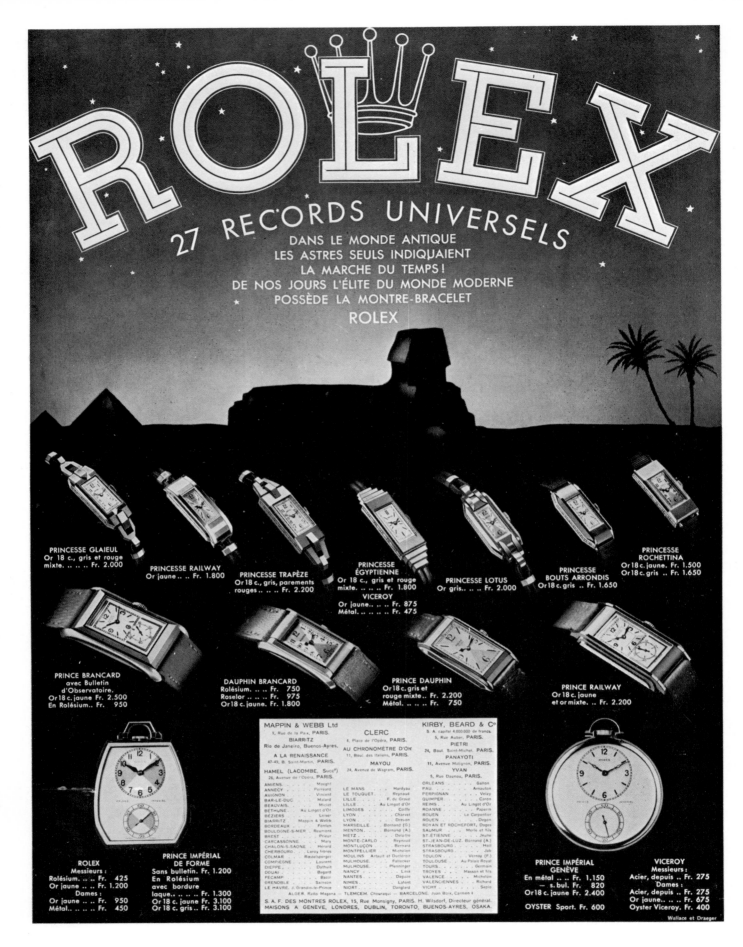

T43 *Rolex advertisement and price list, 1932.*

End of the 18th Century: decorative watches worn on a bracelet documented.

1800-1880: Various forms of armbands with ladies' watches, presumably one of a kind creations.

1880-1910: Ladies' ornamental watches, military and sport watches. The small round pocket watch still sets the pattern.

1910-1930: Experimental phase of the wristwatch. New concepts in technology and design were tested.

1880-1930: Pocket watches were at times worn on the arm. Rebuilding of many ladies' watches.

since 1930: Wristwatch an independent, attainable type of timepiece. Dominance of the wristwatch begins. The pocket watch rapidly loses significance.

Statistics

In a series of publications on clock history the "victory march" of the wristwatch is exactly dated in October of 1927, when Mercedes Gleitze, with a Rolex Oyster on her arm, swam the English Channel. The great advertising success of a Swiss firm impressed many authors so strongly that they called it a new trend. Seldom, though, can watch legends be refuted as easily as in this case, thanks to Swiss export statistics, which, unlike the German, have listed pocket watches and wristwatches separately since 1920. Accordingly, Switzerland exported 7.7 million (75.4%) finished pocket watches in 1920, as opposed to 2.5 million (24.6%) wristwatches. This three-to-one ratio in favor of the pocket watch changed to two-to-one by 1925-26. Barely ten years later, in 1934, the ratio had reversed itself. Now only 3.2 million pocket watches (34.9%), but 6 million wristwatches (65.1%) were exported. This process of replacing the pocket watch with the wristwatch was not to be stopped by either skeptical manufacturers or opposing watchmakers. According to Swiss export statistics, the point of change occurred in 1930, when 6.2 million pocket watches balanced 6.2 million wristwatches. The sporting achievement of the aforementioned Mercedes Gleitze had no decisive influence on this steady development, as the graph on the next page shows.

These Swiss global export statistics show the sales of new watches on the world markets, but they allow no conclusions as to when more wristwatches than pocket watches actually were worn, what percentages of women's and men's wristwatches were sold, what countries were particularly receptive or opposed to the new timepiece, or in what year the watchmakers' repair work was first dominated by the wristwatch.

But when one deduces that for reasons of price, because of the smaller cases, plus the need for decoration, gold and silver cases were used for a considerable majority of women's watches, then the statistics also let one assume what has already been shown elsewhere: that women's watches became the property of the masses before men's. While in 1920 52% of the finished wristwatches exported from Switzerland had cases of precious metal, their proportion was only 29% of the total by 1930.

In 1920 the Enquete branch of the clock industry estimated a probably too conservative yearly consumption in Germany of 2.1 million pocket watches and 1.2 million wristwatches. A few years later the constant question in the trade journals was: "Do you sell more wristwatches or pocket watches?" According to a statement from Helmut Junghans, in 1934 his firm produced 1500 pocket watches and 2000 wristwatches daily. These dates also indicate that after 1930 the wristwatch had passed the pocket watch in German manufacture and sale.

T44 *Only in 1930 did the greatest German watchmaking firm come onto the market with its own movement for men's watches.*

The watchmaker's position

For decades the wristwatch was judged negatively or at least skeptically by the German watchmakers. Only a few of them had already recognized before World War I that a viable new type of watch had begun to establish itself. A Belgian watchmaker had written as early as 1912 that the wristwatch, being so practical and useful, would undoubtedly become more popular among men as well as women. A German colleague. under the influence of the war, came to the conclusion in 1915 that: "Nobody can still doubt that all those who did not want to believe the wristwatch had a future, including all the experts in the watchmakers' shops, have been proved wrong." In the 1880»s it was the makers of large clocks who produced astounding new models. Now the German watchmaker, who during the war and early postwar years could only follow a long way behind the Swiss watch industry, was suddenly confronted with the wristwatch as a permanent mass product. The awareness sank in slowly that rejecting the wristwatch could have similar results to the earlier rejection of fabric regulators and baby alarm clocks.

At first rejected as a short-lived foolish fad or even an insult to the venerable principles of the watchmaker's art, later welcomed as bringing in more business, but generally dreaded in the repair trade because of the small caliber of women's watches, the new technology was ventured into only hesitantly. A basic change in the German watchmakers' standpoint appeared only around 1930. Until then they had doggedly defended the pocket watch. In 1929 the lady's wristwatch was first accepted as one of the masterpiece categories at the German Watchmakers' Convention. In 1930 the editors of the German Watchmakers' Journal offered for discussion the question of what knowledge of wristwatches a qualified assistant should have. A year later, at the urging of watchmaking teachers, a year-long argument began as to whether wristwatch work should be included in apprentices' training. Only in the Thirties did the wristwatch become accepted as an independent unit in the long developmental history of the clock. Consumers and (Swiss) manufacturers had come to this conclusion sooner.

The situation also becomes clear in the sometimes humorous, sometimes drastically self-critical introductions to the first inclusive instructions for repairing wristwatches. These texts include many references to the state of the art at that time, and are therefore quoted as a service to the collector.

The first extensive contribution in a German watchmakers' journal was written by Bruno Hillmann in 1919. It states: "But should anyone be so led astray as to advertise himself as a specialist in repairing wristwatches in hopes of making a good profit, he can be sure of finding himself on the scrap heap within a few years, if he does not manage, after thorough treatment of his eyes and nerves, to earn his pension by sorting baby-alarm covers in a Black Forest clock factory." (The Watchmaker's Art, 1919, page 148.)

Arno Hofrichter (Geneva) carefully checks himself against the authors of renowned watchmaking textbooks before he dares to write: "But what these authors could not teach was the repair of tiny wristwatches with their hidden faults, because the development of this species set in only after their active careers.—Far be it from me to set myself up as their equal in specialized expertise, but I still believe I am justified in handling this theme because I have had the opportunity to observe the manifold metamorphoses of the wristwatch at its birthplace." As for repair work, one "not only may, but must deal with it in practice." (The Watchmaker's Art, 1926, page 62.)

Anton Lechner, who intensively promoted the integration of the wristwatch into the watch-

maker's training, uses the following title for his repair advice: "Leave your father alone, he's making a very small wristwatch!" Then come a string of elementary tips, beginning with the cleanliness of the workbench and the necessary tools. "Nothing more is to be done with a good old-fashioned pair of pliers; you'll scratch the dial, bend the hands, scratch the numbers' lacquer off, and then you'll really lose your balance and put a scratch on it . . ." (South German Watchmakers' Journal, 1933, I, page 12.)

Finally, let us quote Hans Jendritzki: "It is generally said that wristwatches are the watchmaker's problem children. And then the poor quality of the watches is to blame when the watches don't run. To be sure, wristwatches of all calibers are so made that it takes a lot of trouble to breathe the breath of life into them. But how do the finer wristwatches look when they are repaired one or more times? How does it happen that such watches still give trouble after they are repaired? The mediocre quality cannot be to blame then, can it?" (The Watchmaker's Art, 1934, page 115.)

The first specialized book about the wristwatch printed in Germany was written by Bruno Hillmann. It appeared in 1925 under the title: "The wristwatch, its nature and treatment during repair" (48 pages of text, 55 illustrations). The well-

known textbook by Hans Jendritzki, which was often reprinted, first came on the market in 1937 under the title: "Repairing the wristwatch" (107 pages, 78 illustrations). It recognizes the fact that the "Manual of Watchmaking Instruction" by Hermann Sievert, in the 13th revised edition of 1931, has no reference to wristwatches in its text; the wristwatch really had a hard time establishing itself among (German) watchmakers.

The consumer's vote

Women, both style-conscious and employed, decided in favor of the wristwatch before men did. When in 1914 a great French fashion magazine asked its readers what their favorite piece of jewelry was, the answer was clear. Out of 4350 answers, 3437, 79%, named the wristwatch. Other pieces of jewelry, such as pendants, medallions, rings or necklaces received only few votes.

Among the men the experiences of World War I led to a growing worldwide interest in the wristwatch. Critical contemporaries clearly recognized the results: "In the daily press comments on the practicality of this way of wearing a watch have appeared repeatedly, and they have elicited such inspired support that it is useless to think that the soldier on duty will wear his watch differently as a civilian in peacetime .. ." But in comparison to women, the world of men remained more conservative.

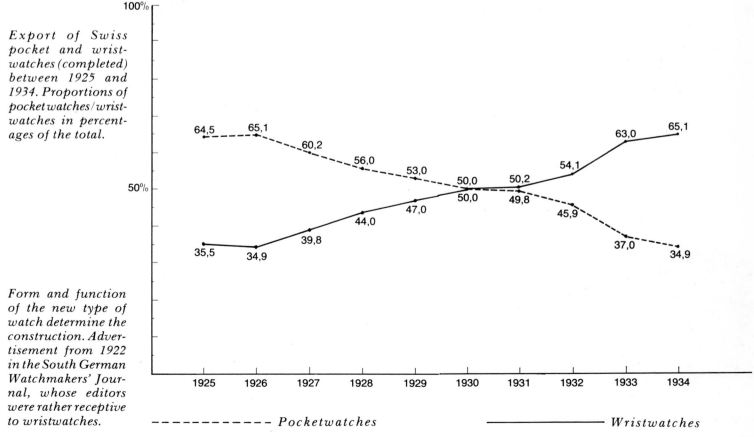

Export of Swiss pocket and wristwatches (completed) between 1925 and 1934. Proportions of pocketwatches/wristwatches in percentages of the total.

Form and function of the new type of watch determine the construction. Advertisement from 1922 in the South German Watchmakers' Journal, whose editors were rather receptive to wristwatches.

– – – – – – – – – – Pocketwatches ——————— Wristwatches

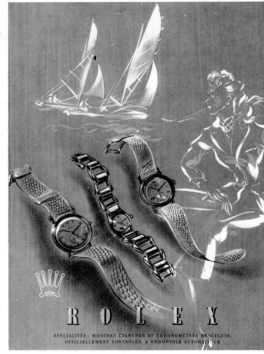

T45 *Women's watches with oval and round Swiss escapement movements. Typical forms circa 1930.*

T46 *Sporting elegance, stressed again and again in advertisements for wristwatches. Advertisements from 1943.*

Many participants in the war turned back to the pocket watch after the Armistice, for it had become something like a symbol of the lost "good old days". The younger generation held onto the more practical wristwatch. Concepts such as modern, sporting and progressive were now linked with the wristwatch, while the pocket watch attracted more conservative buyers. In the long run, this polarization of the products' image hurt the pocket watch and helped the wristwatch.

But the German watch industry wanted to know for sure, and in 1936/37 the Nuremberg Institute for Consumer Research was given the job of making a market study. The result confirmed the assumptions: there were two clearly defined groups, the adherents of the pocket watch and those of the wristwatch.

As one got older one tended toward the pocket watch; that was true of all levels of society. For many the pocket watch was not only a useful object, but also "something living", a "loyal comrade", to which "many memories" were linked.

T47 *Oval English silver case with round Swiss escapement movement. Circa 1920.*

To this group a pocket watch also looked better on a man, it added dignity and class, and was also regarded as a particularly reliable and durable timepiece.

The friends of the wristwatch represented another standpoint; to them practical considerations mattered. The wearer of a wristwatch appears as a modern, progressive-minded person, the opposite of the traditional bourgeois. A teacher formulated it: "If I bought it new, I would buy a wristwatch, because it is in style. My boys always laugh when I pull out my old round pocket watch; they are almost embarrassed." For this generation the watch was not a nostalgic thing, but rather a usable, even consumable item.

The buyer of a pocket watch was the ideal customer; he demanded quality, and the watchmaker could easily build a lasting relationship with him. But according to the Nuremberg Research Institute, this group was rapidly declining. The buyers of wristwatches took an ambivalent attitude to the quality of a watch. One group, especially after unpleasant experiences, bought more impressive watches, the other came to terms with mediocrity and replaced the broken-down wristwatch with a new one in the same price range.

The market research study gave no long-term prognosis. But a watchmaker expressed himself on that subject when he wrote to the German Watchmakers' Journal in 1932: "Our grandfathers lived in the days of the spindle clock, our fathers wore their pocket watches with pride, and even in their early years our children's most fervent wish is for a wristwatch. Perhaps our grandchildren will wear electrically regulated watches on their arms. Who knows what technology will bring us!"

Technological Changes

Phases of development to 1960

Pocket watches and wristwatches resemble each other in the construction of their movements and their form. In wristwatches too, parts and groups are used that are already known from the pocket watch; one need only think of the wheels, the winding, the jewels, or the central system of the small mechanical clock, the connection of escapement and regulation (the balance wheel and hairspring). Only the tuning-fork watch and, shortly thereafter, the quartz watch bring new technological solutions to well-known tasks; electronics replaces fine mechanics.

And yet the wristwatch, in the half-century between 1910 and 1960, became something other than a smaller version of a pocket watch worn on the arm. The new type of watch set new goals in terms of development and production, which then had a positive effect on the making of pocket watches too, as can be seen in terms of shock-resistance or the use of new materials. The constructors blazed new trails, though, when they created specially formed movements for wristwatches or were able to approach the perfect method of self-winding. Even if the bigger mechanical clocks, exposed to the same technology and careful workmanship, will always give better results than the smaller types, the wristwatch has attained a standard of precision and reliability in our century that even renowned experts could scarcely imagine at the turn of the century.

Defining the time limits of a broad process of development with overlappings and shiftings is always problematic; but let us suggest here that the period between 1910 and 1930 can be called the experimental phase of the wristwatch. This can be recognized externally from the experiments with cases and dials, whose high point was reached around 1920, and the gradual transition around 1930 to more subdued, more strongly functional forms.

That is just as true of the technology of the wristwatch. In the latter half of the Twenties the first functional automatic wristwatch of the Harwood system was put into series production; in 1927 the watertight Rolex watch passed a highly respected test, and useful sport watches appeared. In 1933 the development of the Nivarox hairspring was concluded and the problem of shock-resistance was solved. In the same era the sometimes playfully merry search for new movement forms slowed down; its best example was the little Baguette movement of women's watches.

In 1931 the Watchmaker's Weekly published the following overview of Swiss production: "As articles that enjoy particular popularity today the so-called Baguette wristwatches for women can be named, also men's sport watches with shock-resistance, watertight watches for those who enjoy water sports, Notora and calendar wristwatches for business people, wristwatches without hands, eight-day wristwatches and the like. And let us not forget the automatic self-winding wristwatches... An even stronger acceptance in the export trade is shown for chronograph wristwatches." Expressions like unbreakable, watertight or water-protected, anti-magnetic, rustfree and automatic appear more and more often in Swiss watch advertising in the Thirties.

Since it is the main purpose of this book to document the state of technology through selected wristwatches, the introductary text at this point can do without an extended description of the development, especially as individual types of watches and outstanding technologies are still to be portrayed. For the following average observation in the times around 1960 the reports on the Basel Sample Fair were utilized, for this event has developed into an internationally recognized display of the Swiss watch industry's achievements.

T48 Models regarded as progressive in 1932: Second dial in the middle—watertight, shock-resistant sport watch—wristwatch in the shape of a car radiator—jumping hours, turning minute disc, and second dial.

T49 *Baguette movements for small decorative watches. The spatial arrangement of barrel and balance system is typical of this formed caliber.*

T50 *Junghans "Golden Star", ultraflat golden man's wristwatch, German production, though with Swiss AS caliber 1525.*

The basic tendencies can be designated with the following adjectives: the wristwatches are more and more precise and robust, complex and flattened. For men's watches automatic self-winding has gradually been taken for granted, and of sixteen new features announced in 1959, ten concern this type of watch. Automatic men's watches are now, almost without exception, housed in "anti-magnetic" and "watertight" cases, with an unbreakable mainspring and shock-resistant balance-wheel bearings. "The automatic watch now makes even the classic watch's superiority in terms of elegance debatable," says a report on the 1961 clock fair.

The tendency in luxury watches is toward flatter calibers, which allow building the case with as elegant a profile as possible. Particularly noteworthy is an ultraflat 1956 man's watch in a watertight case with a total thickness of 7 mm. There were clear attempts to produce certain caliber watches as chronometers in series of trade quality (1957). The number of timekeeping improvements and variations to suit markets is too great to discuss here; a 1959 watch might be mentioned, the speed of which could be regulated by pressure on a knob without opening the case (Pierce Correctomatic). Watches for aviators, divers, motorists, engineers and doctors, hand and wrist chronographs had places of honor in many displays and outdid each other in watertightness, resistance to magnetic fields and refinements of their measuring abilities (1961).

Among women's watches the automatic winding system was carried farther and realized. The smallest watch of this kind in 1959 had a case diameter of 15.2 mm with sharply reduced height; another automatic movement of 20 mm diameter and 5 mm height was equipped with a direct central second hand and 26 effective rubies. Women's alarm waches and calendar watches naturally are among the offerings, as are sport watches and very small movements of remarkable precision. The technology of the mechanical wristwatch stood in 1960 at the beginning of its last phase of development.

Material research and production technology

Intuition and handworking ability certainly determined the development of clock technology in previous centuries. As wristwatches progressed it was engineering science that came to the fore. The Swiss trade schools, certain research institutes and the development departments of well-known manufacturers have had considerable influence. This is especially clear in material research, the development and testing of new calibers, of new measuring and testing processes, and of the perfection of watch assembly.

The significance of material research for the development of the mechanical wristwatch will be shown here by three examples. The chapter on the balance wheel and the hairspring will include more. Many manufacturers and watchmakers stoically accepted the weaknesses of the steel mainspring: corrosion, magnetism and above all breaking from fatigue, but Reinhard Straumann saw it otherwise. Even in his younger years he envisioned a rust-free, unmagnetic and unbreakable mainspring that combined these qualities with an elasticity comparable to that of the best tempered steel springs.

"During twenty years Straumann strove passionately for the solution of this problem," one of his colleagues wrote. Finally the goal was attained. The Nivaflex mainspring fulfilled all of the conditions he had set; it lasts longer than a mechanical wristwatch does. High-achievement mainsprings of this kind in turn became the reason for the development of special watch calibers with heightened regulating frequency. While the balance wheel of a normal wristwatch makes about 18,000 half-swings, the so-called fast swingers—according to a 1952 graph—make between 19,800 and 21,600 half-swings per hour, and in later years there were automatic wristwatches with up to 36,000 per hour.

In the Thirties constructors were already examining the effect of magnetic fields on the working capability of wristwatches. There were two possible solutions, which could also be combined with each other: replacing steel components, especially of regulators, with less susceptible alloys or building a protective housing to shield the works from magnetic influences. In the IWC "Engineer" of 1956 the creation of a shield against magnetic disturbances of up to 1000 Oersted was accomplished. Normally the influence of 100 Oersted was enough to disturb the regulation of a watch designated as anti-magnetic.

The importance of the lubricants is shown in the oftenpublished words that Breguet is said to have spoken to Napoleon: "Give me the perfect watch oil, Sire, and I'll build you the perfect watch." The watch oils developed in the latter half of the Nineteenth Century were mixtures of neat's-foot oil and liquid paraffin. Their surface tension was certainly sufficient, but they oxidized and became resinous. The small caliber wristwatches particularly required especially high-performance lubricants. One became aware that chemical laws set certain limits for the improvement of classic watch oils, and so new synthesized oils were sought. Around 1950 important researches were completed. But in this respect the development of usable dry lubricants , particularly for the mainspring, should also be noted. These have contributed much to the functional security of the automatic wristwatches.

It would be too much to enumerate all the tools used in manufacture and assembly, or the various machine tools and finishing aids that have had an influential part in the improvement of quality in watches of all price ranges. The hundredth part of a millimeter was the usual standard of size, the thousandth a sufficient measure of tolerance. While formerly it was customary for the assembler or the watchmaker to bring the individual parts to their final form and function, now one strove to achieve the desired final function simply by putting the parts together, without having to rework them.

Only in the regulation, the step-by-step assembly of all parts of the swing system, and the equalization of a required frequency, for example in the subsequent fine regulation, did traditional work processes still have their usual place circa 1960. In these areas automated assembly appeared only later. Wilhelm Keil referred to this goal when in 1957 he advocated "anticipating the regulation in the preparation of parts". An electronic firm, whose program was based on the needs of their watch branch, announced machines in 1966 that would assemble the swing system completely automatically, and others that would set the hairspring onto its pinion.

Interest in high-priced brand-name wristwatches was not to lead to neglect of the lower-priced watches produced in much greater numbers. As can be seen from a market research study, in the mid-Sixties 75% of the men's watches sold in West Germany and 67% of the women's watches were in the price range under 100 Marks.

From the beginning the specialists agreed that in the end only the Swiss anchor escapement was to be used in wristwatches. In the years before

T51 *Reinhard Straumann (1892-1967). With the "Nivaflex" mainspring and "Nivarox" hairspring he created significant elements in the improvement of the mechanical wristwatch.*

T52 *IWC "Engineer", circa 1962. Shielded against magnetic disturbances up to 1000 Oerstedt.*

5 ¹/₄ ‴ Cal. 159

6 ³/₄ ‴ Cal. 160

7 ³/₄ - 11 ‴ Cal. 160

8 ³/₄ ‴ Cal. 106

8 ³/₄ ‴ Cal. 160

10 ¹/₂ ‴ Cal. 108

T53 *Cylinder escapement lasted a long time, even in Swiss watches. Cylinder works from 1937.*

World War II this system of escapement made its way into price ranges that formerly had used only cylindrical workings. From the other side hook-escapement watches, improved by production technology, considerably limited the range of cylinder watches. Yet this means of construction was still produced individually for wristwatches even in 1950. All in all, it can be seen that production technolgy did the less expensive wristwatch even more good than the more pretentious one. This becomes especially obvious in terms of the lifetime of hook-escapement works. The layman still recognizes the difference in quality, but the distance has decreased.

Balance wheel and hairspring

Many influences affect the exact action of a wristwatch, but the regulating organ, the balance wheel with its hairspring, is vitally important. Therefore this complex should be described in detail. Watch collectors all regard the bimetallic compensation balance as a characteristic of better-quality old wristwatches. But in the Thirties the constructors changed their minds on this subject. Since then wristwatches have been equipped with self-compensating hairsprings, and with balance wheels of one metal, and since 1960 increasingly with large ring-shaped balance wheels without screws.

With the help of the compensating balance the irregularities in the running of the watch caused by varying temperatures should be evened out, compensated for. The extent of the temperature's influence is considerable; in an ordinary (not compensated) brass watch with a steel hairspring a temperature increase of one degree Celsius is enough to make the watch lose about twelve seconds in twenty-four hours.

About 90% of this fault is caused by the hairspring, for the elasticity of the spring's steel decreases when warmed. The great masters of the watchmaking art had already recognized this late in the Eighteenth Century, and they built the balance so that they could compensate for the influence of temperature on the hairspring to a considerable degree. So in this concept of construction the balance takes on the job of adapting itself to the conditions of the hairspring and so improving the running of the watch.

The compensating balance consists of two different metals, thus the term "bimetallic watch" is also in use. The two metals, generally steel and brass combined with each other, have different coefficients of elasticity. Brass, with its higher coefficient, forms the outer ring, steel the inner ring and the shank of the balance wheel. As a rule the compensating balance consists of 2/5 steel and 3/5 brass. Very near the shank the ring is cut into in two places. So the ends of the rings can bend in the same way, both halves have to be fully symmetrical and the two metals have to be bound to each other homogeneously. If, for example, the temperature goes up, then the steel spring reacts by lengthening and decreasing in elasticity, which means the clock runs slowly. But at the same time the outer ring of brass expands more than the inner ring of steel, and the free ends bend inward. This bending toward the middle point makes the inert radius of the balance wheel smaller, and the watch, assuming other conditions remained exactly the same, would run faster. The effect of the decreasing elasticity of the hairspring is thus nearly compensated for by the effect of the balance wheel. A fine tuning, the influencing of the radial movement of the free ends of the ring within certain limits, can be achieved by relocating the balance screws set on the outside of the balance wheel. Holes for this purpose are already provided thanks to the technology of manufacturing. Along with them there is a second group of screws, the mass screws. They serve to counterbalance the swinging wheel.

Compensating balances are rather expensive to manufacture and repair, and can easily be misshapen, but another disadvantage, which watchmakers call the secondary error, is more serious. Equalizing the effects of the hairspring by adjusting the balance wheel is not effective through the whole range of temperatures, no matter how fine the adjustment, but works only at one temperature, or two at most.

So if the running irregularities at 20 and 35 degrees Celsius could be almost evened out, the watch would still deviate at other temperatures and run either fast or slow. The cause of this is that with changes in temperature the reaction curve of the balance wheel runs in a straight line, while that of the hairspring bends. To be sure, the two run in opposite directions, but they compensate for each other only tendentially and not completely.

T54 *From the small wristwatch to the alarm clock. Hook escapements indicate cheap watches. Advertisement from 1953.*

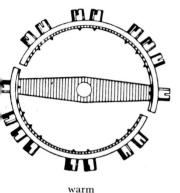

warm

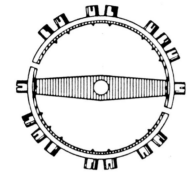

normal temperature

T55 *Positions of the compensating balance wheel at varying temperatures.*

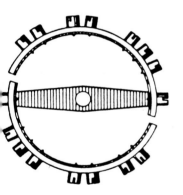

cold

T56 *The classic compensating balance wheel with outer ring of blass and inner ring of steel. Until the advent of new alloys the better-class wristwatch was equipped with a balance wheel of this type.*

This becomes clear through a simple consideration. When a curved line is intersected at two points by a vertical line, then the angles of the straight and curved lines agree only at these two points, while before, between and beyond they differ. The field of variation makes the "secondary error" clear.

This lasting inaccuracy has always bothered the watchmaker and inspired him to refined counter-measures. But the successful solution process appeared only at the end of the Nineteenth Century. Through intensive research Ch. E. Guillaume (1861-1938) was able to create a special steel with 44% nickel content which was particularly suitable for the construction of compensated balances. A balance wheel made of this alloy and brass practically wiped out the secondary error.

Only now did the compensated balance fully deserve its name. The curve of the watch's fast running caused by the balance wheel became a mirror image of the curve of slow running caused by the hairspring. While a watch finely adjusted to two temperatures with the older type of compensated balance always runs three to five seconds fast at the temperatures in between, precision movements with Guillaume balances show a secondary compensation error of only a few tenths of a second. This system, so important for precision timekeeping, still could not be used for portable watches, for it was too costly and too sensitive.

Decisive for the wristwatch was a second idea, that of achieving the equalization of temperature changes not, as before, via the balance wheel, but

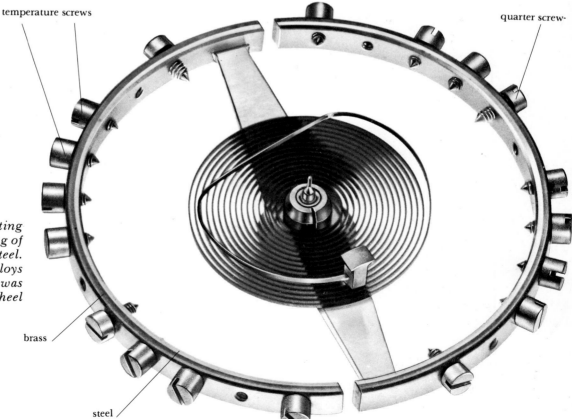

temperature screws

quarter screw-

brass

steel

rather via the hairspring. A regulatory technician from La Chaux-de-Fonds, Paul Perret, made the first attempts, circa 1900, to mount nickel steel hairsprings on monometallic balance wheels. Thereby he learned that the temperature influenced hairsprings of this material much less than he was accustomed to with steel hairsprings. Working with Perret at the beginning, Guillaume followed this phenomenon to its consequences. After intensive laboratory work, in 1919 he found an alloy whose elasticity quotient formed a fully even curve over a wide temperature range. The self-compensating hairspring was discovered. Guillaume called the new alloy Elinvar.

T57 *Charles Edouard Guillaume (1861-1938). Nobel Prize winner in physics, 1920. The results of his research later influenced the development of the mechanical wristwatch.*

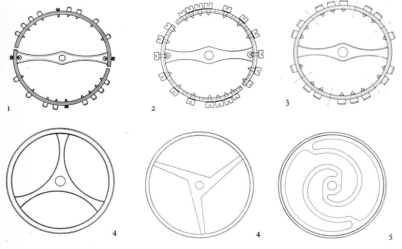

T58 *Various types of balance wheels as of 1969. 1. Cut steel-brass ring. 2. Cut Guillaume ring. 3. Glucydur balance with screws. 4. Ring balances of copper-beryllium (Glucydur) or German silver. 5. Ring balance with shockresistant elastic arms.*

P. Beguin reports: "As a curiosity it can be noted that this invention for quality watches found little acceptance among dealers, for Elinvar hairsprings were not blue. Many watchmakers were convinced that 'white' hairsprings did not belong in good watches. The superiority of the Elinvar hairspring was recognized only after many years." It has nevertheless been estimated that in 1938 about 100 million watches were already fitted with hairsprings of this type.

Even though Elinvar was far superior to the older steel in terms of temperature compensation, still other qualities of steel, such as high elasticity and constant swinging conditions, could not yet be attained. At this point a second period of development begins, which is also linked with the name of Reinhard Straumann. After years of experimenting, in which a special measuring device, called the "time scale" by Straumann, was invented, the Nivarox hairspring could be put on the market in 1933. It consists of an alloy of iron and nickel, similar to Elinvar, but with beryllium added as the main element in improving the elastic and compensating qualities, as well as small admixtures of titanium, manganese and silicium, which have considerably increased resistance to magnetic influences.

The highest—the word is used rightfully here—achievements of the modern hairspring have been described by Helmut Mann as follows: "This alloy is rustfree, insensitive to magnetic fields, possesses the required high elasticity along with low inner friction (deadening), reinforces the constancy of swinging in all situations and throughout heat treatment retains a high degree of stability which assures steady running. Its particular advantage is self-compensation, usually called thermocompensation. That is its ability to bring the thermoelastic coefficients to zero with correct adjustment of all factors in assembly, formation, heat treatment and choice of cross-section."

With that the situation changed completely, compared to what it had been before. The hairspring assured the adaptation to the atmosphere, the balance wheel just needed to function, following the hairspring as a swinging body as exactly balanced as possible. In retrospect one gets the impression that the new type of metal with its fascinating properties struck the watchmakers as rather uncanny, all the more so in a time of transition, for they parted from the old type of balance only hesitantly. The steel-brass balance with uncut rings, along with the monometallic ones of brass or German silver, remained in use.

A pervasive new orientation was seen only after 1935, when the Glucydur balance of hardened beryllium-bronze became known. This metal proved to be particularly resistant during later phases of work such as riveting, balancing or fine adjustment. In addition, the same mechanical properties allowed greater precision in the assembly of the balance, whose ring or arms cannot easily be bent despite their considerably reduced thickness. Now the modern hairspring had found its pendant of equal quality, Nivarox spring and Glucydur wheel, both under various brand names, became the identifying marks of the modern mechanical wristwatch.

One mark of the classic conpensated balance endured longest: the screws around the ring. As P. Beguin could still remark in 1969: "The monometallic balance wheels with screws . . . achieved such good results, and the familiarity of using them is so deeply rooted, that one must almost use force on the regulators when they work with modern ring-formed balances." But the new concept could not be held back.

The Gyromax balance used around 1955 by Patek-Philippe can be regarded as a predecessor. Turnable metal cylinders with slots are set in eight milled openings of a beryllium ring for fine adjustment. Thus it is possible to expand the turning radius of the balance without increasing the weight. Modern ring balances usually have three shanks and have been balanced and regulated by the maker by certain methods. The advantages of the newer type were finally decisive, though: great moment of inertia with relatively light weight, simple means of production, and high stability and resistance to becoming misshapen. In 1968 about 90% of Swiss anchor-balance watches were equipped with ring balances.

Wristwatch caliber

The concept of caliber is not a single standard in watch technology; it can refer to the size, shape or type of movement. The size of the movement is generally measured in Parisian lines (one line = 2.256 mm). A round movement of 10.5 lines thus has a diameter of 23.60 mm; very small movements of women's watches have a size of four or five lines, thus 9.02 to 11.28 mm diameter. The traditional unit of measurement has remained in the language of the trade despite various attempts to replace it with the metric system. The size of the case is the diameter of the front plate, measured in the direction of the winding stem.

Wristwatches and pocket watches also differ in terms of the forms of their movements. Before 1914 wristwatches usually had round movements, and the caliber sizes of Swiss watches ranged from 8 to 16 lines, with miniature decorative watches of caliber 6 being the one exception. After that came a period when men's watches with so-called "formed movements" became about as popular as the round ones. The widespread "Tonneau" movement (French for "cask") was oval with straight narrow sides, and standard calibers of this type had masses of 7.75 by 11 or 8.75 by 12 lines. Finally, following the influence of the automatic watch, the formed movements of men's watches fell out of popularity. But we must note here that men's watches with cases and dials of various form calibers often had round movements, just as round cases could hold formed movements.

The development of women's watches was different. Here the formed movements lived on, though their numbers and styles varied from time to time. There were rectangular, oval and ovoid movements, as well as examples of other geometric forms. Rectangular movements often had their corners angled or their short sides slightly rounded. The longish thin rectangular form of the Baguette movement (French for a small rod) was especially popular in the Twenties and was still made in later years.

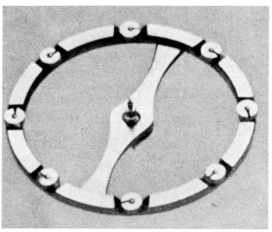

T59 *Highly regarded by specialists, the Gyromax ring balance by Patek Philippe, circa 1955.*

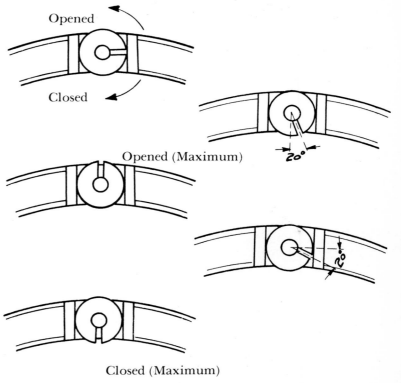

Opened

Closed

Opened (Maximum)

Closed (Maximum)

T60 *Fine adjustment of the Gyromax balance with the help of slotted, turnable cylinders.*

Cal. 4.21

 Cal. 5.16

 Cal. 13.15

 Cal. 12.19

 LONGINES

 Cal. 7.45

 Cal. (13.22) 7.48

 Cal. (15.23) 8.23

 Cal. 8.47

 Cal. 6.22

 Cal. 9.32

 Cal. (20.28) 9.47 **N.**

Cal. 25.17

T61 *Longines wristwatch caliber, from a caliber reference, circa 1938.*

CALIBRE 440	CALIBRES 480 ET 481	CALIBRE 455
6''' PC AM	12,50 PC AM	16 RA SC PC AM
17 rubis	17 rubis	17 rubis

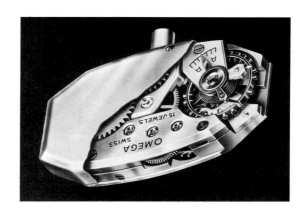

Diamètre 13,50 mm	Longueur 15,20 mm	Diamètre 16,00 mm
Hauteur 3,20 mm	Largeur 12,50 mm	Hauteur 5,50 mm
21 600 oscillations	Hauteur 3,60 mm	19 800 oscillations
	19 800 oscillations	

OMEGA

CALIBRE 244	CALIBRE 252	CALIBRE 302
R 13,5 PC AM	R 13,5 SC PC AM	R 17,8 PC AM
17 rubis	17 rubis	17 rubis

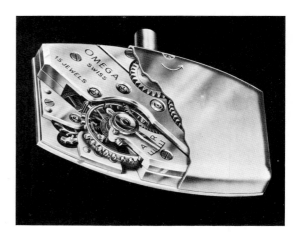

Longueur 17,50 mm	Longueur 17,50 mm	Longueur 22,00 mm
Largeur 13,50 mm	Largeur 13,50 mm	Largeur 17,80 mm
Hauteur 3,25 mm	Hauteur 4,15 mm	Hauteur 3,25 mm
21 600 oscillations	21 600 oscillations	21 600 oscillations

T62/63 *Various Omega wristwatch calibers from the Fifties; at right, one from 1935 with a soft iron cover to protect it from magnetic influences.*

4 $^1/_4$ ′′′ Cal. 67   5 ′′′ Cal. 48   5 $^1/_4$ ′′′ Cal. 61.   5 $^1/_2$ ′′′ Cal. 55

6 $^3/_4$ ′′′ Cal. 46   7 $^1/_2$ ′′′ Cal. 47   7 $^3/_4$-11 ′′′ Cal. 70   8 $^3/_4$-12 ′′′ Cal. 71

9 ′′′ Cal. 54   9/13 ′′′ Cal. 69   7 $^3/_4$ ′′′ Cal. 49   8 $^3/_4$ ′′′ Cal. 42-22   9 $^3/_4$ ′′′ Cal. 50-3
                      seconde au centre

10 $^1/_2$ ′′′ Cal. 39   10 $^1/_2$ ′′′ Cal. 56-3   10 $^1/_2$ ′′′ Cal. 56-22   11 ′′′ Cal. 57-18

Calibres des montres suisses   —   Schweizerische Uhrwerke   —   Swiss Watch Movements

T64 *Calibers of Revue brand wristwatches, 1938.*

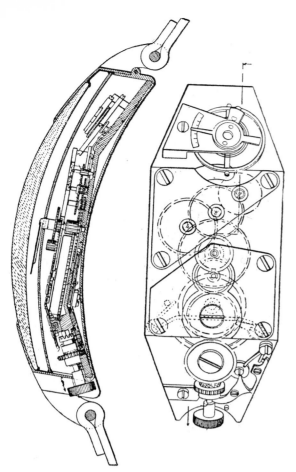

T65 *The "Polyplan" movement by Movado, a construction that follows the bend of the wrist; 1912. Bowed cases were fairly common then, but they usually contained normal round movements. (See also illustrations 27a-e, Illustration Section.)*

T66 *A very popular IWC caliber for women's watches, 1951.*

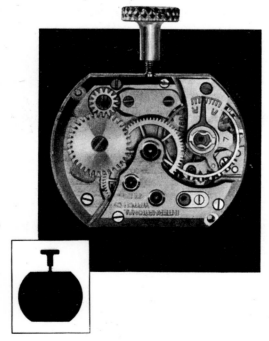

The smallest Baguette movement of 1935 measured 2.25 lines on its shorter sides. In the literature, though, even smaller formed movements for women's watches are called Baguettes, and the typical 5.25 caliber caused watchmakers many a headache at first.

Two types of movements were common in watches of the latter half of the Nineteenth Century, the "Bridge Movement" and the ¾ plate pocket watch. The name of the former indicates that a bridge was provided for each individual moving part. In the ¾ plate watch the balance wheel and anchor had their own bridges, while all the other moving parts were under the ¾ plate. Continuous plates are usually found in wristwatches of the lower and lowest price ranges. More expensive calibers are more oriented to bridge movements; the variety of movement types is also greater than those of pocket watches.

In a 1930 discussion of problems in wristwatch construction, Alfred Helwig compares the open pocket watch to that with a spring lid (the Savonnette). In the one type the winding column is opposite the second dial, in the other, as in wristwatches, at a right angle to it. Definite conclusions for the spatial arrangements of individual parts result from this. Helwig arrives at this statement: Two advantages of the spring-cover watch, "the lesser height of the movement and the healthier arrangement of the moving parts, should be very welcome in the wristwatch." While wristwatches of the earliest period of manufacture were equipped with second dials like those of pocket watches, or else with no second hands at all, later the central second hand established itself. Various transitional types gave way to the space-saving "direct central second" in the power train and thus led to new movement types.

The formed movements of the first generation were usually made of parts from small round movements. Available space sometimes went unused. Later the barrel and balance were made oversize in relation to the power-transmitting parts. In smaller movements this forced the moving parts closer together, sometimes on two levels. A look at many form movements shows the balance in one corner, the barrel in the other.

Two calibers should be mentioned here as examples of the manufacturers' eagerness to experiment: Movado's Polyplan movement (circa 1913) and LeCoultre's Duoplan (circa 1932). In the Polyplan watch not only the case but also the movement fits the curve of the wrist. The available space is used very constructively. From a rectangular ground plate two diagonal side plates descend from the short sides at very obtuse angles. The central piece carries all the moving parts of the watch except the balance, which is set on one side. On the other side are the parts for winding and setting the hands. The anchor is located between the main plate and a bent bridge. Its fork has a slight angle so as to work in the same plane as the balance wheel. Movado modified this idea of having the movement as well as the case fit the shape of the arm in their Curviplan wristwatch, circa 1932.

As the name Duoplan suggests, this movement is built on two levels. The power flow leads from the lower level to beneath a common bridge for the first wheel and the anchor. The balance wheel, of 9 mm diameter, covers almost the whole width of the long, narrow movement (dimensions: 10.5 x 23 mm). "It is astounding how the parts of the usual 11-line man's watch have been built in without creating one compressed or unhealthy point," says a 1933 report. The Duoplan watch also had a new winding system, with the very flat knob partly inset in the back of the case. "Repairs take place before the customer's eyes, because a new movement delivered by the manufacturer is simply put in."

The number of wristwatch calibers can scarcely be estimated. Classifying the Swiss watch movements and settings of 1936 gives us some 3000 calibers. Finishing this documentation took four years and required "countless researches". The "Offocial Catalog of Spare Parts for Swiss Watches" of 1949 and beyond includes in its first volume the most commonly used movements and components of Ebauches SA, in its second those of the other Swiss watch factories from Alpina to Zenith.

The shock-resistant wristwatch

The watch worn openly on an armband is particularly exposed to stress; it leads "a dangerous life", as a Swiss watch expert has said. Therefore this watch must be especially protected from shocks. "It is proved that damage to a watch, mainly caused by shock, occurs to its most sensitive mechanism, the balance. Because of its mass, the delicacy of its pinions, which are set in jewels that can break, the fineness of its adjustment, which must not be disturbed by even a mild shock, the balance is infinitely sensitive," it is stated in a 1935 report.

The increasing demand for robust wristwatches, the so-called sport watches, has doubtless increased the search for practical shock-absorbing. But the problem did not basically consist of creating the "unbreakable watch" or warding off the "strongest shocks", as advertising slogans of the Twenties claimed, but of protecting the especially sensitive parts, above all the pivots of the balance wheel that are so thin in comparison to their own weight, to the extent that they equaled the stressresistance of other parts of the watch. At first the watchmakers were not exactly thrilled by this development, for they lost a relatively lucrative income from the preparation of new balance-wheel arbors.

Until 1930 shock absorbing was one of the unsolved problems of the wristwatch. Help was sought in a variety of ways. If one built especially stable balance pivots, that had its effect on the way the watch ran. "Trumpet-shaped" pivots were indeed shock-resistant, but threatened to destroy the jewels in case of shock. In other cases the balance as a whole was mounted flexibly, protected by flexible parts of the case, or—as in the Wyler system—the balance wheel was equipped with sprung shanks. The difficulty was that not only shocks to the balance wheel from above or below had to be absorbed, but also radial shocks from the sides.

Various processes were used for a long time, especially in lower-priced watches, although tney were not fully satisfactory. It was relatively easy to protect the watch from radial shocks by having a spring-mounted jewel raised by the point of the pivot. Another transitional solution, that of using long flexible pivots, functioned fairly well against axial stress. A blow to the balance wheel was caught by a shock absorber, sparing the sensitive pivot, which only had to counteract the light pressure of the jewel spring. This system worked less well against side shocks. The stable part of the balance mounting met with a limitation from the side, but the pivot, held in a firmly built-in jewel, sagged and finally sprang back into its normal position.

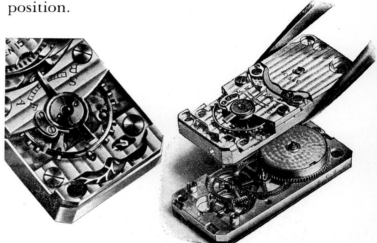

T67 *"Duoplan", the two-step watch. The winding stem is set into the back of the case.*

T68 *Size of the "Duoplan" compared to a normal wristwatch. The individual parts are those of a caliber 11 movement.*

59

More sophisticated types of shock resistance appeared shortly after 1930 and, in terms of concept, lasted quite a long time. Vertical shocks are absorbed in ways similar to that just described. To resist radial shocks the jewel now also gives way. This was made possible in the Incabloc system by mounting the balance jewel in a conical running surface, in the Super Shock Resist system by mounting the jewel in a round spring.

The functional seating of the balance arbors thus attains its goal through the elastic mounting of the balance jewels, which allows them to give way to pressure on the pivot and also to absorb the energy of axial and radial shocks. The most precise return to the original position is achieved through the power of the springs. It is also important to keep the distance and relative position of the jewels constant during the shock, so that the lubrication is not impaired. Modern shock absorbing must be completely centered, quick, and make for as exact as possible return to the original position, and must be renewable as well.

After 1950, when certain patents had expired, there were a great many similar systems that differed only in details. Two firms did the pioneer work. The Du Grenier (Erisman-Schinz) firm built the "Shock Absorber", which only absorbed axial shocks, in 1925, and carried on the develop-

Für höchste Beanspruchung!

Certina LABORA

Die Uhr des Werktätigen

genau
stossfest
wasserdicht
antimagnetisch

KURTH FRERES S.A. GRENCHEN

T69 *Symbolic advertisement for the hard-wearing, shock-absorbing wristwatch of 1944.*

T70 *The elastic case, an early (1915) attempt to protect a wristwatch from stress.*

ment to the "Shock Resist" system and then the "Super Shock Resist", which came on the market in 1933 and was still in frequent use twenty years later. The Porte-Echappement Universal firm was even more successful with their "Incabloc" shock resistance, which also was completed in 1933 after a long period of development. This system was improved in 1938 and could be built into all calibers. The production statistics speak for themselves: 1937: one million, 1952: 25 million, 1981: 700 million. Relatively late, only about 1955, shock resistance found acceptance among such Swiss manufacturers as had made wristwatches of particularly high quality. There had been a fear that this special way of mounting the balance was not compatible with extremely fine adjustment. The problem of shock absorbing became timely again in the Fifties, this time as concerned automatic watches.

The difficulties were then approached from three directions, via sprung rotor pivots, sprung masses of weight or the use of unbreakable components in the rotor mounting. "Development in this direction is still at its beginning, and it offers the constructor a wide field of activity," as H. Kühnhanss wrote in 1954 in the trade journal "The Clock".

Wristwatch chronometers

The development of the wristwatch can be seen most clearly in the way it runs. At first only selected single pieces, later small series and finally larger ones were recognized as being of chronometer quality. Until November 15, 1951 the following definition of the concept was accepted in Switzerland: "A precision watch must be so regular at various conditions and temperatures that it can receive an official certificate of operation." From then on the Fédération Horologère established the standard: "A chronometer is a finely adjusted precision watch at various conditions and temperatures, for which an official certificate of operation was issued."

The observatories and official operational testing agencies are responsible for the testing of high-precision watches. The watches are subjected to a standardized testing procedure there, and when their achievements measure up to the requirements, receive operational certificates with or without qualification. From that the precision of a given chronometer in a certain condition and at a certain temperature can be determined. If one wants to derive a mean result of the various individual tests, one can use the classification number, which weights various results against each other and sets up an "overall score".

The scores of the best wrist chronometers observed at the observatories of Neuenburg and Geneva from 1946 through 1949 can be seen in the following chart. It must be noted that the classification number from Neuenburg decreases with varying exactitude (optimum 0), while that of Geneva increases (optimum 1000).

Year	Neuenburg	Geneva
1946	6.6 (Longines)	797 (Omega)
1947	5.9 (Longines)	835 (Omega)
1948	7.3 (Zenith)	854 (Patek)
1949	7.2 (Omega)	859 (Rolex)

The official testing agencies test more briefly and less stringently than the observatories. The watches consigned to them are intended for the trade; in 1960 there were over 100,000 of them. Over the decades the standards for the title of wrist chronometer have constantly been raised. For a certificate without special notation the tolerances for the criterion of "median daily running in five positions" lay between −10 and +30 in 1920, as compared to −3 and +12 in 1961, for the criterion of "median deviation in daily running in five positions" between +/−15 in 1920 and +/−3.2 in 1961.

Because of the flexible definition of the chronometer concept, Swiss manufacturers of precision wristwatches were, until 1951, often satisfied with having outstanding single pieces or small series tested by observatories and testing agencies, while testing most of their precision watches themselves. The Rolex firm, on the other hand, strove to win official certification for their products. That explains why more than 70% of the 350,000 wristwatches certified by Swiss testing agencies between 1927 and 1954 went out of production. The path of the wristwatch to becoming a timepiece of chronometer quality can also be shown by the example of the Rolex watch:

1910. Official certificate for a wristwatch from a Swiss testing agency.

1914. First A-Chronometer Certificate for a wristwatch from the Kew Observatory.

1936. Series of 500 wristwatches receives certification.

1949. A hundred small chronometer movements receive A-certificates from Kew Observatory.

A further indication of the number of officially tested wrist chronometers is given by the following chart:

Country	1950	1956
Switzerland	circa 30,000	circa 80,000
West Germany	under 100	circa 10,000

Specialists and laymen often do not agree in deciding what is recognized as an exact watch. Defossez outlined the problem as follows: The watchmaker calls a watch good when it runs regularly and as constantly as possible despite changes of situation and temperature . . . The layman does not comprehend this consideration; he believes that a watch should give the right time, even if only approximately . . . He does not value any watch that must often be set, even when the gain or loss is very consistent. So there are two concepts of the precision of a watch: for the wearer it is determined by its daily running; for the watchmaker it is the running variation, or if you will, the unevenness of the running that shows itself."

Année	OBSERVATOIRE DE GENÈVE — Pièce isolée		OBSERVATOIRE DE GENÈVE — Série de 5 pièces		OBSERVATOIRE DE NEUCHATEL — Pièce isolée		OBSERVATOIRE DE NEUCHATEL — Série de 4 pièces	
	3 premières pièces classées	Records absolus	Meilleur résultat de l'année	Records absolus	3 premières pièces classées	Records absolus	Meilleur résultat de l'année	Records absolus
1947	Omega / Omega / Patek Phil.	OMEGA	Omega	OMEGA	Longines / Omega / Longines	Longines	Longines	
1948	Patek Phil. / Omega / Patek Phil.	Patek Phil.	Patek Phil.	Patek Phil.	Zénith / Zénith / Zénith		Zénith	
1949	Rolex / Omega / Patek Phil.	Rolex	Patek Phil.		Omega / Omega / Omega		Omega	
1950	Omega / Omega / Patek Phil.	OMEGA	Omega	OMEGA	Zénith / Zénith / Zénith	Zénith	Zénith	Zénith
1951	Omega / Omega / Rolex	OMEGA	Omega	«	Zénith / Zénith / Omega		Zénith	«
1952	Omega / Omega / Omega	«	Omega	«	Zénith / Omega / Zénith	Zénith	Zénith	Zénith
1953	Patek Phil. / Omega / Omega	«	Patek Phil.	«	Zénith / Omega / Omega	«	Zénith	«
1954	Patek Phil. / Omega / Zénith	Patek Phil.	Omega	OMEGA	Zénith / Zénith / Zénith	«	Zénith	«
1955	Omega / Omega / Patek Phil.	«	Omega	«	Omega / Omega / U. Nardin	OMEGA	Omega	OMEGA
1956	Patek Phil. / Omega / Patek Phil.	«	Patek Phil.	«	Movado / Omega / Zénith	«	Omega	«
1957	Patek Phil. / Patek Phil. / Zénith	Patek Phil.	Patek Phil.	«	Movado / Movado / Movado	«	Movado	Movado
1958	Patek Phil. / Omega / Patek Phil.	Patek Phil.	Omega	OMEGA	Movado / U. Nardin / Movado	«	Movado	Movado
1959	Patek Phil. / Patek Phil. / Omega	«	Omega	OMEGA	Omega / Movado / Omega	OMEGA	Omega	OMEGA
1960	Patek Phil. / Omega / Omega	Patek Phil.	Omega	«	Omega / Omega / Omega	«	Omega	OMEGA
1961	Omega / Omega / Omega	OMEGA	Omega	OMEGA	Longines / Longines / Omega	OMEGA	Longines	Longines
1962	Patek Phil. / Patek Phil. / Omega	«	Patek Phil.	«	Longines / Longines / Longines	Longines	Longines	Longines
1963	Omega / Omega / Longines	OMEGA	Omega	OMEGA	Omega / Longines / Omega	OMEGA	Omega	OMEGA

T74 *Results of precision competition for wristwatches at the observatories of Geneva and Neuchatel. Single pieces and small series were evaluated. Used in an Omega advertisement.*

T75 *Gold "Constellation" chronometer wristwatch with automatic winding and date, and set with jewels, made by Omega in 1960.*

T76/77 *Two chronometer wristwatches made in Germany: Left: Laco chronometer, circa 1955. Right: Bifora "unima" chronometer, circa 1965.*

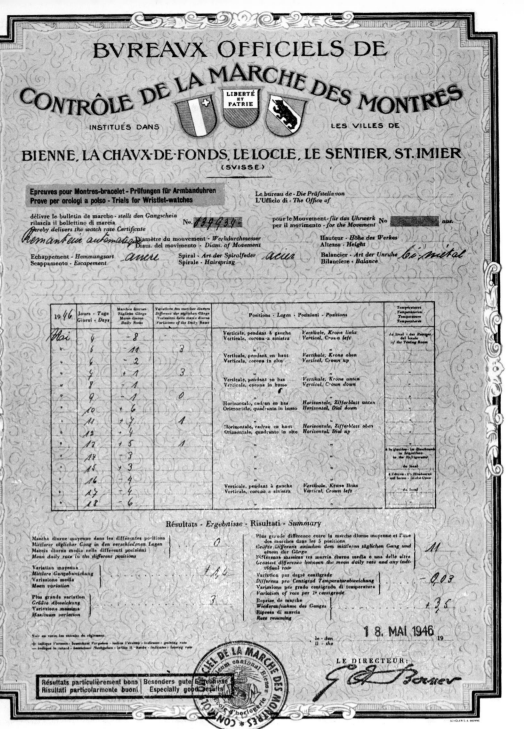

64

CHRONOMETER

Certificat

DIE JUNGHANS-UHR · THE JUNGHANS WATCH · LA MONTRE JUNGHANS

Werk / movement / mouvement	15541	Gehäuse / case / boîte	95447

wurde in der Uhrenprüfungsstelle des Landesgewerbeamts Baden-Württemberg nach den von der Physikalisch-Technischen Bundesanstalt für die Prüfung von Armband-Chronometern aufgestellten Richtlinien geprüft. Die Uhr hat diese Prüfung, die internationalen Grundsätzen entspricht, mit Erfolg bestanden.

has been tested by the Watch Testing Department of the Landesgewerbeamt Baden-Württemberg in accordance with the regulations issued by the Physikalisch-Technische Bundesanstalt for testing wrist watch chronometers. The watch has successfully passed these tests, which correspond with internationally accepted standards.

a été soumise à des épreuves par le Bureau de Contrôle de la Marche des Montres du Landesgewerbeamt Baden-Württemberg d'après les directives établies par la Physikalisch-Technische Bundesanstalt à l'égard de la vérification de chronomètres bracelet. La Montre a subi avec succès cette épreuve qui correspond à des principes internationaux.

Dieser Armband-Chronometer hat das amtliche Prüfungszeugnis	
This wrist watch chronometer has received the official watch rate certificate	5910025
Ce chronomètre-bracelet a reçu le bulletin officiel de contrôle	

UHRENFABRIKEN GEBRÜDER JUNGHANS A.G.

T80 *Early certificate issued on October 30, 1912 by the watch testing agency in Le Locle.*

T81 *Advertisement of the Pierce watchmaking firm, 1943. At this time many watch manufacturers emphasized the quality of their products by showing a certificate (here for the Pierce Chronograph). This did not mean that every Chronograph had received a certificate. It was rather meant to demonstrate what level of accuracy the advertised wristwatches were basically capable of.*

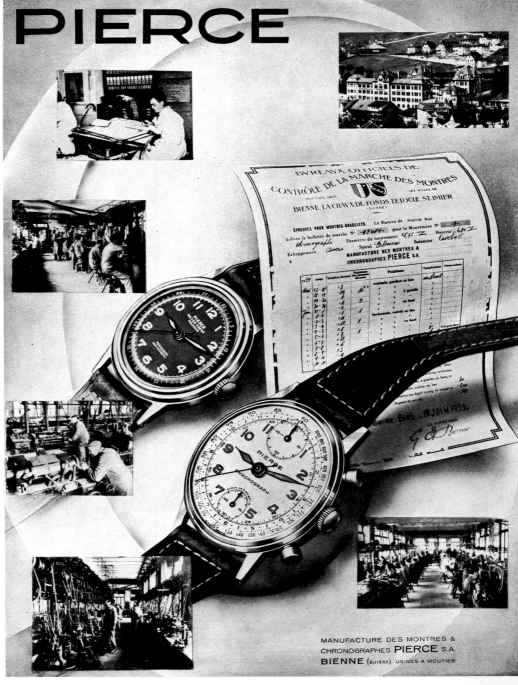

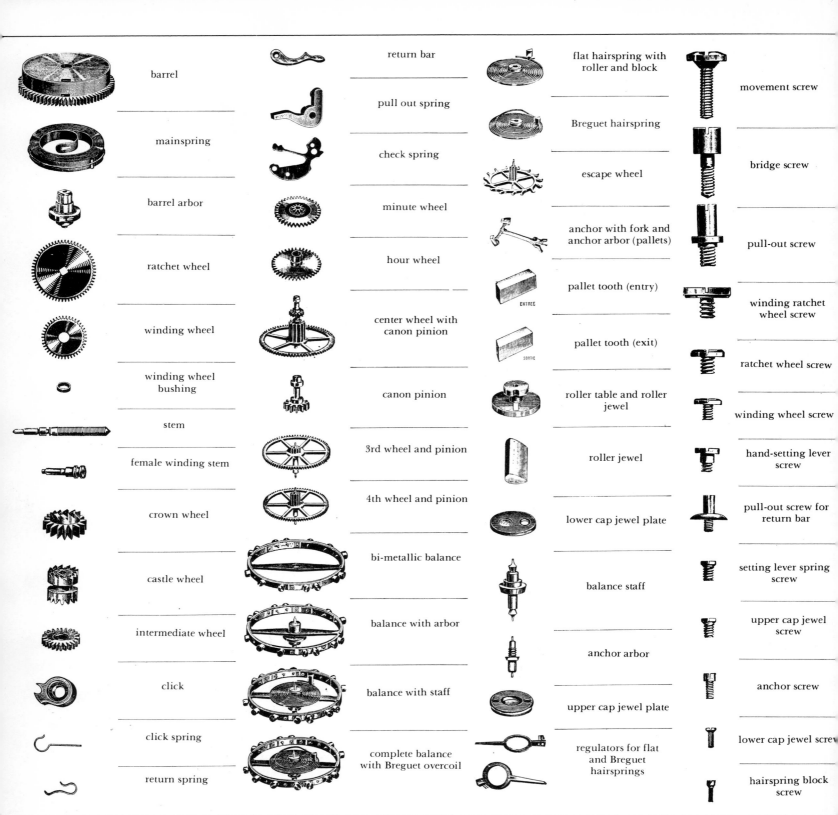

barrel	return bar
mainspring	pull out spring
barrel arbor	check spring
ratchet wheel	minute wheel
winding wheel	hour wheel
winding wheel bushing	center wheel with canon pinion
stem	canon pinion
female winding stem	3rd wheel and pinion
crown wheel	4th wheel and pinion
castle wheel	bi-metallic balance
intermediate wheel	balance with arbor
click	balance with staff
click spring	complete balance with Breguet overcoil
return spring	

flat hairspring with roller and block	movement screw
Breguet hairspring	bridge screw
escape wheel	pull-out screw
anchor with fork and anchor arbor (pallets)	winding ratchet wheel screw
pallet tooth (entry)	ratchet wheel screw
pallet tooth (exit)	winding wheel screw
roller table and roller jewel	hand-setting lever screw
roller jewel	pull-out screw for return bar
lower cap jewel plate	setting lever spring screw
balance staff	upper cap jewel screw
anchor arbor	anchor screw
upper cap jewel plate	lower cap jewel screw
regulators for flat and Breguet hairsprings	hairspring block screw

T82 *Components of the typical mechanical hand-wound wristwatch as of 1938.*

T83 *Junghans wrist chronometer with caliber J85 movement, described more fully at right.*

Construction and function of a classic wristwatch

The construction and function of a "classic" wristwatch in the 1950-60 period of development are especially easy to observe in the Junghans caliber J85. In this movement the high point and simultaneously the end of development of hand-wound movements between 8.75 and 13 lines with central second (standard movement) can be seen clearly.

The steps of development to this standard will be dealt with only to the extent that they need to be understood. Likewise, unusual phases that have fallen out of use will not be explored. Rather the movement, with its points of interest and attributes, shall stand for the approachable final state of the "simple" mechanical wristwatch. There are many similarities with the "classic" pocket watch of the Twenties and Thirties. But the movement varies in so many details from these great ancestors, and all the more in its achievements, that one cannot simply point it out as a miniature pocket watch. In addition, these wristwatch movements clearly point the way to the copmpletion of the picture with automatic winding, so that in this way they already show their own course of development in mechanical watchmaking.

The preparation of over a hundred individual parts with fitting accuracies of down to 1/100 mm and tolerances to 1/1000 mm need not be dealt with here; likewise the actual questions of repair play only a very subordinate role here. For more exhaustive treatments, written from specific viewpoints, are needed for those purposes. The maintenance of these watches should be limited to cleaning neglected watches, checking for wear and tear, and replacing defective parts with original spare parts or units such as a complete balance wheel. Moreover, the points of wear remain the same throughout the lifetime of the works, at least in terms of wanting good steady running at reasonable prices. More extensive repairs, or even "improvements" to the watch, which could be quite sensible in earlier generations of factory-made watches, or in part even necessary, usually lead to the worsening of better-quality wristwatch movements.

The Junghans caliber J85 represents the development of a round watch movement of its era. With a workplate diameter of 11.5 lines or 25.6 mm, the movement consists of the following marks of quality:

Swiss anchor escapement, precision regulatory apparatus (gooseneck fine adjustment), shock-resisting system, 17 functioning jewels, central second in the power flow, coupling winding, barrel and wheel bridges, balance mount and small anchor mount.

The movement was put on the market early in the Sixties by Junghans of Schramberg, as a chronometer with watertight steel, doublé or gold cases, with official test certificates. At that time the retail price was about 160 Marks (with steel or double ¿accent¡ case). Cost factors and the stepwise development of electric and electronic watch types gradually served to push the good, reliable mechanical wristwatch out of the market.

The plate

The basic carrying piece of the whole movement, the stable ground plate, was made of brass in about 200 work processes and gilded to protect it from oxidation. On the exploded diagram one can see a great number of screw holes, view holes and seats for the wheel train, hand-setting and winding mechanisms. One also notices the bored-out places to attach the bridges, mounting blocks, dial and other parts. The mounting pins that used to be pressed into the plate have been replaced by high points that were left when the plate was machined.

The movement

The powerplant of the watch consists of a brass barrel with teeth around the outside, a cover, and inside the mainspring, nowadays of unbreakable "Nivaflex spring steel". In the center of the barrel is the barrel arbor.

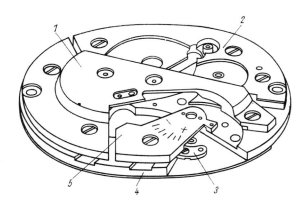

T84 *Movement layout of a small watch: 1. Wheel bridge; 2. Barrel bridge; 3. Anchor mount; 4. Movement plate; 5. balance mount.*

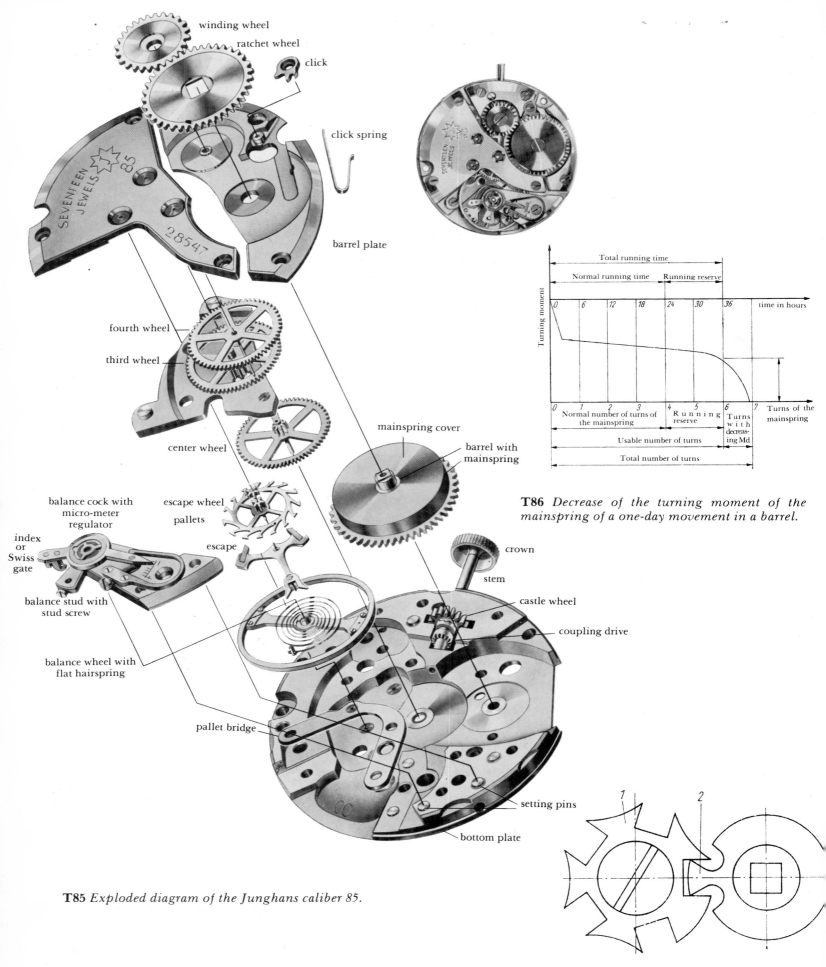

winding wheel

ratchet wheel

click

click spring

barrel plate

fourth wheel

third wheel

center wheel

balance cock with
micro-meter
regulator

index
or
Swiss
gate

escape wheel

pallets

escape

balance stud with
stud screw

balance wheel with
flat hairspring

pallet bridge

mainspring cover

barrel with
mainspring

crown

stem

castle wheel

coupling drive

setting pins

bottom plate

T85 *Exploded diagram of the Junghans caliber 85.*

SEVENTEEN JEWELS 85

28547

Total running time

Normal running time | Running reserve

| 0 | 6 | 12 | 18 | 24 | 30 | 36 | time in hours

Turning moment

| 0 | 1 | 2 | 3 | 4 | 5 | 6 | 7 | Turns of the mainspring

Normal number of turns of
the mainspring

Running
reserve

Turns
with
decreas-
ing Md

Usable number of turns

Total number of turns

T86 *Decrease of the turning moment of the mainspring of a one-day movement in a barrel.*

T87 *Maltese cross mechanism to limit the varying mainspring drive moments, with one cross and two fingers.*

1   2

68

The mainspring is attached to the barrel outside and the arbor inside via hooks and eyes. This system is dimensioned so that the spring is fully wound with about seven full turns, i.e., tensed between the two points of attachment. When fully wound, the spring, tightly coiled against itself, should fill half the barrel.

The basic characteristics of a mainspring, or of the spring and drive moment of the watch provided by the mainspring, can be read from the spring indicator line.

According to the typical indicator line, the fully wound mainspring delivers a disproportionately great drive moment, when about half wound a relatively even one, which decreases strongly with further relaxing of the spring. For this reason it would be ideal to use only the middle tension span of the mainspring to run the watch, in order to have it run evenly.

For better timepieces (pocket watches, marine chronometers, large clocks) one formerly tried to keep the driving force constant by using fusee and chain. In wristwatches this mechanism, which uses up energy as well as space, could not be used.

Only in exceptional cases has a Maltese cross mechanism been used to compensate for the varying moments of mainspring drive. Through the development of new spring materials it has been more practical to extend the running duration of a wristwatch to about 46 to 48 hours. Since the hand-wound wristwatch is wound once every 24 hours as a rule, the sharp drop in a mainspring's drive moment in its very relaxed condition no longer matters.

The disproportionately large power of the fully wound spring is considerably counteracted through the form of the outer spring hook and the winding ratchet.

The mainspring barrel is set into the works and covered by the barrel bridge, which holds it in place. The spring wheel is screwed onto the square section of the barrel arbor. Its teeth mesh with those of the crown wheel, which is held by a counter-clockwise screw because of its movement direction. When the watch is wound, the crown wheel is turned by the clockwise movement of the coupling wheel driven by the winding stem. The locking click meshes with the teeth of the spring wheel and prevents the wound-up mainspring from unwinding. The click is pushed into position by the locking spring, which at the same time allows the watch to be wound.

The shape of the click (in this case with three teeth) lets the mainspring relax slightly by itself when the winding stops, until the teeth of the click can lock into those of the spring wheel. In this way the reduction of the fully wound mainspring's drive moment is attained.

While the swing system reacts on a variably strong drive with only as little as possible variation in amplitude and thus in running changes, a further compensation for the uneven spring indicator line—one of the main problems in the construction of precisely running hand-wound watches—is attained.

The winding mechanism

When the winding stem is pressed down (its normal position), the winding spring of the coupling shaft is pulled open. When the winding stem is turned clockwise, the coupling drive that fits over the square section of the winding stem uses its angled teeth to turn the coupling wheel.

The mainspring is wound via the coupling, crown and spring wheels. Thanks to the angled teeth and their relation to the coupling bar and its spring, the stem can be turned counterclockwise to an unlimited extent, which means that one can wind the mainspring by a steady left-right turning of the knob.

The outer third of the winding stem includes a perforation to engage the angled lever. When the angled lever screw is tightened, it holds the winding stem in the watch, and when the stem is pulled out, the lever moves with it and causes a change in the coupling drive's contact. In this second position its straight spur teeth mesh with those of the hand-setting wheel. Thereby, with the help of the hand-setting apparatus (still to be discussed), the clock can be set. The angled lever spring makes this possible. The arrangement and attachment of these parts is best done on the front side of the plate, so that the winding and setting functions take place on the dial side of the plate.

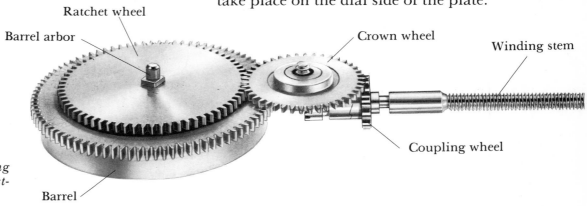

Ratchet wheel

Barrel arbor

Crown wheel

Winding stem

Coupling wheel

T88 *Wheel train of the winding system of a hand-wound wrist-watch.*

Barrel

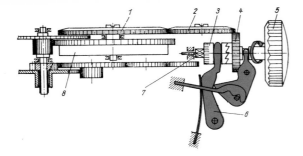

T89 *The winding coupling of a wristwatch in its position when the watch is being wound: 1. lock wheel; 2. crown wheel; 3. coupling drive; 4. coupling wheel; 5. winding knob; 6. coupling lever; 7. square block and pivot at the end of the winding stem; 8. mainspring barrel.*

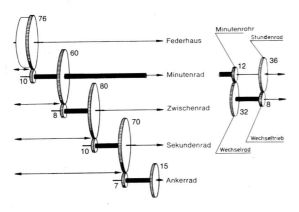

T90 *Layout of the wheels and hands of the caliber J85, with numbers of teeth on the wheels and pinions.*

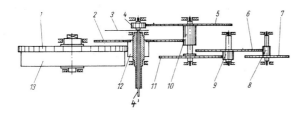

T91 *Wheel assembly for indirect drive of a central second hand: 1. first wheel; 2. second wheel; 3. sliding spring; 4. pinion of the second hand outside the power flow; 4'. long forward pivot for mounting the second hand; 5. third wheel; 6. fourth wheel; 7. anchor wheel; 8. anchor wheel pinion; 9. fourth wheel pinion; 10. third wheel pinion; 11. lower third wheel; 12. bored-out second wheel pinion; 13. barrel.*

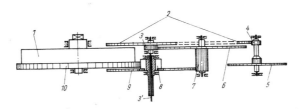

T92 *Wheel assembly for direct drive of a central second hand: 1. barrel; 2. fourth wheel; 3. fourth wheel pinion (in the power flow); 4. anchor wheel pinion; 5. anchor wheel; 6. third wheel; 7. third wheel pinion; 8. bored-out second wheel pinion; 9. second wheel; 10. first wheel; 3'. long forward pivot for mounting the second hand.*

The wheels

The wheel train translates the slow turning of the barrel into the fast turning of the anchor wheel and transmits the necessary spring moment to the escapement and balance. Normally four steps are necessary, since for each step there are 60 to 100 teeth on the wheels and 5 to 10 teeth on the pinions. The wheels are numbered in English terminology, beginning with the first (in German the barrel) wheel, then the second (minute), third ("smallbase" or "between" wheel), fourth (second) and fifth (escape or anchor) wheels.

The drives and the arbors with their mountings, the pivots, are made of hardened and polished steel, the cogwheels generally of brass. The pivots are usually seated in synthetic rubies. In this way a harder material always comes into contact with a softer one. With proper lubrication, friction and abrasion can be kept to a minimum.

The teeth of the barrel wheel mesh with those of the second wheel's pinion, which is bored out so that the pivot for the central second hand can lead through it.

The upper mounting of the barrel arbor is a perforation in the barrel bridge. Because of the low turning speed and the relatively great diameters, the barrel mountings are not highly stressed and therefore are usually not jeweled.

The second or minute wheel is riveted to the second pinion, and meshes with the third pinion. The third wheel, riveted to it, meshes with the fourth wheel's pinion, whose long pivot passes through the bored-out section of the second pinion and arbor. This small pinion is not visible in the diagram, because it is covered by the fourth wheel.

The anchor wheel, held against the wheel bridge by its mounting, is driven by the pinion of the fourth wheel.

In this arrangement the central second hand is brought into the power flow. One also calls it a "direct central second". This means of driving has been in common use for some thirty years, replacing the interim solution of having the central second hand driven from outside the power flow, which in turn superseded the eccentrically positioned second hand. In the eccentric arrangement the wheels and pinions were simply set next to each other and the upper pivot of the fourth wheel lengthened so the second hand could be mounted on it. The boring out of the second wheel's arbor was not necessary. With the central second hand outside the power flow this basic conception was maintained. But the third wheel's arbor carries on its pivot, which is lengthened to the rear, an additional wheel, flying or mounted under an additional bridge or mount, which drives another gear whose long spindle passes through the bored-out second wheel arbor.

This system requires a sliding spring to minimize the contact between wheel and spindle.

Numerous manufacturers, such as Omega, used this more involved and not always reliable system even long after the "direct central second" became established.

In terms of the height of the watch movement, the direct central second drive was a major contribution to the creation of flat watches with central second hands.

The swing system of the watch is driven via the anchor wheel.

The mounting of all the wheel assemblies must be so exact that the correct engagements will always be reestablished under all conditions after the watch has been dismantled and reassembled. This explains why plates, bridges and blocks require a material strength appropriate to the function of the watch. Very flat, sometimes too flat, movement constructions often cause trouble, if not in the original construction, then in use or when repaired.

The caliber J85 has a height of 5 mm, but there are reliably functioning watches with a height of 2 mm.

The mounting jewels for the pivots are pressed into cylindrical perforations of the plates, bridges or mounts. They can be replaced easily when necessary. In old watches of high quality the mountings were often held in chatons which were sometimes screwed in.

At times additional mounting jewels are used in wristwatches, especially on the anchor wheel pivot, to reduce axial play. Such jewels do not usually improve the watch.

T95 Manufacturer's advertisement for upper and lower jewels for watches, 1938.

In order to be able to suggest better quality in a watch in terms of a higher number of jewels, duly noted on the face, manufacturers equipped their movements with a multitude of jewels, partly without function, sinmply screwed onto the plates with small covers. Normally, though, a good non-automatic wristwatch uses 15 or 17 jewels: two bearing and cap jewels for each of the balance pivots, two bearings for the anchor pivot, two pallet jewels for the anchor, one balance lever jewel; the rest are mountings for the wheels. For the third, fourth and fifth wheels six jewels are needed, which adds up to fifteen jewels. If the pivots of the second wheel are also mounted in jewels, these two bring the total to seventeen jewels, which will satisfy the highest demands.

T93 Cyma movement with indirect central second hand (driven outside the power flow).

T94 Movado formed movement with three screwed chatons.

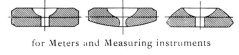
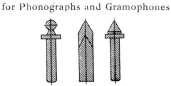
T96 International Watch movement with screwed chaton for the second wheel.

T97 Movement with a three-armed jewel plate. The top jewels have no function but are just there to provide a higher number of jewels for publicity.

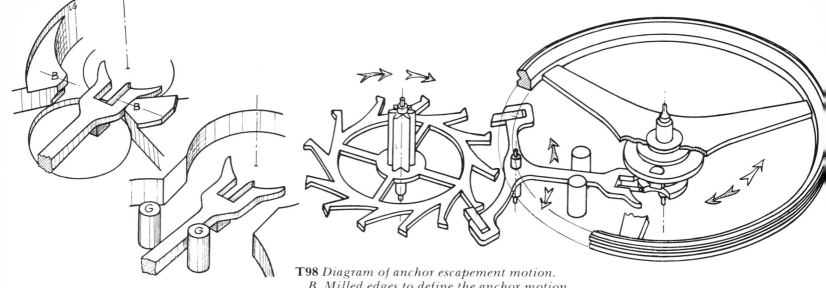

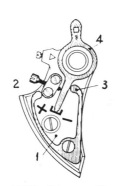

T98 *Diagram of anchor escapement motion.*
B. Milled edges to define the anchor motion.
G. Curb pins to define the anchor motion.

T99 *Fine adjustment setup for the regulating indicator: 1. Balance mount; 2. Fine-threaded screw for moving the regulating indicator; 3. Oppositional pressure (gooseneck) spring; 4. Regulator.*

TOUT POUR L'EXPORTATION
ASSORTIMENTS À ANCRE
L. JEANNERET-WESPY
SOCIÉTÉ ANONYME
LA CHAUX-DE-FONDS
SUISSE

T101 *Manufacturer's advertisement of 1938, with assortment of parts for anchor escapament with flat hairspring.*

T100 *Simple regulating indicator with spring key.*

The escapement

The energy of the wound mainspring makes the escapement function and replaces the friction energy that the swing system (balance wheel and hairspring) and the wheel train of the watch need. The wheel train thus has the job of transmitting the driving force from the mainspring to the swing system as constantly and economically as possible.

The highly developed mechanical wristwatches of the years since 1950 use only one escapement system: the Swiss anchor escapement. It consists of anchor wheel, anchor, balance wheel with spiral and plateau, regulatory equipment including the arbors, pivots, bearings, and the shock-resistance syetem. The anchor, with its two pallet jewels, intervenes in the anchor wheel's motion. The anchor is linked with the balance wheel via the anchor fork, which contacts the lever jewel and safety roller with its tines and the safety hook. In this way the driving force of the watch is transmitted to the balance wheel and the escapement function is simultaneously induced. The anchor movement is defined by two curb pins on the plate. For economic reasons these were often replaced by milled edges on the plate or the anchor mount. The curb pins, though, offer the advantage of being easier to adjust if necessary. But as production standards rose, the necessity for a supplementary adjustment disappeared. In the first decades of factory-made watches, because of the comparative lack of precision in the manufacture of watches, this adjustment had been important in the quality of the end product.

The balance system *(swing system)*

The balance system consists of the following parts:
—Balance ring
—Balance arbor with its pivots
—Plateau with lever jewel and safety roller
—Hairspring with spring roller and spring stud.
—Regulator with its arms

In all except the very simple wristwatches the balance wheel is located between the plate and the separate balance mount, so that the balance system can be removed from the movement for adjustment or repair without dismantling the whole watch.

All modern wristwatches have a self-compensating Nivarox hairspring, so that the balance no longer needs its own temperature compensation, as was required in the balance swing systems of earlier precision watches. (See pp. 52 ff)

The outer end of the hairspring is attached to the hairspring stud, which is held by a screw in a perforation of the balance mount. This means that the balance system can be detached from the balance mount by loosening this screw.

The regulator is attached to the balance block over the balance bearing. The regulator is movable, which allows a precise adjustment of the watch. In the caliber J85 the regulating indicator, with the help of a "gooseneck regulator assembly", is moved via a visible fine-threaded screw, which allows very subtle adjustment of the regulating indicator. The gooseneck regulator offers, among others, a facility for fine regulation. Most wristwatches, though, have no such setup for fine regulation other than the regulating indicator.

Very fine watches, for example those of Audemars Piguet, Patek Philippe, Vacheron & Constantin or Rolex, in part possess a fully free-swinging hairspring. The adjustment of their running is done with the help of mass screws on the balance ring, as in marine chronometers.

In our example the hairspring passes through the two curb pins at the outer end of the regulator, the hairspring bar and the spiral key. The active length of the hairspring to the hairspring roller can be changed via the spiral key by moving the regulating indicator. Lengthening the active spring length causes the watch to slow down; shortening causes it to speed up.

T102 *Parts of anchor escapement with raised hairspring.*

T103 *Universal movement, still without shock resistance.*

T104 *Zenith movement with Incabloc shock resistance.*

The play of the hairspring blade between the two limits of the spiral key must be equal. When at rest, the spring must not lie against either of the regulator arms, or be held fast between them, which would cause damage to the spring if the regulator were moved. A neat and exact passage of the spring through the key is one of the necessary requirements for good regulatory capability and thus for good running, which in turn forms the basis of fulfillment of chronometer testing conditions.

The passage of the spring through the spiral key and its attachment are especially critical spots in the swing system, and their careful formation defines the capability of the whole watch to a great degree.

How problematic the spring's passage is can be seen in the fact that for a change in running of one minute a day the active length of the hairspring need only be changed approximately one millimeter. Thus the passage of the spring through the key must not be changed by moving the regulating indicator either.

Aside from faults in the direction of the spring, deviations in the running of the watch can be caused by faulty choice of spring attachment points, changes in the driving force, changes in the friction coefficients of the balance pivots and the lubricating quality of the oil.

As a rule, temperature fluctuations do not lead to serious changes in the running of good wristwatches, because of the already described compensations. Likewise changes in air pressure generally have a negligible effect on the swing system.

A good watch should always show constant running independent of the conditions of use. Depending on its wearer, a wristwatch goes through several thousand position changes a day and is more or less strongly speeded up by arm movements, which can lead to a change in the breadth of the swing and thereby to a fault of isochronism, even if only in milliseconds. The cumulative effect of all these fluctuations can in the end make for a disturbing inaccuracy in running.

Good watches are made so that disturbing influences which have a negative effect on the running of a watch compensate for each other. In this matter one can mention the carrying compensation of Grossmann and the Caspari theorem, according to which the manufacturers proceed from the assumption that the watch will be worn on the left arm.

The shock-resistance system

It has already been mentioned that, especially after the relevant Erisman-Schinz and Porte-Echappement patents expired, there came a veritable inflation in the variety of shock resistance system arrangements and constructions.

From the late Fifties on, no manufacturer except those of the simplest wristwatches could afford not to build shockresistant movements into his watches.

The presence of a shock resistance system was usually proclaimed on the face. The manufacturers particularly liked to adorn the watch face with the name of a renowned shock resistance system such as "Incabloc" or "Super Shock Resist". Over the years this ceased to be in style, since the presence of a shock resistance system went without saying.

After thoroughgoing technical observation, the efficacy of many of the shock resistance systems that have been used must be in doubt. They do not meet the demands made on them as to protection from vertical and radial shocks, while still allowing unproblematic oil retention, to the degree that one is accustomed to in good systems.

Which shock resistance system is used in a wristwatch can be seen when one opens the rear cover and looks at the balance mount. When shock resistance is present, the cap jewel of the balance wheel is held in place by a spring. With experience, or by comparison with the illustrations in a guide book, one can recognize the type.

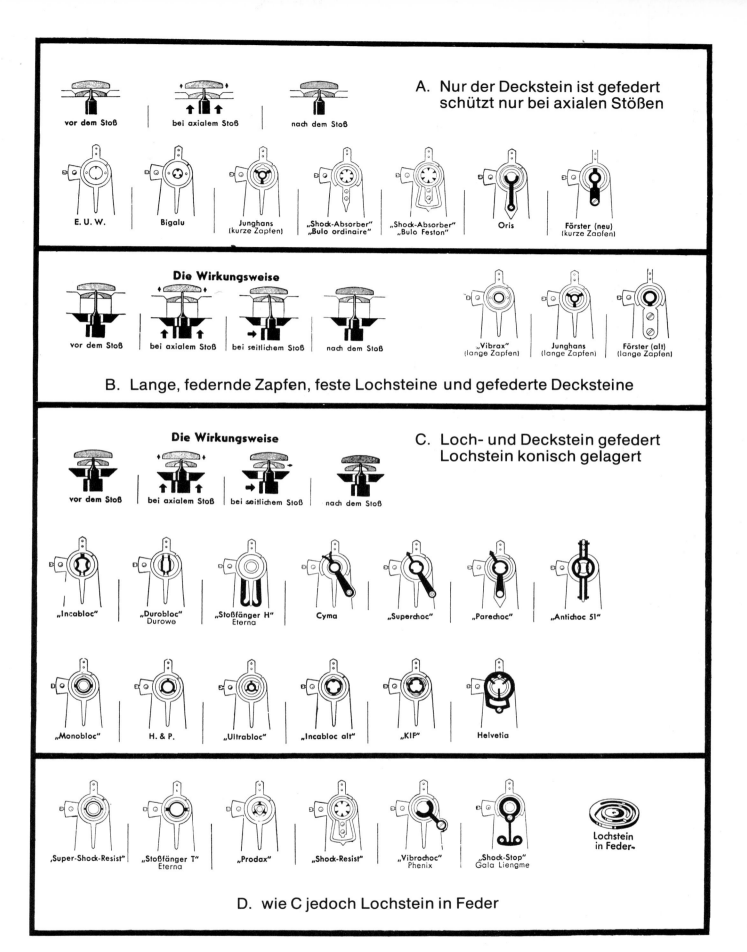

A. Nur der Deckstein ist gefedert schützt nur bei axialen Stößen

vor dem Stoß | bei axialem Stoß | nach dem Stoß

E. U. W. | Bigalu | Junghans (kurze Zapfen) | „Shock-Absorber" „Bulo ordinaire" | „Shock-Absorber" „Bulo Feston" | Oris | Förster (neu) (kurze Zapfen)

Die Wirkungsweise

vor dem Stoß | bei axialem Stoß | bei seitlichem Stoß | nach dem Stoß

„Vibrax" (lange Zapfen) | Junghans (lange Zapfen) | Förster (alt) (lange Zapfen)

B. Lange, federnde Zapfen, feste Lochsteine und gefederte Decksteine

Die Wirkungsweise

C. Loch- und Deckstein gefedert Lochstein konisch gelagert

vor dem Stoß | bei axialem Stoß | bei seitlichem Stoß | nach dem Stoß

„Incabloc" | „Durobloc" Durowe | „Stoßfänger H" Eterna | Cyma | „Superchoc" | „Parechoc" | „Antichoc 51"

„Monobloc" | H. & P. | „Ultrabloc" | „Incabloc alt" | „KIF" | Helvetia

„Super-Shock-Resist" | „Stoßfänger T" Eterna | „Prodax" | „Shock-Resist" | „Vibrochoc" Phenix | „Shock-Stop" Gala Liengme | Lochstein in Feder

D. wie C jedoch Lochstein in Feder

T105 *Various shock resistance systems and their functionings; state of the art in 1953. A. Only the cap jewel is sprung, protecting only from axial shocks; B. Long springlike pivots, firm hole jewels and sprung cap jewels; C. Cover and hole jewels sprung, the latter set conically; D. As C, but with the hole jewels sprung.*

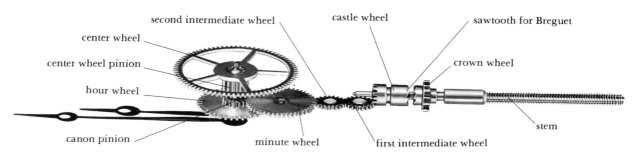

second intermediate wheel · castle wheel · sawtooth for Breguet · center wheel · crown wheel · center wheel pinion · hour wheel · canon pinion · minute wheel · first intermediate wheel · stem

T106 *Hand assembly of a wristwatch, including setting mechanism.*

T107 *Breitling wrist chronograph with twelve-hour dial; the hour hand makes two full revolutions in 24 hours.*

T108 *Breitling wrist chronograph with 24-hour dial; the hour hand makes only one full revolution in 24 hours.*

Shock resistance systems are hardly ever repaired nowadays. With a few operations one can easily replace the whole defective system, which is a better guarantee of proper functioning.

The balance wheel

The balance wheel should have as low a weight as possible so as to keep friction and danger of breaking to a minimum; on the other hand, it should have a high moment of inertia, so that the arc of its swing is influenced as little as possible by the motion of the watch and external disturbances. It must also be stable, simple to produce and thus to adjust, so that its center of gravity lies at its geometric center.

Today's watches almost exclusively use simple monometallic ring balances with two or three balance shanks, while in previous years balance wheels with screws were used. The swinging time of the system derives from the moment of inertia of the watch and the righting moment of the spring.

Both factors together allowed, until circa 1950, only the so-called normal swinger with 18,000 swings per hour, or five half-swings per second

(2.5 Hz). But watches made after 1950, such as the caliber J85, for example, also usually had normal swinging. After that, though, increasing numbers of "fast swingers" came into use, with speeds of 19,800, 21,600, 28,800 or even 36,000 swings per hour. Fast swinging is less sensitive to external disturbances, but demands better measures of elasticity in the hairspring materials, higher driving energy from the mainspring, and lubricants that are equal to the speed.

The body and spindle of the balance wheel form a main element in the swing system. The balance block, plateau and spring roller are fastened to it. The form of its pivot essentially depends on the type of shock resistance system used.

The hairspring

The hairspring has already been described as a particularly sensitive part of the swing system. In this respect one must look at its total treatment. Variations and manipulations of hairsprings should be done only by the suitably trained expert.

If a hairspring is defective, the whole swing system should be replaced, if possible, by a new one adjusted at the factory and suited to the system, to maintain the good functioning of the watch. The correct location of the watch's center of gravity derives from the cooperation of balance wheel and hairspring; in addition, static and dynamic equilibrium of the whole system is indicated.

The hands

The under-the-dial mechanism of a wristwatch with a central second hand is simple in terms of construction and function. It consists of the minute tube, the change wheel with its spindle, and the hour wheel. The bored-out minute wheel arbor is a constructional specialty. The long pivot of the second wheel arbor can be passed through it. The central second hand is attached to the outer end of the pivot. To assure exact running and disturbance-free functioning of the watch, the steel pivot must be able to move in the boring without friction. The minute wheel, making one revolution per hour, could carry the minute hand directly on its spindle if it did not need to be set.

So that the watch can always be set, the minute tube is set on the pivot of the minute wheel arbor. The drive from the minute wheel to the minute tube (formerly called the quarter tube), works with the help of a friction (sliding or rubbing) coupling.

The minute tube. via its spindle, meshes with the changing wheel. Its spindle contacts the changing-wheel bar, which is pressed into the front of the plate. The changing wheel spindle drives the hour wheel with its tube, to which the hour hand is attached. The transition from the minute tube to the hour wheel is usually in a 12:1 ratio, so that when a minute wheel has turned twelve times, the hour wheel has made one revolution. There are some special watches in which this ratio is 24:1, that is, the hour wheel revolves once in 24 hours. In such cases the hour hand shows all 24 hours of the day.

Setting the hands is done after pulling out the stem; the changed position of the angled lever connected to it affects the coupling spindle, the setting wheels, and the changing wheel and its spindle. The watch's hands can be moved in either direction this way, whereby the watch generally stops when the hands are turned backward, because the clockwork has to work against the coupling. It is usually not possible to adjust the second hand, yet some movement calibers (including the J85) include a device that stops the balance wheel, in which a small spring lies against the balance and stops it when the winding stem is pulled out. If the stem is pulled at the moment when the second hand is at the number 12, the minute hand can be set precisely and the watch started exactly at the tone of a time signal by pushing the knob in. In this way one achieves a watch time that is exact to the second.

The calendar

By using additional intermediate wheels the turning of a number disc is made possible, so that a change in the day indicator occurs after every 24 hours or two revolutions of the hour hand. If the watch is also to indicate the day of the week, another dial is needed, which also moves once every 24 hours.

A variety of constructions for changing the day of the week and month have been patented. At first they required several hours to change the position of the indicators gradually without influencing the running of the watch too strongly. One often finds transitional arrangements that take power from the movement constantly throughout the day, store it in a spring, and concentrate it around midnight to change the indicator(s).

Great progress toward easy handling of wristwatches, including those with calendars, was made by various means of correcting the date quickly by using the winding stem. In a middle position the stem acts directly on the indicator.

Showing the month or the phase of the moon is in principle not much more difficult. Further translations are required, as are manual or automatic correction facilities for the various month lengths and leap years.

T109 *View under the dial of a calendar watch with apparatus for gradual date change after 10:00 P.M.*

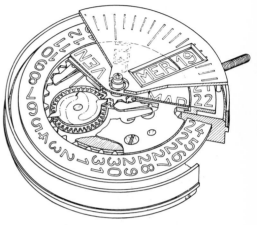

T110 *View under the dial of a calendar watch giving day of the week and of the month.*

Pillar movements for wristwatches

The pillar movement creates an arrangement that is easier to construct but has the same functions as the massive movement. All principal functions and details have already been described, so that here we need only mention the atypical simplifications.

The basic plate is a stamped sheet-metal part of sufficient thickness (about 1 mm for sheet brass or iron), with as few machined curved or flat surfaces as possible. It includes perforations for the lower mounting of the power train and the movement, as well as the escapement and balance system, plus screw-holes for the winding parts. Three or more pillars are attached to this plate, defining the distance from it to a second plate which is screwed onto the pillars; hence the name of this type of watch.

The power system with the most often-used back-and-forth winding is a simpler arrangement of the already described coupling winding in massive movements. The disadvantages are greater abrasion and, resulting from that, a shorter lifetime than the massive construction.

In winding position the winding spindle is moved by the square block of the winding shaft and moves the winding wheel and ratchet wheel via the intermediate wheel. This ratchet wheel is a movable cover of the barrel, which carries the inner hook for the winding spring on a central tube. The locking spring contacts the outside of the ratchet wheel directly. The barrel arbor is made as a screw. One can screw it through the upper plate. So dismantling the barrel to replace the mainspring can by done simply by loosening this one screw. The barrel and the ratchet wheel are then removed from the movement sideways between the pillars.

When the stem is pulled out, setting the hands takes place via the second position of the winder. The angled lever is activated by an incision in the winding stem to arrest the winder, so that its contact with the ratchet wheel is disconnected, and setting the hands can be done by the setting wheel via the intermediate changing wheel. The setting wheel moves the hour and minute wheels, which are linked by a friction connection with the minute wheel.

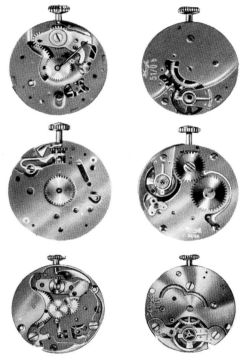

T111 *Kienzle pillar works of 1956: above, caliber 51 with hook anchor; center, caliber 54/7 with hook anchor; below, caliber 48/15 with "Kienzle anchor" including patented profiled jewels.*

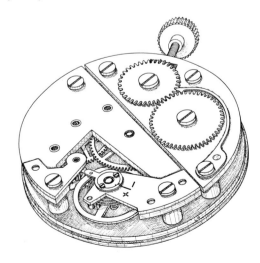

T112 *Diagonal view of a pillar movement with hook anchor.*

78

The wheel train, consisting of the usual first through fifth wheels, is mounted under a covering plate that extends almost completely over the works. The minute wheel, linked with the hands, is centrally mounted. In the Roskopf system this construction is simplified even more, so that a central minute wheel, and thus one of the running wheels, was not needed. From the setting wheel a spindle, firmly linked with the barrel cover, led to the hand apparatus. This Roskopf system offers a disconnection between the coupling and the back-and-forth winding concerning the directions of winding and of setting the hands.

The front pivot of the second wheel is lengthened for the eccentric second hand, while for the central second hand arrangements like those of the massive movement are used. The central second outside the power flow was achieved by means of a bored-out minute wheel arbor and perforated second pivot, and the central second hand within the power flow (the direct second) was the result of variations on the usual arrangements. They have to stay as simple as possible, and require as few additional parts as possible, in order to keep the cost of assembly low.

The escapement and balance system of pillar movements

The escapement and balance system with Swiss anchor escapement—hook anchor escapement in very simple watches—is very similar to those of massive movements. The anchor is mounted against the base plate with a simple anchor block. On the plate bars are placed to limit the anchor's motion. The balance system is built much as in massive watches.

The assembled works are not as stable as those of massive movements, but with proper adjustment and care the results of running a pillar watch can be about as good as of a watch with massive movement. For that reason a number of constructions have been developed in the last few decades in which clear differences between the two different types of construction are scarcely possible. Elements of massive and pillar movements have been combined and put to use.

With very simple hook anchors the balance mounting is not fitted with hole and cap jewels; steel bearings, or occasionally synthetic rubies and steel points, are used on the balance spindles. Movements of this kind—in part automatically mounted—are produced at such low prices that for this reason alone it does not pay to repair them. If worse results, with deviations of about a minute per day, are typical of such watches, then it is mainly because of the cheap hairsprings used, which do not have the good qualities of the aforementioned Nivarox springs.

Simple watches of this type of construction can be regarded as reliable timepieces, but unfortu-

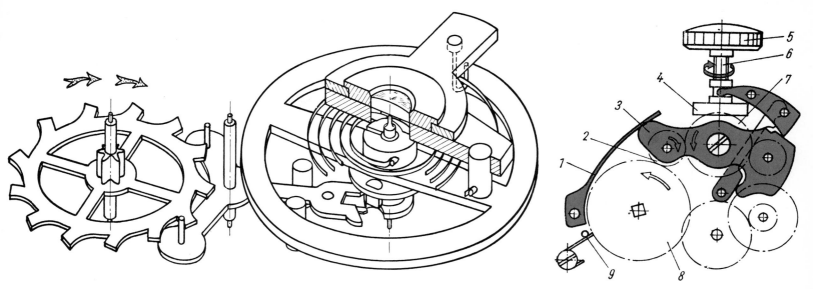

T113 *Schematic drawing of a hook anchor escapement.*

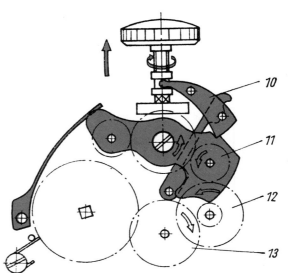

nately their lifetime and possibility of being repaired are reduced.

The wristwatch with cylinder escapement

Along with the jeweled and hook anchor escapements there is a third type used in wristwatches: the cylinder escapement.

This type of watch escapement, invented at the beginning of the Eighteenth Century, turns up most often in very early or very cheap newer wristwatches.

In Germany in particular, the cylinder escapement was produced until the Forties.

In its usual form the movement with cylinder escapement is similar to that with anchor escapement. But on close inspection it becomes clear that the "anchor" of the cylinder watch is directly in the balance wheel spindle. This spindle consists of A threaded steel tube. It is mounted with two plugs with trunnions that, as in the anchor watch, often run in jewel mountings. The watch with cylinder escapement also has a cylinder wheel instead of an anchor wheel; this is noticeable because of its highly set teeth.

For many reasons the running attainments of a cylinder watch are far below those of a watch with anchor escapement; thus the cylinder escapement has been given up in view of the ever-increasing demand for watches as exact as possible.

T114 *Back-and-forth winding: top, winding position; bottom, setting position. 1. winding spring; 2. winding wheel; 3. Rocker; 4. Winding spindle with square hole; 5. winding knob; 6. winding shaft; 7. middle wheel; 8. ratchet wheel; 9. ratchet spring; 10. angled lever; 11. hand-setting wheel; 12. changing wheel with spindle; 13. Hour wheel.*

T115 *The cylinder escapement: A. lower movable mount; B. balance wheel mount; C. cylinder wheel mount; E. second wheel; K. lower covering plate; P. plate; R. Regulating indicator; S. upper covering plate; X. cylinder wheel; Z. cylinder; r. buffer on the balance mount; e. swing pin on the balance ring.*

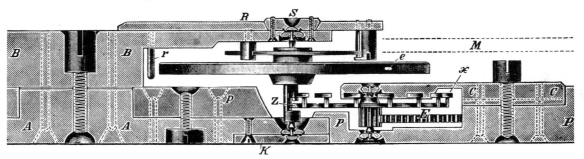

79

Automatic watches

Self-winding pocket watches

The automatic watch fascinates, perhaps because there is something of "perpetual motion" about it, a movement that just runs and runs, apparently without problems. Earlier generations must also have felt this way; otherwise the "montre perpetuelle" concept would not have come into use for the pocket watch with automatic winding.

Abraham Louis Perrelet (1729-1826) was the first to turn this idea into reality. Around 1770 he built the first pocket watch with automatic winding, finding in the process a solution, later called the rotor principle, that influenced the development of the automatic wristwatch decisively too. Perrelet mounted the swinging mass of the winding system centrally and did not limit the swinging arc. Just as in later wristwatches, both directions in which the rotor swung were used to wind the drive spring. Two latch wheels set next to each other equalized the movements. This rotor principle, though, seems not to have proved itself very well in the pocket watch, where the moving impulses are generally up and down. In any case, Perrelet's concept was not taken up by other masters who built self-winding pocket watches.

Abraham Louis Breguet (1747-1823) also worked on this technical problem. He created many forms of the pocket watch with automatic winding, which he named "Perpetuelle", and all were based on his chosen principle of construction. Unlike Perrelet, he decided on an up-and-down swinging weight on a lever arm. In the later Perpetuelles that he built, Breguet was able to decrease the winding system's need for space considerably, so that these watches were flatter. In comparison with other watchmakers, he built relatively many pocket watches of this type, 31 pieces just between 1787 and 1791, a few of which, to be sure, were completed only after 1800.

The idea of the automatic pocket watch was especially alluring toward the end of the Eighteenth Century, as shown by the individual pieces preserved in museums and collections. The swinging masses take various forms; Breguet's were heart- or hammer-shaped, and they were often made of gold or platinum because of their high specific gravity.

The production of larger series of automatic pocket watches came about only near the end of the Nineteenth Century. The "Perpetuale" of Lohr can be pointed out as an example. This system, patented in England in 1878, was produced in

T116 *Automatic pocket watch with rotor, by Louis Perrelet, circa 1770. Only a century and a half later was this concept taken up again in the consitution of modern automatic wristwatches.*

T117 *Lohr's "Perpetuale", circa 1890. The lever arm with swinging weight is clearly seen. This winding system works only by up-and-down motions, appropriate to its being carried in the pocket.*

T118 *John Harwood (1893-1965). His invention, the automatic Harwood system wristwatch, decisively influenced the development of the automatic wristwatch.*

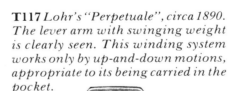

Switzerland from 1884 on. The effective element was again a one-armed lever with a swinging weight, mounted at a right angle to the watch, a kind of seesaw like that of the pedometer. A square shape was chosen for the case of Lohr's watch because it would set as vertically as possible in the pocket, so that the winding system could function fully.

Automatic winding remained a curious rarity in the pocket watch, more a technical joke or a refined accessory than a general procedure. It was different with the wristwatch. Unlike the pocket watch, it was often not laid aside at night, so that regular winding did not easily become a habit. This presumably strengthened the wish to own a watch that wound itself.

Then too, one wears the wristwatch on a part of the body that changes its position constantly. Depending on activity and temperament, one moves one's left arm from 7,000 to 40,000 times a day. It was a problem for the pocket watch that the moving impulses often were not sufficient to wind the spring; for the wristwatch ways had to be found to dampen the mechanism sufficiently from all too vigorous motions so that they would not damage the watch and, in particular, the winding system. Pocket watches with automatic winding were gentlemen's watches and often quite sizable. But the later phase of the mechanical wristwatch also included the decorative automatic watch for the lady.

The Harwood system

In 1922 trade journals were already telling of a wristwatch with automatic winding that was being developed in England, and on October 16, 1923 John Harwood (1893-1965) and Harley Cutts applied for a patent in Switzerland as well; it was granted on September 1, 1924, as number 106,583. In 1926 Harwood went into partnership with A. Schild AG. He also received much support from Walter Vogt, founder of the Fortis watch firm. Schild developed the first Harwood system automatic watch and Fortis AG presented the new device at the Basel Clock Fair. Today it is generally accepted that Harwood's patent provided the concept that opened the way for the later worldwide spread of the wristwatch with automatic winding.

As a soldier in World War I Harwood, a trained watchmaker, recognized the unreliability of the wristwatches then available and asked himself how to improve the situation. Like many another inventor, he did not dwell on what had already been done in the field, but searched independently for a solution. He had to overcome many difficulties before he was able to persuade Swiss manufacturers to take up his ideas.

"John Harwood, unlike most inventors, was not satisfied to offer ideas or approximate sketches; he made a prototype of his automatic wristwatch, which was well thought out and masterfully constructed . . . Along with his prototype he brought along the drawings of all the special parts for his system, thereby making the manufacturers' job much easier," Peter Aebi reported in the New Watchmakers' Journal in 1966. At first Harwood chose a round movement of 10.5 lines as his basis. On account of the winding system it was housed in a caliber 13 case. A few months later he made a second prototype, a movement of 8.75 lines in an 11 case.

A new feature of his invention was the particular way of transmitting the swinging weight's impulse to the winding wheels inside the closed case of the watch. Harwood located the movable winding weight very stably in the center of the movement, on both the bridge side and the dial side. The center of movement is the arbor of the minute wheel. The moving part of the winding mechanism, shaped like a segment of a circle, can describe an angle of about 130 degrees. Too-vigorous movements of the swinging weight make it contact buffers on both ends, rather like the well-known railroad spring buffers. In this watch the automatic winding works in only one direction.

A steel plate, turning around the same axis as the swinging weight, is linked to the weight by spring pressure. A regulating screw allows it to even out the power of the friction between the two elements. When the watch is to be wound, the friction plate accompanies the swinging weight and transmits the power to the mainspring via various inter-

T119 *The Harwood watch, easily identified by the lack of a stem winder and by the dot over the 6. The hands are set by pressing the glass. When a red dot appears, the power connection between the works and the hands is in effect.*

T120 *A look inside this automatic watch. The two buffers at the sides of the swinging weight are readily visible. The cogwheel at the top serves to set the hands through the glass, which cannot be seen here.*

mediate components. The more strongly the spring is wound, the stronger its resistance becomes. From a certain point on, the connection between the plate and the swinging weight becomes a sliding coupling. The mass swings farther without being able to transmit the power, so that the mainspring cannot be overwound.

But Harwood did not want to create only the automatic wristwatch, but also the dust-free watch case. To make this case as impervious as possible, he omitted the winding stem and used a watch glass that could be turned in either direction to activate a complex setting mechanism. A red dot, in the place where the second hand was usually attached, shows after setting to indicate that the power connection between movement and the hands exists again. His aligned concept of sheltering the movement from outside influences was certainly right, as other developments of the time show, but this solution of Harwood's did not catch on because it was obviously too complex.

Even today there are differences of opinion as to why the Harwood automatic watch was not a success. Too-high price, management errors, and above all the effects of the world economic crisis, say some, while others note technical production difficulties and conceptual weaknesses. Problems arose, especially because of the many screws that

were to hold the automatic movement together. Insufficiently tightened screws in works with buffered swinging weights loosen in time and fall into the works. Then too, the Harwood, because it lacks a special winding apparatus, can only be set in motion when the mainspring has wound down by vigorous shaking, and it needed even more vigorous motion to keep it going for twelve hours.

Haywood was not the first to construct a wristwatch with automatic winding. In 1922 the Leroy system wristwatch already existed. According to the fashion of the times, watches of this kind were built into pointed-oval cases, giving the swinging weights relatively little freedom of movement. Individual attempts were made to combine long, narrow works with winding elements set to the side. Another attempt consisted of using the mass of the movement itself for winding via a lever or ball drive, making the movement movable in its longer dimension inside the case ("Rolls", "Wig-Wag"). The moving space was limited to a few millimeters, and the position of the dial had to be changed.

Another of Harwood's ideas was for a wristwatch that could be wound by a spring bow on the case (Autorist). Later considerations led to utilizing the motion of outer parts of the watch, such as closing a protective lid, for automatic winding, an idea

T121 *Earliest known construction of an automatic wristwatch: the Leroy system of 1922. Left, front view; right, works. Unlike the Harwood, only a few examples were made.*

T122 *The automatic watch with swinging weight limited at the side was the prevailing solution of the Forties. In the illustrated example from 1944 a spiral spring is the damper.*

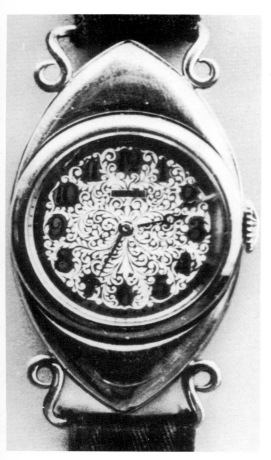

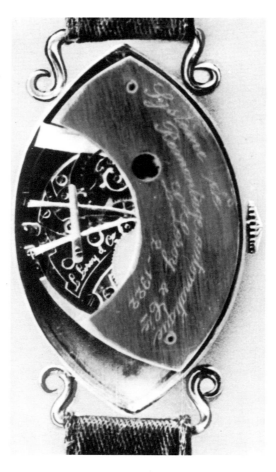

82

that was realized in similar form in many box-watches. Another concept sought to press a movable lid against the watch while wearing it on the wrist in such a way as to set the winding apparatus in motion. All in all, there were many ideas, but scarcely a progressive solution and only small production statistics. Thus today the first automatic watches—save for the Harwood itself—are extremely hard to find.

The following list of early automatic wrist-watches may be of interest to the collector:

1930 Rolls
1931 Glycine
1931 Wig-Wag
1931 Autorist
1931 Rolex Perpetual

Among those listed the Rolex Perpetual holds a special place. Its conception led to the second phase of automatic watches. The rotor principle chosen in 1931, which had also been Perrelet's choice 150 years before, was to be a decisive landmark of the perfected automatic wristwatch of later decades. The improved watch with automatic winding also showed that, despite interesting attempts, the wristwatch that ran for eight days could not establish itself.

On the way to perfection

The Englishman John Harwood and the German Hans Wilsdorf (1881-1960) stand at the beginning of the history of the wristwatch with automatic winding as its innovators. In retrospect it can be seen that the Thirties were characterized by internal preliminary work and individual, rather short-lived projects. The next decade brought proof of the workability of the automatic watch, while the breakthrough on the watch market took place after 1950. This developmental process can no longer be attributed to individual persons or factories, but appears as a unified achievement of the entire Swiss watch industry. Hundreds of patent applications within the relatively short span of fifteen years indicate the almost passionate search for workable solutions.

The experts were at first in agreement as to how the automatic watch of the future should be made, but the technical and economic conditions allowed only a gradual striving for this goal. It was agreed that this watch should be less sizable, above all flatter, a problem that Breguet had already tried to solve in the pocket watch. The justification of this requirement in Harwood's example is clear, for the parts of the automatic winding take up almost twice as much room as the actual movement: the watches had movements twice as high and, because of the greater diameter of the swinging weight, approximately tripled volume.

This striving for a flatter watch at first hindered the acceptance of the technically desired rotor principle, for where was one to find room in the case for certain parts of a watch with a limited swinging weight? Only gradually were ways found to set the automatic part into the case. Now the automatic wristwatch was no longer twice as high, but only a good third higher than the usual watch, How far this development toward ever-flatter (and simultaneously ever-smaller) automatic wrist-watches was pushed is documented by a construction of Jean Lasalle (Geneva, 1978). This caliber had a diameter of 20 mm and a height of 2.08 mm.

A further requirement was the simplification of construction and repair. Therefore the automatic works were set up as a closed unit, a block that could be removed quickly from the movement, worked on separately, and reinstalled simply. Constructors' efforts to limit the number of individual parts of the winding point in a similar direction. The reduction of these parts from sixteen to seven was reported in 1954 by Mido for his Powerwind system; only three screws fasten the simply built automatic part to the basic movement, as Girard Perregaux reported of the Gyromatik in 1956.

The question of working security takes on a new dimension psychologically in the automatic watch. Disturbances are particularly feared exactly because one imagines one has a perpetually, "eternally" running watch. One wanted to be modern and yet secure in conventional technology; therefore the automatic wristwatch should also be capable of being wound by hand—a conceptual anachronism, as Harwood already knew.

This demand was also supported by the manufacturers, all the more so in that the connection of winding and hand setting was already customary in the wristwatch. Economic considerations are also involved, for as many parts of existing calibers as possible should also be usable in the watch with automatic winding. All too often watches made to be hand-wound were simply equipped with additional automatic winding. Later both possibilities, hand and automatic winding, were already considered when a new caliber was being designed.

It took some years before the mistrust of the automatic watch had disappeared. This also explains why the consumers in early times valued a watch with a central second hand—because one could see at a glance whether the watch was still running. The development of automatic watches with winding indicators, like those of marine chronometers, between 1950 and 1955 points in the same direction. Zodiac and Jaeger-LeCoultre introduced this in 1948/49, and in 1954 Buren offered the smallest automatic movement with a winding indicator.

These fears naturally had a real basis, for in the early years there were many weak points: in

T123 *In 1931 Rolex used the rotor principle and steadily improved its functioning ability. A notable specialty: the automatic watch in a watertight case (Oyster Perpetual). A 1941 advertisement.*

T124 *Felsa automatic caliber with rotor turning 360 degrees, 1944.*

T125 *Dial and movement of the first automatic wristwatch by Patek Philippe, 1953. The rotor is made of 18 karat gold.*

watches with limited swinging space there were the buffering spring elements, with the rotor the central position of the swinging weight. Often the material of the steel pinions could not stand the demands on it, or the location of the winding wheels, to name just a few examples. In addition, the non-automatic watch had become more and more reliable over the years, and the automatic watch had to catch up.

A few words still need to be said about the precision of the automatic wristwatch. In theory their advantages include the fact that the mainspring is always at the same strength, so that a relatively even spring power can work. It took a lot of effort, though, before an automatic type was found that proved capable of resisting the actions of a lively wearer and yet reacted sensitively on less vigorous people. The anticipated running reserve often could not be attained, that is, the spring was only half-wound. Heavier swinging weights were to help. At first brass shells were filled with lead, later swinging weights were made of metals with heavier specific weights than the 18 karat gold that was also in use.

Early automatic watches had no basic movement separate from the winding system; only gradually were works and winding paired. This increase in the diameter of the movement in turn allowed greater size for the barrel and balance. Then the general progress in watch technology came to benefit the high-quality basic movement. Around 1950 the automatic watch was in a price range about 80 to 100% higher than a comparable hand-wound watch.

In the last years before World War II systems with centrally located but laterally limited swinging weights were regarded as the standard solution, using swinging distances of 120 to 150 degrees. The automatic winding usually worked only in one direction. In a publication of the Le Locle Watch Museum, automatic movements of this kind made in the decade between 1938 and 1948 were documented as representative of the Swiss watch industry:

Year	Brand	Works diameter (lines)	Height (mm)
1938	A. Schild	11.25	5.20
1939	Eterna	12	5.30
1942	Eterna	9.75	4.50
1943	Cyma	10.5	6.00
1943	Omega	13	4.55
1944	Tissot	12.5	5.05
1944	A. Schild	11	5.50
1947	Certina	11.5	5.45
1948	Zenith	13	4.90

Deviating special forms were developed by Buren (1944) with decentral swinging weight, and by Pierce (1945). Here the moving mass was successfully governed by two pillars in a system based on the construction of stamping machines.

Three basic extra parts mark the wristwatch with automatic winding: swinging weight, reduction apparatus and winding limitation. In all but a few special cases the swinging weight of the wristwatch was located centrally. Differences exist

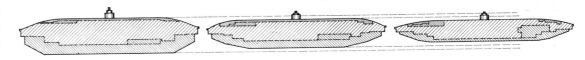

in terms of whether this weight describes an arc or a full circle (rotor). Both types can be laid out so that two directions, or only one, can be used for winding. The reduction apparatus has the task of turning the fast but relatively powerless motion of the swinging weight into a slower but stronger and more effective turning of the mainspring.

To prevent the overwinding of the mainspring, the Harwood solution of using a sliding spring was refined; better materials and lubricants have helped. The outer end of the spring is not hooked to the wall of the barrel, but pressed through an inserted dragspring. It is the mainspring that brakes, while the dragspring serves to increase the pressing. A similar effect is achieved by thickening the outer end of the mainspring, or by using a differential drive.

After 1950 the rotor working in both directions became more and more popular. Thereby the free turning of the swinging weight could be done away with. Sliding bearings were replaced by ball bearings with 5 to 7 balls, which could be held at proper intervals by a distance cage. The Eterna of 1949 was the first automatic watch with a rotor on ball bearings. The advantages of this solution are undeniable: the swinging weight is mounted unbreakably, the ball bearing does not wear itself out, unlike an axle, and the rotor reacts sensitively to changes in condition.

The use of the rotor that works effectively in both directions required complex changes in the winding works. A sensible and at the same time sturdy mechanical equalizer was necessary to reverse the impulse in one direction, as the mainspring can only be wound in one direction. Several solutions were possible, including change drives, couplings working in one way, or eccentric drives.

The essential stages of development of the functionally true automatic wristwatch can be summed up in three representative movements:

1931   Rolex Perpetual   7.5 mm high
Oldest automatic wristwatch with rotor, Winding in one direction, Relatively small basic movement, Indirect central second hand, Impermeable case, A concept pointing into the future.

1942   Felsa   5.80 mm high
First movement with rotor effective in both directions, Movement and swinging weight greatly alike in mass, Simple separation of winding and basic movement, Direct central second hand, The most influential model of the post-1940 era.

1953   Patek-Philippe   5.40 mm high
First automatic wristwatch of this brand; 18 karat gold rotor, Self-winding, equipped with 12 jewel bearings, Various ball bearings, High storage ability in a short time, Gyromax balance without screws, The high-karat achievement of the Fifties.

An informative documentation of Swiss automatic movements of the times before and after 1950 was published by Prof. B. Humbert, of the Biel Watchmaking School, in the Swiss Watchmaker's Journal. From 1953 on the study was continued over several years. Functions of the various movements are described very thoroughly and illustrated by many drawings. The same author published all of these reports in book form in 1960. In 250 pages the presentation deals with more than 100 automatic calibers, with 300 illustrations.

In the following years too there appeared many new variations of the automatic wristwatch. A particularly interesting new treatment was the Mikro-Rotor that was built into calibers 12 and 12.5 in the late Fifties. While the classic rotor needs a large turning circle, which requires a second working level above the basic movement, the micro-rotor was integrated into the actual movement, rather like a balance wheel of rather large diameter. Self-changing calendars in watertight and dustfree cases with central second hand, and sometimes also winding indicators, were already part of the usual equipment of highquality automatic watches before 1960. In the following years automatic winding appeared in connection with other complexities, in wrist chronographs and alarm watches, or in wristwatches with "eternal" calendars.

Beyond that, the tendency toward flat, even ultra-flat, automatic movements increased, so that total heights between two and three millimeters were attained.

Step by step the automatic wristwatch became a consumer product for everyone, increasing quality along with sinking price. One Swiss factory has made over 20 million pieces in one automatic caliber alone. In addition, lower-quality movements (Roskopf movements) were equipped with automatic winding. In the automatic watch, technically ever further refined, and linked with progress that could be achieved in production, the watch manufacturers saw their most effective means in the competition with electronic watches for a portion of the market. As for the mechanical watch's future, the answer was still to be heard in the mid-Seventies: the automatic wristwatch is the future.

The woman's automatic watch

The wide variety of formed movements for women's wristwatches inspired various attempts to achieve automatic winding with the help of a laterally mounted swinging weight. This led to a long list of patents but, just as in other considerations of combining formed movements with round swinging weights, to no lastingly useful solutions. The automatic woman's watch too is thus built on a round basic movement.

The basic problem, that a technical system's degree of effectiveness decreases when the dimensions are reduced, had long been known, and not just by watch technicians. The winding effect of a swinging weight changes not only in linear terms, but in the square of the diameter reduction. Thicker swinging weights, one possible solution, had the fatal side effect of making the small watch look even bulkier. The other way seemed more rewarding: increase the usable production as a whole. So the rotor working in both directions became common in women's watches sooner than in men's.

The ball-bearing rotor was originally intended for women's watches and was transformed to men's watch calibers only two years later. Further positive effects were achieved by minimizing transitional losses, such as by using other parts instead of a ratchet under spring pressure, which absorbed a relatively large amount of energy.

Individual automatic calibers usable for women's watches before 1950 were relatively large and measured between 9.25 and 9.75 lines. From them arose two standard sizes, movements of 7.75 caliber and, in the Sixties, also those of 6.75. The most commonly used caliber of women's automatic watch was the 7.75, which after 1960 had a total height between 4.30 and 4.80 mm. Over the years various manufacturers could meet the challenge of making the smallest automatic wristwatch. In 1967 a six-line movement by A. Schild won the title.

Women's watches in general are less popular among collectors. For the technically versed admirer, though, the woman's automatic wristwatch from its early predecessors to its latest phase of mass production can be a charming collector's item.

Technology of self-winding watches

In discussing the hand-wound wristwatch it was noted that a spring tension as constant as possible was an essential requirement for the regular running of a mechanical watch.

The automatic winding represents an important step on the way to fulfilling this requirement, as its various stages of development will show.

After 1950 a winding system had finally prevailed in which a rotor can turn without limit in both directions and wind the spring in the process.

Differences appear in various brands because of rotor size and position (central rotor, eccentric central rotor, microrotor), the mounting of the rotor (journal or roller bearings), and the kind of drive that converts the two-way motion of the rotor into one winding direction (cogwheel, free-running or eccentric converter).

The winding mechanism generally is made of the following parts:

1. Driving force (swinging weight or rotor)
2. Conversion drive
3. Reduction drive.
4. Automatic lock.
5. Apparatus for preventing the overwinding and breaking of the mainspring.

These components will now be examined more thoroughly, and important technical aspects will be explicated.

The driving force

In automatic winding the free-turning rotor has replaced the formerly-used pendulum-type swinging weight.

The rotor must have as great a weight as possible, but must not be too thick or take up too much space, and must be free to turn without touching the movement or case.

Since the wristwatch is exposed to particular mechanical pressures, the rotor must be mounted so that its free and easy motion is possible under all wearing conditions, and so that the rotor and mounting are insensitive to shock.

To give the rotor, usually a half-round segment, as much mass as possible, the rotor ring is generally made of a heavy alloy such as tungsten.

Especially fine products also use 18- to 21-karat gold, which has a high specific weight.

The rotor is mounted on either journal or ball bearings. Regarding journal bearings, we must differentiate between:

—Systems in which the rotor is attached to an axle, both of whose pivots are set in bearings such as jewels (T 128). This method has the disadvantage of great height, which counteracts the building of flat wristwatches.

1943
Caliber 13''
Swinging mass with spring buffers. Winding in one direction. Small second hand.
Height 4.55 mm.

1944
Caliber 12½''
Swinging mass with spring buffers. Winding in one direction.
Height 5.05 mm.

1944
Caliber 12½''
Off-center turning of the mass. Similar construction to step counter systems. Height 5.20 mm.

1945
Caliber 11''
Linear motion of winding mass. A toothed rod winds the mainspring via the winding wheel. Height 5.00 mm.

1947
Caliber 11½''
Swinging mass with spring buffers. Winding in one direction. Height 5.45 mm.

1948
Caliber 9¼''
Rotor on roller or ball bearings. Winding in both directions. Height 5.35 mm.

1950
Caliber 12''
Swinging mass with spring buffers. Winding in one direction. Height 5.70 mm.

1952
Caliber 7¾''
Rotor on roller or ball bearings. First caliber of the Etarotor type. Second out of the center. Three million produced. Height 5.30 mm.

1953
Caliber 12½''
Rotor with two winding directions. System with setting drive. Second out of the center. Height 6.05 mm.

1956
Caliber 12½''
Micro-rotor integrated into the movement. Two winding directions. Height 4.30 mm.

1959
Caliber 11½''
Rotor with two winding directions. Ball bearings. Height 5.40 mm.

1959
Caliber 13''
Rotor mounted on the outside of the movement. Two winding directions. Height 4.50 mm.

1959
Caliber 12½''
Rotor with two winding directions. Winding wheel system with planetary drive. Modular construction. Height 4.50 mm.

1962
Caliber 12½''
Micro-rotor integrated into the movement. Two winding directions. Extra flat. Height 3.20 mm.

1963
Caliber 6¾''
Rotor with two winding directions. Winding wheel system with planetary drive. Modular construction. Height 4.25 mm.

1964
Caliber 6¾''
Rotor with two winding directions. Ball bearings. Click spring wheels. Height 4.60 mm.

1966
Caliber 11½''
Setting action with small ruby cylinders. Height 5.20 mm.

1969
Caliber 13¾''
Chronograph module movement with integrated micro-rotor. Height 7.70 mm.

1971
Caliber 11½''
Rotor with one winding direction. Modular construction. Height 5.20 mm.

1972
Caliber 7¾''
Rotor with two winding directions. System with click spring wheels. Height 4.85 mm.

1976
Caliber 12''
Rotor with one winding direction. Modular construction. Height 6.50 mm.

1977
Caliber 11½''
Rotor with two winding directions. Setting action. Modular construction. Height 5.40 mm.

T127 *Wristwatch movements with automatic winding from 1943 to 1977, all equipped with Incabloc shock resistance.*

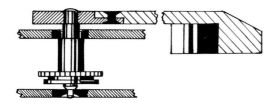

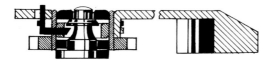

T128 *Rotor mounting on an axle with both pivots set in jewels; ball bearing mounting of the rotor; rotor mounting on a firm turning axle.*

IWC

T129 *Drawing of an eccentric conversion.*

T130 *Drawing of a cogwheel conversion.*

—Systems in which the bearing housing is pressed into the rotor and the turning axle is stiff (T 128).

The ball-bearing rotor mounting was developed by Eterna and patented for this firm. It combines robustness and ease of turning. (T 128)

A cogwheel, pinion or eccentric cam conducts the motion of the rotor to the winding wheel assembly.

Conversion drive

It has the task of polarizing the right and left turning of the rotor into the direction needed to wind the watch. Here we must differentiate three groups of conversion drives:

—Cogwheel conversion (T 130)

In this system a pair of teeth make contact with the rotor drive so that the turning motion is carried over a conversion wheel, or the two directions over two conversion wheels, to the first wheel of a reduction drive.

—Free-running conversion

In free-running conversion the two turning directions are carried over a ratchet and roller system, converted to the one direction right for winding, and this is transmitted to the reduction drive.

—Eccentric conversion (T 129)

Here an eccentric cam is fastened to the center of the rotor, passing the turning of the rotor in both directions over a connecting link and two stop-and-start ratchet levers fastened to the movement, to a diagonally toothed lock wheel. This automatic winding was developed and patented by, among others, IWC Schaffhausen.

In simpler automatic watches the converter is omitted and only one turning direction of the rotor is used to wind the watch. In the opposite direction the rotor runs free.

T132 *Sliding coupling to avoid the overwinding and breaking of the mainspring: 1. mainspring; 2. sliding stud; 3. barrel; 4. hook with sliding stud; 5. mainspring stud; 6. mainspring arbor.*

T131 *Examples of rotor mountings: left: eccentric arrangement; center: planet rotor integrated into the movement; right: central rotor mounted in ball bearings.*

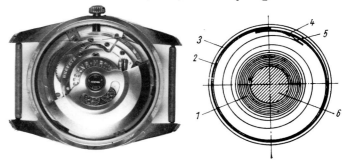

Reduction drive

The rotor is set in fast turning motion by the wearer's arm motions, but very little power is produced. If the rotor, via the converter, were connected directly with the ratchet wheel on the barrel, the rotor would stop turning, for to wind the spring a higher turning moment is needed than can be produced with the direct help of the rotor.

For this reason a reduction drive is inserted between the converter and the ratchet wheel. This drive reduces the rotor motions to small but powerful motions sufficient to wind the mainspring. As long as all dimensions are correct, each motion of the rotor leads to a small turn of the ratchet wheel and thus winds the mainspring. Depending on its construction, one full turn of the rotor gives 1/30 to 1/200 turn of the rachet wheel.

The automatic lock

Even though early wristwatches with automatic winding did not allow manual winding of the mainspring by the stem, the wish to wind the automatic watch by the stem was always there. To do that, the automatic lock must uncouple the automatic mechanism during manual winding and thus prevent a transmission of power to the rotor.

Over the years many systems for the separation of rotor and barrel were developed.

The mainspring

In watches with automatic winding the overwinding and consequent destruction of the mainspring must be prevented. This is usually done by sliding studs located on the outer end of the mainspring. These are sliding couplings made of spring steel about 1.5 times as thick as the mainspring. They are somewhat longer than the inner circumference of the barrel and have a hook on which the mainspring hangs.

If the mainspring is fully wound by the automatic winding, the stud slides on the inner wall of the barrel and so protects the mainspring from overwinding, while at less than full winding it acts like an attachment of the spring to the barrel wall. For the sliding stud to work properly, the inner wall of the barrel and the outside of the sliding stud are treated with lubricant containing molybdenum sulfide.

For ease of repairing automatic watches, the winding mechanism in modern constructions is usually built as a module which can be detached from the movement as a unit by loosening a few screws.

Though in their early years automatic wristwatches were in part fit for only limited everyday use, since 1960, and even earlier in Switzerland, their many improvements have led to their taking over an ever-growing portion of the watch market.

T133 *Movement with automatic winding by a central rotor. Right: polarizing the rotor motions by an eccentric converter. Left: Movement with automatic winding by a swinging weight. Winding occurs in only one direction.*

T134 *Kienzle Automatic, caliber 57/15, with Kienzle anchor motion, in which the self-winding unit can be removed from the movement by loosening three screws.*

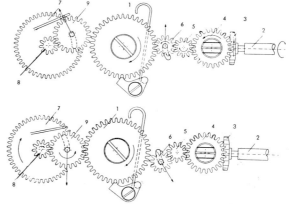

T135 *The difference between hand winding and automatic winding. The process of hand winding in an automatic movement: winding stem 2 and wheels 3 to 6 turn in the directions shown by the arrows. Wheel 6, because of its turning moment, is brought independently into contact with wheel 1, and wheel 9 swings out of contact with wheel 6. The process of automatic winding: the rotor turns wheels 7, 8 and 9 in the directions shown. Wheel 9 makes contact with wheel 1 and wheel 6 swings out of contact with wheel 1.*

Special types of wristwatches

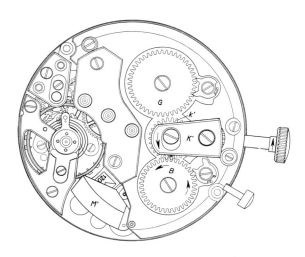

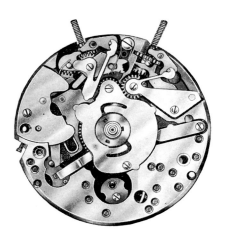

T136 *Vulcain 120 caliber alarm wristwatch with two spring barrels for watchworks and alarm. A stem is used to wind it.*

T137 *Front and rear views of an alarm wristwatch caliber by AS.*

Alarm watches

The first "complication" of a mechanical clock was probably a waking alarm, even before a striking mechanism had appeared. The first wristwatch with an alarm was also developed rather early, 1912/14, by the Eterna firm. Two problems had to be solved before this type of watch could do its job: the miniaturization of the alarm apparatus and the attainment of a certain fulness of sound. Difficulties even inspired attempts to create, instead of the audible, the tangible alarm watch, which touched one's wrist with a small staff or gripper at the set time. But this version was not to catch on.

Around 1947 the Vulcain firm, using the English name of Cricket, developed an alarm wristwatch whose fullness of sound was amazing. The watch sounded for some 25 seconds, about as loudly as a small travel alarm clock. The effect was attained by means of a double cover. The bell is mounted in the case similarly to that of a back-wall bell alarm clock, with the movement sealed off. A second cover envelops the bell from outside; four long slits in it let the sound out.

By 1950 the technical problems were solved and the alarm became a more and more frequent addition to the wristwatch. The Memovox wristwatch of LeCoultre (1950) deserves mention; when worn on the arm it rings very softly, but when put down its freely vibrating case cover develops a loud enough sound to wake one. The Pierce Duofon watch of 1956 offered a further refinement. This wrist alarm can be set in one of two degrees of loudness. The one, a strong ringing, serves to wake one; the other, a hum, gives a discreet warning at the set time. A small window in the dial shows whether it is set for waking or signaling.

Many alarm wristwatches have two separate spring barrels for clockwork and alarm; in others one spring does both jobs, for example, in the Venus 12.5 caliber of Ebauches (1956). The running reserve amounts to 56 hours before and 38 hours after the alarm has rung for 22 seconds. There is also a tendency to make alarm wristwatches flatter, more elegant, and at the same time more useful and easier to repair. Further developments worthy of note include the Memovox Automatic of LeCoultre (1951) and the watertight Alarm of Paul Buhré (circa 1955). In 1958 the Vulcain house created a miniature model for ladies, the Golden Voice alarm watch.

The technology of alarm watches

In the alarm watch the normal wristwatch is fitted with alarm works. In the past thirty years various types of alarm watches have been developed. The pallet includes the alarm itself, hand winding, and a spring barrel. Automatically wound watches have only a mainspring barrel, so that the automatic winding serves both the watch and the alarm. A calendar is included in some new alarm watches.

All alarm wristwatches include the following parts:

—The alarm drive in the form of a spring housing. It can be either a barrel of its own or the mainspring, which then drives both the watchworks and the alarm works.
—The wheel works of the alarm. Its job is to turn the slow movement of the spring with a high turning moment into a higher rate for the balance wheel of the alarm.
—The alarm escapement, consisting of a balance wheel and an anchor. A hammer is attached to the anchor, and the escapement converts the turning of the wheels into the back-and-forth motion of the hammer.
—The alarm signal. It is made by the hammer striking a sounding body (bell, case bottom, case edge).
—The alarm-setting mechanism. It makes the alarm sound at the right time. The alarm watch usually has a central alarm-setting hand or disc. The alarm can be set by using a stem.
—The shutoff apparatus. It links the alarm works with the watchworks. Its essential parts are the alarm setting wheel with its tiller, the shutoff bar, the shutoff spring and the shutoff lever. The last is connected with the alarm anchor axle and thus with the hammer.
A nose on the shutoff spring blocks the alarm works by stopping the pendulum movement of the hammer. At the set time this nose is beyond the reach of the hammer, so that the alarm rings.
—The on-off mechanism. By pressing or pulling a knob or stem the alarm process is interrupted by stopping the balance, anchor or hammer. Many manufacturers include a window in the face with an indicator to show whether the alarm is on or off.

In general, the basic movement of the alarm wristwatch does not differ from those of the simple wristwatch. Wheel trains and other parts of normal watch calibers are used.

In quartz watches, even more often than in mechanical ones, and for considerably lower prices, various functions are combined in one watch. The electronic watch with calendar, alarm, chronograph and small calculator is an example.

T138 *Advertisement for an alarm wristwatch, from 1958.*

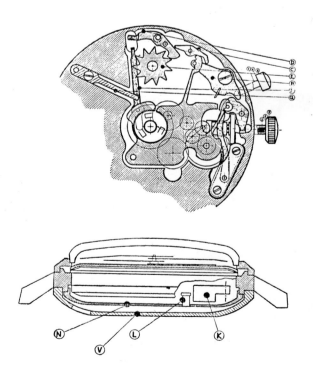

T139 *Cutaway drawing through the house of a Vulcain Cricket alarm wristwatch: K. Hammer; L. Striking point for the hammer; N. Membrane; V. The actual bottom, with holes to let out the sound.*

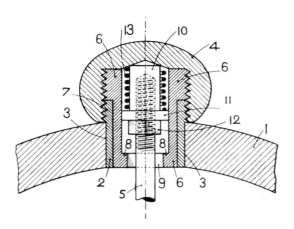

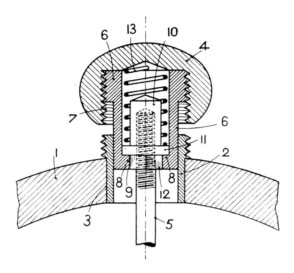

T140 *Making the winding stem of the Rolex Oyster watertight. The decisive patent was issued in 1926. Illustration from 1935. 1. Case; 2. Tube fastened into the case; 4. Stem knob; 5. Stem; 6. Casing; 7. Thread of the knob; 8. Casing attaching point; 9. Square casing block; 10. Cap; 11. Cap attaching point; 12. Square block of the cap; 13. Screwshaped spring.*

Watertight wristwatches

Aside from automatic winding, no added feature of the wristwatch has attracted as much interest as the watch in a watertight case. Water tests of all kinds have caught the public interest and become favorite requirements for selling the product: a wristwatch in a goldfish bowl, on the outside of a diving tender, as a timepiece for expeditions on, above and below the ground, where it is tested in many ways. "Water-resistant", "watertight", "100% watertight" or "extra-watertight" were the terms used, each one of which meant something different, so that official testing procedures and norms were requested.

But the initiators were not looking for the watertight wristwatch so much as for the movement shielded as perfectly as possible from all external influences. John Harwood expressed these considerations very memorably: "Then I continued my work, carefully put the tiny works back into their case, and followed their travels in my mind. I saw the watch on its owner's arm as it traveled on through life; I asked myself how it would be wound; I saw it stop, or saw various bits of dust slip in through the winding stem hole . . ."

In a 1935 Rolex advertisement the following words were used: watertight, dust-tight, tropic-resistant, gas-tight, airtight, snow-tight, thus hermetically sealed, permanently sealed against all damaging influences. In other words, the original precision of the wristwatch should be held constant as long as possible. Even before the turn of the century patents were granted for the means to hermetically sealed pocket watches. But only in the wristwatch were they put to practical use.

The watch must be made watertight in three areas: glass, case and winding stem. Making a tight fit without damaging the glass was a problem that was even harder to solve with the rectangular glasses of formed watches than with round ones. Special types of glass also had to be created to stand such temperature variations as occur in swimming activities during the summer.

The second difficulty, the closing of the case, was treated in various ways. If the two pieces, the case and the bottom, were fitted very precisely, they could be screwed, as was done with Rolex watches. Other manufacturers used caulking materials of various kinds: gum, cork, leather or later plastic. Another solution was to make the bottom and middle of the case out of one piece; this was the Wyler firm's method. In 1940 there were about fifty so-called watertight cases, which usually could be

T141 *Hans Wilsdorf (1881-1960). As chief of the Rolex firm he influenced the technical and economic development of the wristwatch for decades.*

opened only with special keys, and whose construction, despite instructions, often required much intuition.

But the main problems were in the area of the winding stem, for the winding and setting controls were constantly being moved and thus could not simply be sealed. "The winding knob and its stem must turn without too much friction and also be capable of moving in and out without damaging a permanent seal. Watertight stuffing-boxes, rings and lips have proved themselves," Professor Glaser wrote in 1974. The Rolex firm was the first to succeed in building a practically watertight watch industrially. The decisive patent for making the stem watertight was granted in 1926.

Once again, as so often in the history of the watch, the true significance of the new development was not recognized. Only Hans Wilsdorf, proprietor of the Rolex firm, came up with the idea. The "Oyster" appeared in 1926/27, the "Oyster Perpetual" in 1931. Even in hindsight one must agree with the Swiss editor who formulated in 1935: "One can well say that the Rolex Watch Co. did the whole Swiss watch industry a great service, first by solving the technical problems and then by creating customers for the watertight watch." A special development began with the diver's watch, whereby Rolex, with its "Submariner" (1953), again led the way.

T142 *The sporting achievement of Mercedes Gleitze, who swam the English Channel wearing a Rolex Oyster in 1927, was utilized commercially.*

T143 *Wrist chronograph by Breitling with 30-minute indicator, circa 1915.*

T144 *Above, two wrist chronographs with a case form very popular around 1938, by Doxa. Below, face and rear views of a chronograph movement, circa 1938.*

Chronograph wristwatches

The term "chronograph" has become accepted for pocket watches and wristwatches that also fulfill the functions of a stopwatch. This concept is erroneous insofar as nothing about the wrist chronograph has been registered in writing, unlike the original chronographs which permanently record lengths of time. The first chronographs were presumably recording short-time watches.

In terms of its purpose, a well-functioning, sufficiently large wristwatch must be equipped with an additional apparatus that enables it to time the start of an event or the time span of a process precisely. The indicator must be clearly legible, so the chronograph hand (stopwatch hand) generally takes the form of a central second hand. The time since the beginning of the measured process is recorded in passing and can be read from an added minute hand, sometimes also from an added hour hand.

Pure stopwatches, even in the age of the wristwatch, have retained the form of the pocket watch, but pocket chronographs, on the other hand, have been replaced by wrist chronographs. Of course the technological knowledge and construction have come from the pocket watch, but the wrist chronograph already has its own history. The first experiments go back to before World War I. As early as 1910 the Moeris firm advertised a stopwatch worn on a leather strap. In 1915 the Revue Internationale d'Horlogerie reported of a "Chronograph-Bracelet" of the Breitling firm with a central chronograph hand and a 30-minute indicator. The first "watertight" wrist chronograph was offered by Mido in 1937.

A decisive historical point was reached in 1969 with the origin of the automatic wrist chronograph. The Chronomatic, developed between 1965 and 1969 jointly by Breitling, Hamilton-Burén and Heuer-Leonidas in cooperation with the Dubois & Dépraz machine works, is a good example. This chronograph with automatic winding (planetary rotor) counts minutes and hours and also includes a calendar. The height of the movement is 7.70 mm. In 1969 too, Zenith-Movado placed a chronograph movement with a central rotor mounted in ball bearings (caliber 3019 PHC), a calendar, and a height of 6.50 mm on the market. In 1973 the Ebauches SA brought out the caliber 7750 Valjoux automatic chronograph movement with a central rotor. But the micro-mechanics did not end here. Just a few years later, in addition to 13'' and 13.75'' calibers, there was already a movement of 11.5''.

Chronographs are complicated mechanical systems. Since the functions are generally to be controlled by two push buttons without disturbing the running clock, a lever mechanism is needed, and even at second glance it is still confusing. In terms of the control of this lever mechanism we can differentiate between chronographs with and without a switching wheel (T 147).

The chronographs without a switching wheel were developed from those with one in the early Fifties for economic reasons. In the last fifteen years the so-called "economy" chronographs, starkly simplified in terms of control and adjustment, have appeared. There are three basic forms of mechanism for transferring power fron the running wheel to the chronograph, and numerous variations. The following attempt to classify chronographs is therefore limited to their characteristics that are recognizable even to the layman.

There are genuine and non-genuine chronographs. The first go on functioning as watches when they are used as stopwatches; they have permanently running works and immediately pull the sweep hand back to zero when the timing is finished. Non-genuine chronographs no longer show the right time when they are used as stopwatches. Neither stopping the sweep hand nor setting it at zero can be done without influencing the running of the works.

T145 *The prestige of the classic stopwatch in pocket-watch case, then indispensible at sporting events, shall be taken over by the wrist chronograph. Advertisement from 1943.*

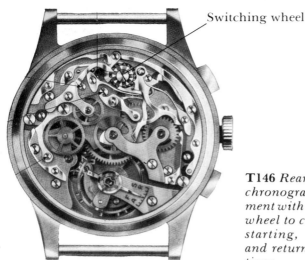

Switching wheel

T146 *Rear view of a chronograph movement with switching wheel to control the starting, stopping and returning functions.*

8180	8139
8340	8270
8350	8020
8219	8290
8100	8000
8325	8060
8080	8320

8350	8140
8180	8270
8325	8020
8220	8200
8070	8290
8100	8000
8345	8060
8355	8080
8335	8320

T147 *Schematic drawings: above, a chronograph movement without switching wheel; below, a chronograph movement with a switching wheel.*

To make a genuine chronograph out of a watch, the works and the chronograph mechanics must be linked when necessary, but also be separable. Not all watches with complicated dials, push buttons and central sweep hands qualify as genuine chronographs.

The suitability of a chronograph for certain time measurements can be recognized externally by the number of hands and buttons. Watches with one button can be used only to measure one event without interruption. Starting, stopping and resetting to zero follow in unchangeable order. On the other hand, chronographs with two buttons allow the timing of a process with any number of interruptions. The single stopped sections are added up mechanically. By 1945 most wrist chronographs were already equipped with two buttons.

The most complicated type of chronographs—with two buttons and two hands—chronograph hand and sweep hand (Rattrapante)—can be used for the simultaneous timing of several processes that begin at the same time but last for different lengths of time. While the chronograph hand runs on until the end of the timing, the sweep hand can make intermediate stops. By pushing the button again the sweep hand can be made to catch up to the chronograph hand so that both again show the same time. This type is complex and resultingly expensive; thus for the sake of completeness the less common special form, the "Mono-Rattrapante", should be mentioned. Here one hand essentially fulfills the functions of both by stopping and then springing ahead to the point that it would have reached if it had not been interrupted.

The ways the buttons work are not the same in all brands and calibers, even though certain unities exist, so that everyone must get acquainted with his own chronograph. The chronograph hand of most models revolves once in a minute, and the division of the dial allows the reading of fifths of a second. The minute indicator can react in various ways. Either it jumps from one minute to the next or it runs steadily like the minute hand of a watch. But the "half-immediate" recording, in which the change begins about five seconds before the minute ends, is most often used.

Wrist chronographs are basically special watches for work and sport, for pilots, divers and racing drivers, for doctors and engineers. Appropriate dials allow the watch to be used as a tachometer (speed indicator), telemeter (distance indicator), or pulsometer (pulse indicator) as well, to name just a few examples. The desired indications can then be read directly. Many special wrist chronographs have several dials and also a ring-shaped calculator, making them versatile measuring and calculating devices. Naturally it takes training to use them.

In closing, a few notes on the accuracy of wrist chronographs: The transition wheels to be set are pressed against each other and wear themselves out. Wheel contact and balance swinging can result in brief delays, all the more so as there are limits to the fineness of the wheel teeth, Naturally the accuracy of the timing cannot be better than that of the basic watch, whose running is influenced by the workings of the additional wheels. But there are also chronographs with chronometer qualification, one more proof of the striving for perfection in the last phase of development of the mechanical watch.

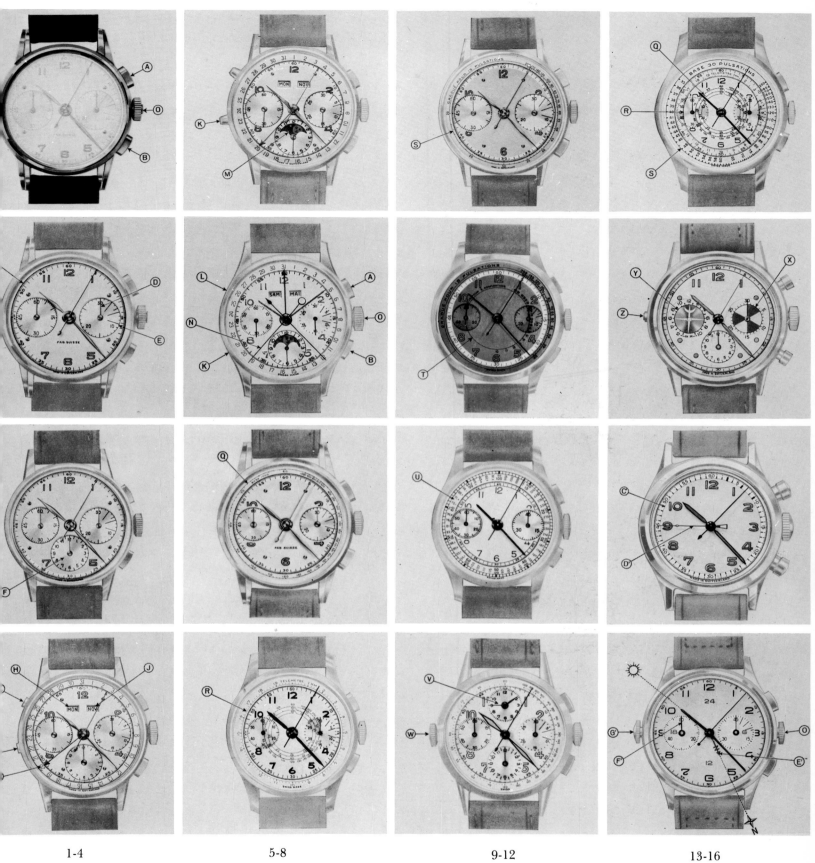

1-4   5-8   9-12   13-16

T148 *Chronographs, Top to bottom:*

1A. Starting button; B. Return button; O. Hold button;
2. Chronograph with 30-minute indicator;
3. Chronograph with 12-hour indicator;
4. Chronograph with calendar;
5. Chronograph with calendar and moon phase indicator;
6. Chronograph with double hands;
7. Tachometer chronograph;
8. Telemeter chronograph;
9. Pulsometer chronograph;
10. Breath counter chronograph;
11. Production counter chronograph;
12. Memento chronograph;
13. Multipurpose chronograph;
14. Season chronograph;
15. Chronograph with central total indicator;
16. Chronograph with orientation indicator.

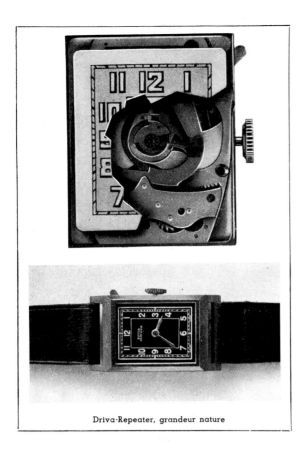

Driva-Repeater, grandeur nature

T149 *In the age of electrification wristwatches that strike the hour have not found many buyers. Driva Repeater with hour and quarter striking, 1930.*

T150 *Wristwatch with a calendar, which had to be set by hand, circa 1930.*

98

Chronograph wristwatch technology

For a more thorough explanation of the genuine chronograph, we can begin with a movement with indirect central second hand (outside the power flow). To the fourth wheel pivot of the watchworks, which is lengthened to the back, a first transition wheel is attached. It is in constant mesh with a second transition wheel carried on the setting lever. With this lever's help the second transition wheel can be brought into contact with the fine-toothed central wheel by releasing the chronograph with the start button. On the forward end of its pivot the central wheel carries the chronograph's second indicator. On its rear the central wheel bears a switch heart with the help of this and the return lever the adjusted central chronograph hand can be brought back to the starting position (zero) by pushing the button.

A minute counter adds up the revolutions of the central chronograph hand and shows them on a minute indicator on the dial, usually near the 3. Chronographs deal in various ways with hour counters that add up the revolutions of the minute counter. In this way measurements of 1/5 of a second to 12 hours are possible. Via switch hearts and return levels these indicators can also be brought back to zero.

Wristwatches with "complexities"

If one compares wristwatches and pocket watches in terms of complexities, one will see that almost all the complexities known to the pocket watch have also been realized in the wristwatch. The main goal was often to challenge the creative ability of renowned manufacturers or the technical skill of individual watchmakers, rather than to achieve commercial success. A typical example is the tourbillon watch developed in 1954 by the Patek firm. The same is true of watches with minute repetition. The attempt to create a reasonably priced wristwatch that struck the hours and quarter hours (Driva Repeater, 1937) obviously found little accord with the public.

The development of calendar watches, which Humbert catalogued impressively in the Swiss Watchmakers' Journal in 1951/53, is a different matter. To be sure, the wristwatch with "eternal" calendar is the exception. In a report to the Basel Fair in 1958 it was said: "The wristwatch with an everlasting calendar, which shows the date completely accurately without manual assistance, regardless of whether the months have 28, 29, 30 or 31 days, is presented by Patek-Philippe as an exclusive item . . . As a real collector's and enthusiast's piece it can be produced at a price of about 3250 Swiss francs." As a further development in 1958, Patek offered the eternal calendar with central second, and in 1967/68, in a 12« movement, the eternal calendar with automatic winding. Audemars Piguet and Gérald Genta also produce wristwatches with "eternal" calendars today.

But even the choice of calendar wristwatches with four indications—date, weekday, month and moon phase—is fairly wide. After Humbert, the following firms had developed their own calibers by 1953: Cortébert, Jaeger LeCoultre, Movado, Omega, Audemars Piguet, Record, Universal, Vacheron. Five calibers by Ebauches SA can be added.

At this point it might be mentioned that does not apply to calendar watches alone. As Humbert wrote in 1951: "As far as the caliber of the Ebauches is concerned, one small detail is worth remembering. Ebauches often sells the same caliber to several firms. These movements are finished in popular or traditional styles, according to the jewels, balances, hairsprings etc. used in them. The rebuilder often receives calendar watches for repairs, which bear a factory name, but the raw works were bought from Ebauches."

Technologically there is in calendar watches the problem of using additional wheels to create transitional relationships which release a switch only at a desired time. For the simplest type, the day indicator, the switching process can work only after 24 hours, that is, after two revolutions of the hour wheel. But the real difficulties are not in the transitions, but in providing appropriate possibilities for correction. A third setting of the winding apparatus is necessary to reset the watch manually to correct the calendar for months with fewer than 31 days.

It would be best for the even running of the watch to take the power for changing the calendar from the watchworks continually, spreading the process over a long period of time. But this is opposed by the buyer's wish always to be able to read the exact date clearly in the window of the dial. For that reason the preference is for fast-change mechanisms that allow a rather jumpy change. But it must be assured that the energy storer will not be strained too much, or else the watch might stop.

In the late phase of the mechanical wristwatch, watches that give the date are quite common; those with date and day of the week, common enough. This indicates another difference between pocket watch and wristwatch. Newer mechanical wristwatches are fitted with special features much more often than pocket watches are. There are many examples of this, not only in the area of military and expedition watches, but even in production for the ordinary market. An automatic watch with central second hand, calendar date and certificate of reliability is, to be sure, above the standard of the usual mechanical wristwatch, but in the late phase of micromechanics it is nothing more than a particularly outstanding product of the watchmaker's art.

T151 *Man's wristwatch with automatic winding and "eternal" calendar by Patek Philippe, 1970. Under-the-dial view; the calendar discs are mounted on their own plate. Automatic movement, caliber 27-460 Q, 37 jewels, free-swinging self-compensating Breguet hairspring, Gyromax balance, ball-bearing rotor of 18 karat gold, winding in both directions.*

The outer form

Case, hands and dial

While the expert can find important indications of a watch's age and quality by examining the movement, the beginning collector is more attracted to the outside. Case and dial offer him better information for an evaluation. Even at the beginning of our century it was customary to put the brand name of a watch on the dial. Along with the maker's name, technical features are often named, such as "automatic" or "chronometer quality". It is noticeable that renowned firms rarely mention the number of jewels on the dial (though usually on the back plate). The widespread notion that the number of jewels can be decisive in determining the quality of a watch can be accepted only with reservations.

T152 *Tissot hinged case of 1937.*

Movement and case should go well together, and in many wristwatches they do. But often enough one finds surprises: mediocre movements in impressive cases are found, and more rarely an uninteresting case will hold a good movement. In the decisions of the watch factories, the cases made by specialized supplier firms play an important role.

At this point it seems to be important to insert a warning to the beginning collector. The stamped parts of old cases, sometimes held together by hinges, can be opened easily in comparison with the modern cases that are screwed together. But while opening the dust cover of a pocket watch brings the interesting rear plate into view, the open wristwatch shows only its dial. So it is natural to take out the movement. But consider that the winding stem to which the knob is attached reacts very sensitively to being used as a lever, and many works are fitted so tightly into the case that even light pressure during removal or insertion can lead to damage.

While the development of watch movements is basically a matter of technical progress and necessary rationalization in production, the design and production of the case are primarily based on matters of style.

To stay competitive, watch manufacturers must more or less strongly follow the dictates of prevailing styles and try to match the taste of the buyer.

Until about 1910 the wristwatch resembled the round shape of the pocket watch. After that an experimental phase began, sometimes leading to very daring case and dial designs. In the General Journal for Watchmakers these tendencies were described ironically by a contemporary in 1914 with the following words: "There is no doubt that we stand before a new stage of development of the pocket watch. The boring, everlasting roundness of their form cries out for help; it can no longer stand its popularity . . . oval, rectangulaj, hexagonal and other basic forms of movement and case should also have their rights, and that's what, with its singing—the wristwatch has brought about" (parodying the song "Die Lorelei"). And the watch glasses were made in equally curious shapes. At that time smaller wristwatches had Arabic numbers, while larger ones often had hard-to-read Roman numerals on the dial. There was a notable preference for a red number 12; the high point of this style was around 1915.

From the mid-Twenties on more subdued styles prevailed, and decoration was subordinated to function, except in special women's watches. Men's watches tended to take rectangular forms, with sometimes round, sometimes rectangular dials showing. Women's watches were dominated by round basic forms in many variations, along with slim rectangular watches with formed movements, particularly the Baguette. Roman numerals rarely appeared on wristwatches any more. Around 1935 it was briefly the fad to replace the numbers on the dial by lines. Some special forms also came on the market at that time, such as the digital watch or the "Duodial" with separate main dial and second-hand dial.

Around 1940 the classically simple rectangular watch reached the high point of its development. It was often made with a black dial.

Along with these external aspects, the passing years brought increasing desire for useful, practical features such as dust- and watertightness, resistance to wear, and at the same time stylish appearance.

The watch manufacturers answered with round wristwatches having screwed-on bottoms (beginning with the Rolex Oyster), or screwed rectangular watches whose movements were often encapsulated or sealed with an impervious substance.

But the complicated watch of this era, which was later to become a normal form, already required a round form at this time. Rectangular cases, despite many attempts, are hard to make impervious; formed movements hindered the development of the automatic watch.

From the mid-Fifties on the simple round shape dominated the market for men's watches, and to a lesser degree for women's. Samuel Guye characterized this development in 1956 in these words: "Fashion requires very simple lines for the case, flat and very flat watches with big dial openings, and not overloaded dials with markings and hands as clear as possible." Numbers were fully or partly replaced by lines on the dial. The mechanical wristwatch of the late phase had found its face.

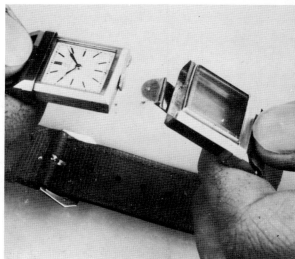

T154 *Watertight man's watch by Omega, 1936. The case is made of two parts that slide together.*

T 155 △

T155 *Wristwatch with tablet-form case, meant to make viewing the dial easier. Omega 1935.*

T156 *Watertight wristwatch by Nivea, 1941. For protection against water the movement was itself encapsulated again.*

T 156

101

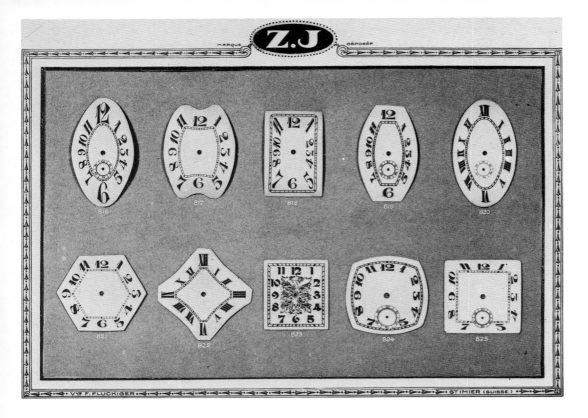

In this era various firms (such as IWC, Roamer, Wyler) decided on one-piece bowl cases covered by a glass. To remove the movement once the glass was off, the winding stem was made in two pieces. The outer part could be taken out of the case by pulling hard on the knob. After that the movement could be removed from the front. Other firms (such as Heuer) developed special cases with spring latches, that could also be guaranteed as watertight.

To open these various cases, the hobbyist needed not only specific knowledge of the inner nature of wristwatches, but also a wide assortment of special tools (wrenches, holding tools, etc.).

Above all, one had to realize that, after opening and reassembling a "watertight" wristwatch, one cannot assume that the watch is still 100% watertight. This is guaranteed only with the most careful handling according to the manufacturer's instructions. In addition, new sealing materials should always be used.

As a costly material for wristwatch cases, gold remained generally preferred over the years. The same is true of the gold doublé watch. Silver, though, which oxidizes and looks tarnished, lost popularity rapidly after 1930 and had become quite uncommon by 1945. Wristwatches with burnished steel cases were made only in the early years. The popularity of Tula silver watches ended in the Twenties. The era of the practical watch with a chromed case began around 1930; like many gold-plated cases, it did not stand up to hard use. In certain places the basic metal showed through, or the chrome came loose from the metal under it. There were even chromed silver cases.

In the early Thirties cases of stainless steel were limited to high-quality watches, as this material was very hard to work and thus expensive. But by 1945 the cases of medium-quality Swiss wristwatches were also being made almost exclusively of this robust and good-looking material. To avoid damage, stainless steel bottoms were later used for goldplated watches as well.

Materials with particular technical qualities or esthetic effects were also used for wristwatch cases. The unscratchable cases of Rado or the titanium cases of IWC can be mentioned as examples.

In the most recent times one also finds plastic cases, which can be produced very practically and economically. Changes of many kinds have also been made to the dials, the "faces" of the watches, likewise in terms of fashion, but also for practicality of production, as with the cases.

In the earliest years it was enameled dials that dominated the appearance of wristwatches, but from the Twenties on, more and more metal dials, with galvanized or painted surfaces, were used. The divisions were printed, raised, engraved, etched or stamped.

At this point it is necessary to mention the wristwatch with luminous dial and hands. Like the watches used in the two World Wars, many sporting wristwatches were heavily treated with luminous paint. But in the Fifties the problems of using radioactive materials were better understood. Legal regulations, along with buyers' keener awareness, have caused the practical and once very popular wristwatch with luminous dial to become quite insignificant since 1960, apart from some special uses.

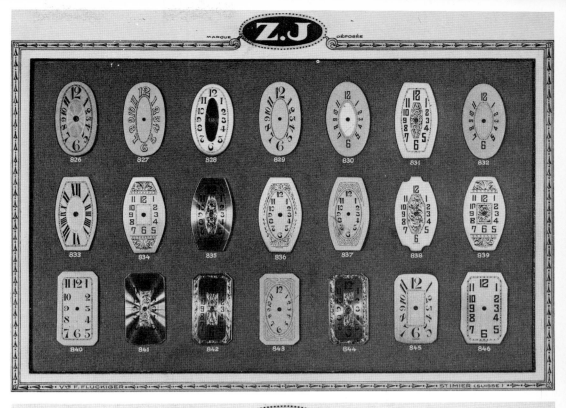

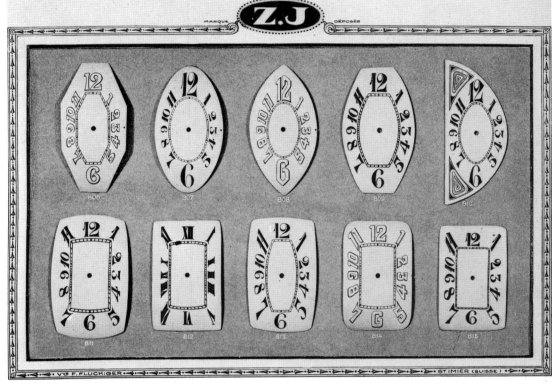

T157-159 *The "Storm and Stress" era of the wristwatch, as seen in examples of dials. From an advertisement, circa 1920.*

Finally, low-priced wristwatches of the most recent times have been made with plastic dials.

The manufacturers of high-priced wristwatches often gave their products "faces" of precious metals or with precious jewels.

Around 1925 most wristwatches had pear-shaped hands; also in use were cathedral hands, Breguet hands and, as a fourth variation, "modern" forms. Watches with luminous dials were fitted with skeletal hands resembling the pear-shaped ones. In the following years a great many imaginative hands appeared. Many types soon disappeared, while others showed a tendency to become "classic". Around 1960 the so-called dauphine hands were replaced by various bar forms. Many old wristwatches no longer have their original hands. In many cases even an alert layman can notice the mixing of styles; in others even the specialist may not be sure.

The face of a watch often determines its chance of selling; this is true of the watch market in general as well as the collector's market. Love at first sight for a certain wristwatch, aside from all technological and economic rationale, is often inspired by the external impression of case, dial and hands.

103

2001   5¹/₂''' Platin m. Brill.

2019   8³/₄'''
guillochiert, mit Alt-Gold-Auflage

2002   5¹/₂''', Plat. m. Brill.

2003   Alt-Gold   8³/₄'''

2020   8³/₄''', Alt-Gold

2011   6³/₄''' cis., 16 Rubin

2004   8³/₄'''   graviert

2021   8³/₄''', mirage grav.

2012   6³/₄''' cis., 16 Rubin

2005   8³/₄''', mirage, graviert

2022   8³/₄''', mirage grav.

2013   8³/₄''' cis.

2006   8³/₄''', mirage pol.

2023   8³/₄''', pol.

2014   8³/₄''' cis.

2007   8³/₄'''

2024   8³/₄''', pol.

2015   8³/₄''' cis.

2008   8³/₄''', Jll.

2025   8³/₄''', pol.

2016   6³/₄''' pol., Anker und Cylinder

2009   6¹/₂''', ovales Werk

2026   8³/₄''', Jll.

2017   6³/₄''' pol., Anker und Cylinder

2010   6''', ovales Werk

2027   8³/₄'''

2018   6³/₄''' pol., Anker, 16 Rubin

104

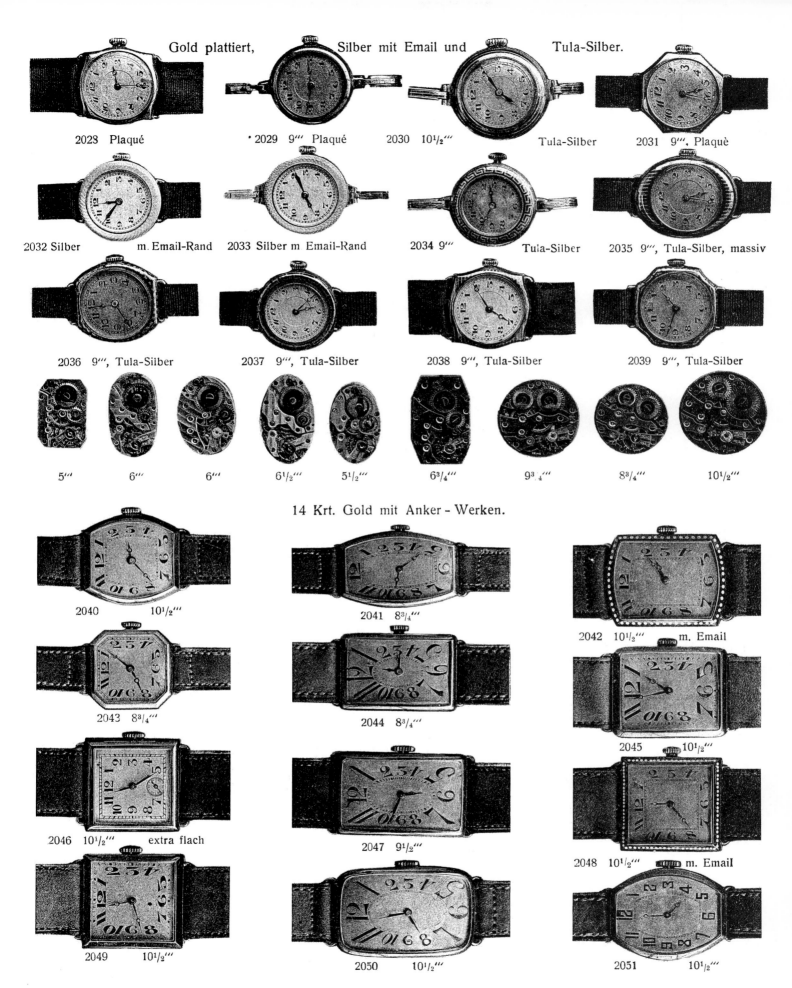

Gold plattiert,   Silber mit Email und   Tula-Silber.

2023 Plaqué   · 2029 9''' Plaqué   2030 10¹/₂'''   Tula-Silber   2031 9'''. Plaquè

2032 Silber   m. Email-Rand   2033 Silber m Email-Rand   2034 9'''   Tula-Silber   2035 9''', Tula-Silber, massiv

2036 9''', Tula-Silber   2037 9''', Tula-Silber   2038 9''', Tula-Silber   2039 9''', Tula-Silber

5'''   6'''   6'''   6¹/₂'''   5¹/₂'''   6³/₄'''   9³/₄'''   8³/₄'''   10¹/₂'''

14 Krt. Gold mit Anker - Werken.

2040   10¹/₂'''   2041 8³/₄'''   2042 10¹/₂'''   m. Email

2043 8³/₄'''   2044 8³/₄'''   2045 10¹/₂'''

2046 10¹/₂'''   extra flach   2047 9¹/₂'''   2048 10¹/₂'''   m. Email

2049   10¹/₂'''   2050   10¹/₂'''   2051   10¹/₂'''

T160 *Two-page advertisement of Franz Bauermeister, Berlin, 1923.*

Von Armbanduhren und ihren Formen

Von Fritz Leuthold

eim Aufkommen der Armbanduhren gab es nur wenige Muster, die sich an die bekanntesten geometrischen Figuren anlehnten. Die Gehäuse waren meist vollformig, d. h. Glasrand, Mittelteil und Boden waren gleich geformt. — Die Anstöße der Gehäuse werden unterschieden in Haken (*anses*) für Rips- oder Lederband und Böckchen (*plots*) für Zugband.

Bei der Benennung der Gehäuseformen gibt es verschiedene Grundbezeichnungen.

Gouge bedeutet immer eine Einbuchtung.

Guichet ist ein extra breiter Glasrand.

Biseau bedeutet facettierter Glasrand.

Cannelé rippenähnlich wie bei Geldstücken.

Nachstehende Bilder mit Formbezeichnung und Größenangabe stellen die bekanntesten der vollformigen Gehäuse dar. Es gibt natürlich noch viele andere Formen, die jedoch meistens nur geringfügige Unterschiede aufweisen.

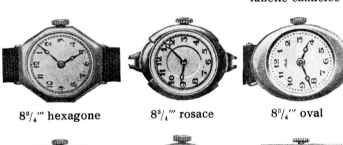

8³/₄''' rund; lentille   8³/₄''' rund; guichet   8³/₄''' empire; lunette cannelée

8³/₄''' hexagone   8³/₄''' rosace   8³/₄''' oval

8³/₄''' Viereck, geschnittene Ecke; carré, coins coupés   8³/₄''' médaillon   8³/₄''' carré, biseau

8³/₄''' Viereck, runde Ecken; carré, coins ronds   8³/₄''' Segment   8³/₄''' carré cambré

8³/₄''' Sechseck; hexagone   8³/₄''' Achteck; octogone   8³/₄''' Tonnenform, tonneau

8³/₄''' Kreuz; croix   8³/₄''' Lyra   8³/₄''' gouge

Verschiedene Herren-Uhrgehäuseformen haben den Damen-Armbanduhren als Muster gedient.

8³/₄''' rund; lunette gouge   8³/₄''' rund; lunette pommes   8³/₄''' rund; lunette gouge perlée

Die schon erwähnten Anstöße (*cornes*) für Ripsbanduhren gibt es in vielen geschmackvollen Ausführungen.

Die Entwicklung der Mirage-Form

An den ersten Mustern erkennt jeder, daß diese nicht schön waren, da das Rund des Gehäuses zu stark hervortritt, was eben durch die Bemusterung des Glasrandes verhindert werden soll, zumal auch das Fassonglas unvorteilhaft wirkt.

Zum Rundglas zurückgekehrt, wird das Aussehen viel besser.

Graviert und evtl. mattiert oder gefärbt sieht die Uhr noch viel vorteilhafter aus, da die meisten Muster Entwürfe der einzelnen Fabrikanten sind und in vollformigen Gehäusen gar nicht gemacht werden können. Aus diesem Grunde ist es nicht möglich, die einzelnen Muster zu benennen, da das viel zu weit gehen würde. Es laufen daher alle Muster unter dem Namen „Mirage".

Mirage-Formen

Nachstehende Bilder zeigen drei Uhren mit gleichgroßen Werken. Die Gehäuse haben gleiches Aussehen und sind nur im Bau verschieden. Die Größenunterschiede fallen stark auf zugunsten der Mirage-Form, die bedeutend kleiner aussieht als das vollformige oder gar das Illusion-Gehäuse.

Illusion   Mirage   Vollform

Das Geschäft in länglichen Damen-Armbanduhren hat stark nachgelassen. Es folgen nachstehend einige Grundformen.

5¼''' Rechteck, eingebuchtete Ecken;   5¼''' Rechteck mit Anstoß;
rectangulaire, coins gougés   rectangulaire, tank

5½'''   5½'''
Tonnenform; tonneau   Rechteck; rectangulaire

6½'''   6½'''
Rechteck, geschnittene Ecken;   oval
rectangulaire, coins coupés

Herrenkalotten werden in letzter Zeit wieder gern gekauft, nachdem der Artikel ziemlich zwei Jahre still gelegen hatte. Die Formen sind einfacher geworden, allerdings werden die Gehäuse teilweise graviert und mattiert. Reliefzahlen werden auch oft verlangt. Der Bau der Gehäuse ist der gleiche wie bei den Damen-Armbanduhren. Das zweiteilige Gehäuse findet viel Verwendung zum Teil auch bei runden Uhren. Flache Ausführung spricht sehr an, und längliche Formen sind vielfach leicht gewölbt und der Armbiegung angepaßt.

10½''' Tonnenform mit Anstoß;   8¾''' Rechteck mit Anstoß
tonneau tank   rectangulaire tank;

Um runde Gehäuse größerer Art extra flach zu gestalten, werden kleinere Werke eingesetzt und mit einem breiten Werkring umgeben. Es ist selbstverständlich, daß ein solches Werk bedeutend flacher ist als ein größeres, das der Gehäusegröße nach eigentlich dazu gehören würde.

Tonnenform; tonneau   rund, ziseliert, mit Anstößen

Viereck geschweift;   Viereck mit Anstößen;
Carré cambré   Carré tank

Damit sind die hauptsächlichsten Formen der heutigen Armbanduhren nebst ihren deutschen und französischen Bezeichnungen erwähnt. Wir entsprachen mit der Zusammenstellung einem besonderen Wunsche aus dem Leserkreise, da hin und wieder doch Zweifel über die Bedeutung der Katalogangaben bestehen. Wir hoffen, daß die Zusammenstellung den Verkehr zwischen Lieferanten und Einzelhandel erleichtert. Der Artikel mußte sich zwar auf die wichtigsten Formen beschränken, enthält diese aber doch in so genügender Zahl, daß auch die Namen der nicht aufgeführten Formen leicht erklärlich sind.

Hinsichtlich der Gehäuseformen und ihrer Bezeichnungen für Taschenuhren verweisen wir auf die Veröffentlichung in Nr. 15 der Uhrmacher-Woche vom Jahrgang 1922, die außerdem auch Erläuterungen technischer Art enthält, Bezeichnungen der Werkteile usw. In umfangreicherer Weise als es in einem Zeitungsartikel möglich ist, sind die fremdsprachlichen Bezeichnungen in Moritz Großmanns Taschenwörterbuch für Uhrmacher (Deutsch-Französisch-Englisch) enthalten, das bei der Benutzung ausländischer Kataloge wertvolle Dienste leistet.

T161 *Reprint of an article from "Watchmaker's Weekly", 35th year, Leipzig, 1928, no. 11, pp. 165-166. Title: Of Wristwatches and Their Forms.*

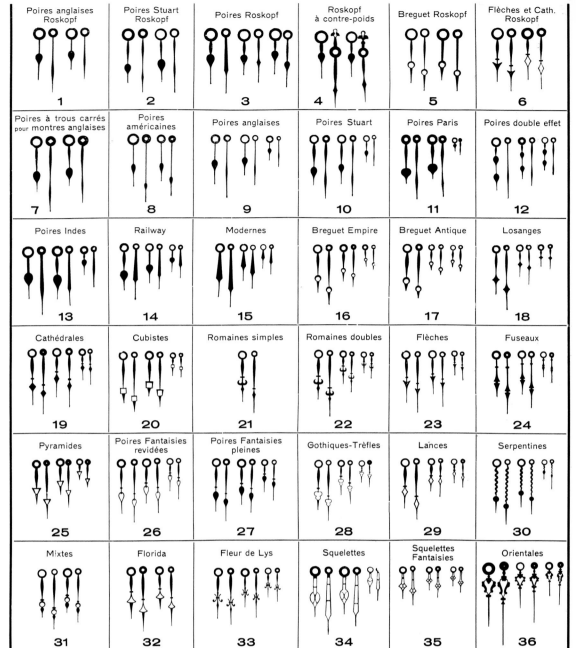

Poires anglaises Roskopf	Poires Stuart Roskopf	Poires Roskopf	Roskopf à contre-poids	Breguet Roskopf	Flèches et Cath. Roskopf
1	**2**	**3**	**4**	**5**	**6**
Poires à trous carrés pour montres anglaises	Poires américaines	Poires anglaises	Poires Stuart	Poires Paris	Poires double effet
7	**8**	**9**	**10**	**11**	**12**
Poires Indes	Railway	Modernes	Breguet Empire	Breguet Antique	Losanges
13	**14**	**15**	**16**	**17**	**18**
Cathédrales	Cubistes	Romaines simples	Romaines doubles	Flèches	Fuseaux
19	**20**	**21**	**22**	**23**	**24**
Pyramides	Poires Fantaisies revidées	Poires Fantaisies pleines	Gothiques-Trèfles	Lances	Serpentines
25	**26**	**27**	**28**	**29**	**30**
Mixtes	Florida	Fleur de Lys	Squelettes	Squelettes Fantaisies	Orientales
31	**32**	**33**	**34**	**35**	**36**

T162 *Wristwatch of the Seventies by Dugena, in a plastic case.*

Louis XV	Louis XVI	Louis XVI Roskopf	Louis XV Roskopf	Houx	Squelettes-Cœurs
37	38	39	40	41	42

Dessins Gothiques	Dessins variés	Cerfs-volant	Bâtons Demi-Squelettes	Bâtons forts	Bâtons étroits	Bâtons extra-minces
43	44	45	46	47	48	49

Index	Index	Index	Index	Index	Index-Squelettes
50	51	52	53	54	55

Index-Squelettes	Index-Squelettes	Index-Squelettes	Index-Squelettes	Index-Squelettes	Index-Squelettes
56	57	58	59	60	61

Index	Index	Index	Index	Feuilles	Feuilles fortes
62	63	64	65	66	67

Hirondelles	Hirondelles revidées	Losanges revidés	Losanges mixtes	Modernes mixtes	Index Z	Feuilles revidées
68	69	70	71	72	73	74

1 2 3 4 5 6 7 8 9 10 11 12 13 14 15 16 17 18 19 20 21

T164 *Chart of hand types for pocket and wristwatches. Simple hands were preferred for wristwatches. Until 1930 type 9 (Poires anglaises) was widespread, as were 16 (Breguet Empire), 15 (modern) and 6 (Cathedral Roskopf).*

T163 *Rolex "Oyster" case in its present form.*

T165 *Golden bracelet with means to attach a woman's pocket watch. Gold enamel watch with cylinder movement, circa 1840.*

T166 *The watch is clamped between springy wire bows—a "patented solution" of 1891.*

Watchbands and variations

In the wristwatch, watch and band form a unit. Watchbands should be secure and comfortable, durable and stylish, requirements that cannot always be harmonized in practice. Even though the band contributes significantly to the total impression, it plays a secondary role to the watch. This is, of course, not true of some types of ornamental watches.

Here it is possible for the watch itself to be of less importance than precious stones or the goldsmith's art, or in borderline cases to be a decorative element of the band. This is obvious in many striking art-deco creations of the mid-Twenties, when watches with small dials were built into cases which blended into an artistic unit with the band. A more exact description of these and other ornamental watches would not fit into this book,

since the discussion would have to go into art history and types of materials. But in our century there has scarcely been a type of arm jewelry that has not somehow been combined with a watch. Of course it is hard to draw a dividing line because bracelets of high quality have often had small watches of similar quality built into them, as can be seen by looking at the catalogs of Patek Philippe and other leading watch manufacturers.

The variety of watchband forms is strongly systematized. Even before 1900 there were metal bands of gold, silver, tula, doublé and steel; later stainless steel and chromed bands were often used. Leather straps also came into use quite early. Like metal bands, they have remained popular to this day, while textiles and, later, plastics have been less important.

In terms of how they are worn, one can differentiate between the firm band, which must be opened when the watch is taken off, and other types which can be slipped over the hand. The watch on a massive bracelet belongs to the latter type just as much as the flexible band of links. The spring-opening bracelet, which can be pushed sideways over the hand, can be named as a special type. This type already existed before 1900; a few appeared around 1925 and again, especially for men, after 1950.

There are also differences between men's and women's watchbands. The smaller and lighter women's watches usually allow slimmer bands that are more strongly influenced by fashion, though fashion trends can also be noted in men's watchbands. A final difference is between normal types that are firmly attached to the watch and other designs that have allowed the watch to be worn either on the arm or as a pocket watch.

The following chronicle is chronological, summing up watchband types mainly according to when they appeared. The period after 1960 will also be included, as the main forms of watch bands in use today were developed in the formative years. Individual novelties of later years will also be noted.

The journal editor M. Loeske, renowned in his day, in a 1926 article looking back over the watches of the previous fifty years, wrote of watchbands: "The first wristwatches were set in stiff oval bracelets of doublé, silver and gold. Then for a while bands in chain form were popular." To avoid the discomfort caused by stiff bracelets, "bands with flexible shear-shaped links were introduced around 1890."

After 1900 the first band appeared that presumably had been developed expressly to meet the special requirements of the wristwatch: the slim to moderately wide expanding link band ("spring-pull band"), at first with a few relatively long links, later with many short, stiff ones. Since 1908

link bands made by German and Swiss firms have been stressed strongly in advertisements. The next stage of development was completed when, shortly before 1920, the "flexible, flat-spiral" band came on the market; at first it was hooked and fastened right onto the bow of the watch.

The following years saw, above all, the perfecting of the well-known basic types of metal bands. Special types of linkage were developed to make it possible to pass the band quickly over the hand and have it close securely. The disturbing holes between the links of the shear bands disappeared. It became possible to create flexible bands without soldered or riveted links. The fine-link elastic band was made so that, in fitting, individual links could be added or removed quickly and easily. Non-weakening springs assured the long-sought "gentle pull" that the band exerts on the arm without causing pressure.

Pigskin was the preferred material for leather bands before 1914, sometimes with closing seams. Men's watches had slimmer bands than today. A leather band was usually run through both bows and behind the watch, so that there was a layer of leather, fitting the form of the watch, between arm and watch. But the modern way of fastening two short straps, one on each side of the watch, was also practiced then. For a long time it was customary to fasten the leather band by gluing and sewing; in other cases it was riveted or buttoned on. The clasp of the leather band has changed little; a special form was the push-button clasp popular around 1920. The watchmakers hesitated to add leather bands to their stocks. Even in 1928 it was said in the Watchmaker's Weekly: "Sewing a two-part band onto a wristwatch is a simple job, but this work is comonly left for the saddler."

Between 1920 and 1940 many women wore their watches on cloth bands of rep, moiré or brocade. Black was the most popular color, and at times so was sky blue. The cord band, made of cloth aeround 1930 and later of leather, was one of the short-lived types, and so was the band of plaited nylon or perlon that came out in the early Fifties and was very popular for a time.

Much thought was devoted to finding types of armbands that would allow chiefly the woman's pocket watch, and the man's as well, to be worn on the arm without being rebuilt. The most popular type for both sexes for work or everyday use was the wide leather capsule band, whose lifetime extended for half a century, from 1880 to 1930. As early as 1896 the German Watchmakers' Journal mentioned the "well-known leather armbands with watch capsules." Even men's pocket watches with movements of 20-line diameter were worn then in lumpy leather cases on the arm. At times the watch glass was even protected by having a wire mesh screen put over it. These armbands were sold by saddlers. A watchmaker of the time even claimed that the real impulse to wear the watch on the wrist came not from the watch industry, but from the leather trade.

Other possibilities of changing the pocket watch consisted of hanging them inside a kind of springy wire cage or attaching them between two metal rings. Another model, consisting of a metal capsule on a doublé band, points to the fact that even today every woman's watch, whatever metal it may be made of, is made to look like a gold watch. Finally we must mention the various system of holding the watch between four clawlike elements which were fastened in place after being adjusted.

A specially worked model of this kind was praised in 1913 by a jeweler in these words: "In whatever size and height you want, these cleverly constructed watch holders which can be adjusted by one push of a lever to ten different positions, let you insert the watch absolutely securely and comfortably and take it out just as easily." In another advertisement, jewelers and watchmakers were urged to convert the pocket watches in their stocks, which could no longer be sold because wristwatches were in style, in this manner.

The journal "The Watch" dedicated a 1963 special edition to the watchband because the editors felt the band was an important factor in the modern conception of the wristwatch as well as in the progress of practical use of this type of watch. At that time barely fifty West German firms manufactured this article, though it had become a big seller even in the watchmakers' shops.

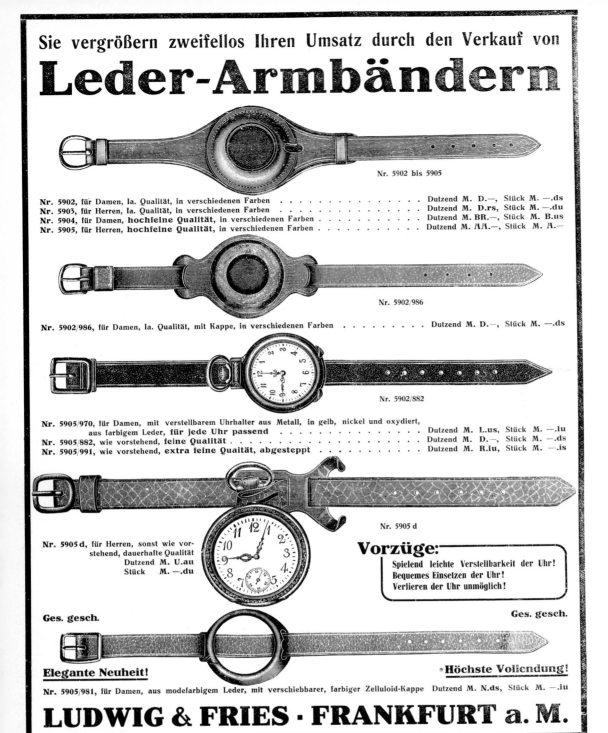
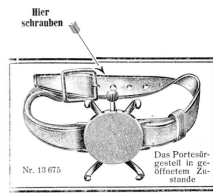

Hier
schrauben

Nr. 13 675

Das Portesûr-
gestell in ge-
öffnetem Zu-
stande

Nr. 13 675
Das Portesûrgestell mit Uhr

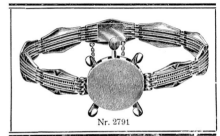

Nr. 2791

T170 *The "Portesûrgestell", another of the many systems for converting pocket watches to wristwatches. It is no accident that most of the devices shown here date from 1913, for the demand was amazingly high in that year. This says something of the popularity of the wristwatch shortly before the outbreak of World War I.*

T168 *The leather capsule band, probably the most practical way to wear a pocket watch as a wristwatch, had a long commercial life between 1880 ans 1930. A 1913 advertisement.*

T169 *A combination of leather band and metal bracket, 1913.*

Opened

Closed

T171 *Brackets that can be adjusted to the size of the watch, combined with an elastic link; 1913.*

112

T172 *An unusually wide link band for the lady, a slim leather band running behind the watch for the gentleman. Wearing the watch on the inside of the wrist was just as uncommon then as now.*

T173 *Watch and armband types of 1913. The small elastic link band of metal was common for women's watches, the slim leather band for men's.*

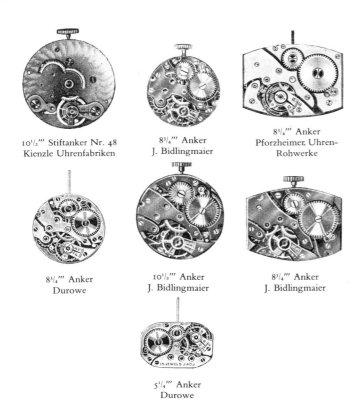

10½''' Stiftanker Nr. 48
Kienzle Uhrenfabriken

8¾''' Anker
J. Bidlingmaier

8¾''' Anker
Pforzheimer. Uhren-Rohwerke

8¾''' Anker
Durowe

10½''' Anker
J. Bidlingmaier

8¾''' Anker
J. Bidlingmaier

5¼''' Anker
Durowe

T175 *Wristwatch movements produced in Germany. Various manufacturers and levels of quality, 1934.*

T176 *"Tutima" wrist chronograph, Glashütte, the last wristwatch developed in Glashütte before World War II.*

T177 *Advertisement from 1953, when the German wristwatch industry was expanding.*

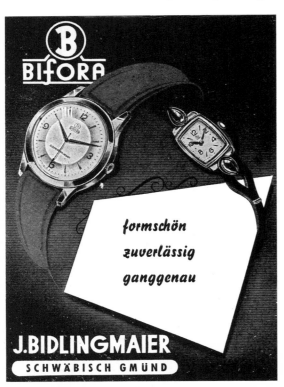

B BIFORA

formschön
zuverlässig
ganggenau

J. BIDLINGMAIER
SCHWÄBISCH GMÜND

watches made for the market. In 1930 the German Watchmakers' Journal commented: "The 'Tutima' wristwatch of Glashütte is the first wristwatch completely produced in Germany; it is built by the newest production methods at the Uhrenroh-Werke-Fabrik (Urofa) of Glashütte. It is made in 8.75-line size, round, for ladies' and men's wristwatches in three qualities that differ very little from each other . . . The 'Tutima' has been on the market for some time and has found much acceptance among watchmakers." "Tutima" was originally the trade mark of the Uhrenfabrik Glashütte AG (UFAG). The "Urofa" caliber 54, a women's formed movement of 5.25 lines, turned out to be especially successful.

The firm of J. Bidlingmaier in Schwäbisch Gmünd also began quite early (1928) to produce movements for their own use, and so deserves to be named here. Special attention among German watchmakers was attracted not only by the round 8.5- and 10.5-line wristwatch movements of Junghans, but also by the first movement from the Pforzheimer Uhren-Rohwerke GmbH (PUW), a 15-jewel, 8.75 line, anchor-balance, formed movement for men's wristwatches, and later by Urofa caliber 58, a space-utilizing movement of 9 by 13 lines with a second hand.

The level of 1934 is shown here as documented by a chart from the German Watchmakers' Journal. According to it, the following firms had developed wristwatch works of their own manufacture or assembly:

Manufacturer	Lines	Form	Escapement	Jewels
Thiel Brothers,	12	round	hook anchor	—
Ruhla	10	round	hook anchor	3
Junghans Brothers,	10.5	round	anchor	15
Schramberg	8.75	round	anchor	15
	10.5	round	cylinder	1 or 6
	8.75	round	cylinder	6
Kienzle Watch Fac-	13	round	hook anchor	—
tory, Schwenningen	12	round	hook anchor	—
	10.5	round	hook anchor	4
Müller-Schlenker,	12.5	round	hook anchor	—
Schwenningen				
Schätzle & Tschudin,	9	round	cylinder	10
Pforzheim				
Uhren-Rohwerk-Fabrik,	8.75	round	cylinder	10
Glashütte	10.5	round	anchor	7/15
	8.75	round	anchor	11/15/16
	5.25	oval	anchor	11/15/16
J. Bidlingmaier,	10.5	round	anchor	7/15
Schwäbisch	8.75	round	anchor	7/15
Gmünd	8.75	tonneau	anchor	7/15
	5.25	oval	anchor	7/15
Kasper & Co.,	8.75	round	cylinder	2/6
Pforzheim				
Herm. Friedr. Bauer,	8.75	round	anchor	7/11/15
Pforzheim				
Maurer & Reiling,	10.5	round	cylinder	0 to 10
Pforzheim				
Pforzheimer Uhren-	8.75	tonneau	anchor	15
Rohwerke GmbH,				
Pforzheim				
Durowe GmbH,	8.75	round	anchor	7/15
Pforzheim	5.25	oval	anchor	7/15

A chart of the calibers (form and size of movements) used by German watch factories was published in installments in 1939 by the journal "Watchmaker's Weekly". The list includes manufacturers, trade marks, sizes and caliber numbers, front and back views of the individual movements, and in a few cases additional data. It shows that round movements of 8.75- and 10.5-line sizes were especially widespread, as well as 5.25-line movements for women's watches and 7.75x11- and 8.75x12-line sizes for men's watches.

There is scarcely any evidence at hand regarding development during the war years. Presumably only a small part of the available manufacturing capacity was devoted to watch production, primarily for military use, while another part was used to make technologically related war materials such as detonators and automatic controls. In 1941 the Glashütte watch industry developed for military use a wrist chronograph that later had to fulfill high demands in series production.

The times since 1945

After World War II the German wristwatch industry again needed to make contact with the developments in Switzerland. It had to catch up to nearly a decade of progress, both technologically and commercially. Even though the German firms had gained much experience in production technology during the war years, the change in production from various war materials to wristwatches and the change to a planned economic approach to competing for markets were not easy. Numerous factories turned to wristwatch production: Mauthe of Schwenningen began production in 1946, Kaiser of Villingen in 1950. The German watch manufacturers' goal was to meet domestic demand for reasonably priced wristwatches, gradually raise standards of quality, and build up export trade as well. In 1961 in Pforzheim and Schramberg, Schwenningen and Schwäbisch Gmünd, 7.5 million wristwatches were produced, of which 2.8 million (37%) were exported.

In the early Fifties there was more news of new manufacture of popular calibers, in which round movements tended to win out over formed types at all levels of quality. In 1950 much attention was drawn to the "space-utilizing movement" for women's watches made by the Pforzheimer Uhren-Rohwerke (PUW), a 5.25-line formed movement in which overdimensional parts were used for the anchor and anchor wheel. As in 1939, in addition to higher-grade watches, millions of reasonably priced wristwatches with hook anchor escapements were produced. In medium-quality women's watches the cylinder escapement was finally replaced by the jeweled anchor. In this class 15-jewel pillar movements dominate, increasingly equipped with shock resistance and modern springs.

The first men's watches with automatic winding came onto the market in 1951/52, the Bidlingmaier "B-Automatik", the "Junghans-Automatik" and the Lacher "Laco-Duromat". All three models used winding systems with two-way rotors in movements of 10.5 lines. The Junghans watch also had a winding indicator. "The remaining field of the complex watch is comparatively easy to occupy," said a 1953 report. There were simple calendar watches (Parat, Förster), simple wrist chronographs (Hanhart, Junghans), and since 1951 the "Minivox" alarm wristwatch, also by Junghans.

Percentages of the Watch Market in Individual
Price Ranges 1967/68

Brand	up to 30 DM	30 to 60 DM	60 to 100 DM	100 to 150 DM	150 to 200 DM	over 200 DM
Kienzle	33.7	20.0	11.7	10.3	4.3	6.0
Junghans	5.4	13.1	11.7	9.1	4.3	12.0
Dugena	1.5	5.4	12.6	12.4	11.7	16.0
Anker	11.8	8.3	6.1	7.9	8.5	5.0
Zentra	2.5	4.6	7.1	6.2	11.7	7.0
Timex	3.4	9.2	2.1	1.2	1.1	—
Bifora	under 1%	1.5	3.8	1.2	3.2	—
Others	20.6	20.9	26.5	39.7	36.1	44.0
No Data	21.1	17.0	18.4	12.0	19.1	10.0
	100.0	100.0	100.0	100.0	100.0	100.0

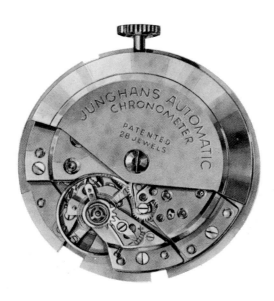

T178 *A highest-grade product of German wristwatch production after World War II: the J83 chronometer movement with automatic winding, by Junghans. In production from 1958 to 1967.*

A few years later the basic situation had changed, even though the variety of Swiss offerings and the technical refinement of the leading Swiss manufacturers could not be equaled. After 1955 the man's automatic watch was an established part of German manufacturers' programs. Less costly production was to invite new levels of buyers, as with the "Volksautomatic" series introduced by Kienzle in 1956. Wristwatches became flatter, technically more advanced and more reliable. The direct central second hand prevailed, as did the woman's automatic, the man's automatic with complexities and the wrist chronometer.

Research shows that "German watches are thoroughly capable of meeting higher demands", and the German Hydrographic Institute of Hamburg upgraded its testing to suit the higher Swiss criteria. One year later Junghans brought out a wrist chronometer with automatic winding, probably the highest achievement of German constructors in the realm of the mechanical wristwatch. In the same period, 1957/58, two watch factories, Laco-Durowe and Uhren-Werk-Ersingen (Epperlein), reported electromechanical wristwatches. A new technology made itself known.

"What does a German wristwatch now amount to?" the reader might ask at the end of this chapter. The answer must remain open. The purist must demand that a watch be produced in a factory with its own development and manifold production of parts, though concessions are allowed in the case and dial, but movement and case numbers should be equal. Another might call every watch sold under a German factory or trade name a German watch. It must be pointed out, though, that only the specialist can have exact information, even with the many Swiss watches, as to which parts of the watch were made in the home factory and which were bought from other firms. Before World War I, after all, most cylinder wheels for Swiss watches were made in France, and many cases came from Pforzheim. The decision as to what can be called a German watch is left to the collector's judgment.

T179 *Wristwatch movement with electromechanical drive, Landeron caliber 4750, of 1960.*

On the way to the quartz watch

In the same period when the problem of winding the mechanical wristwatch seemed to have been solved by high-performance mainsprings and refined automatic systems, when hairsprings were developed to the point that, as Professor Straumann reported in 1962, "the influence of their own failure on the running of the watch is about 10% less than other failures that disturb running," when even in small-series wristwatches without regulation deviations of about 30 seconds a day could be striven for, the laboratories and development departments in various countries were working intensively on a new technology. In retrospect, three stages of development can be seen clearly: the electromechanical wristwatch, the tuning-fork watch, and the quartz watch.

Again, as so often in the history of the watch, skepticism at first prevailed and the impact of the new developments was undervalued. In 1957 Professor Keil came to the following conclusion: "These reports [of electric wristwatches] have had a sensational effect and shaken up the watch industry, but they are more representative of a desire for sensation at any price than of facts resting on a foundation of a technically and economically satisfactory solution to a problem."

Today we know that a good two decades of intensive developmental work sufficed to catch up to the head start of the mechanical portable watch with its nearly 500-year history. If at first the question was heard as to what chance the electric watch had against a highly developed fine mechanical technology, the subject changed by the mid-Seventies. The mechanical watch took a defensive position; the electronic quartz watch began to take over the markets. A few dates will show the stages of this technological breakthrough:

1952: Lip (France) and Elgin (USA) inform the press of developmental progress in the field of the electro mechanical wristwatch.

1957: Hamilton (USA) begins series production of an electric wristwatch.

1960: Bulova (USA/Switzerland) brings the tuning-fork "Accutron" wristwatch developed by Max Hetzel onto the market; the Ebauches SA electromechanical 4750L caliber is ready for production.

1962: Founding of the Swiss Centre Electronic Horloger (CEH) research center.

1967: Prototype of a quartz wristwatch achieves a new precision record in competition at the Neuenburg observatory.

1970: Two million Bulova Accutron sold; various firms display quartz wristwatches as the Basel Fair.

Two basic technical problems had to be solved before electric wristwatches could be produced. The first was the creation of lasting and capable miniature batteries, for a wristwatch whose source of energy had to be changed constantly was not a saleable product. That was Max Hetzel's verdict on which problems came up during the construction of the tuning-fork watch: that batteries meant to run a watch for a whole year ran down after two months. Even experts had not thought that such low use of power could bring on an inner short circuit.

The second problem makes the link between watch production and general technical development even clearer. The question was what contact system was able to function economically and without abrasion through the approximately 100 million contacts that take place in an electric wristwatch. The previous electrotechnology had to give up; only the semi-conductor system of the transistor brought a solution of the problem. But now the road was free for new development.

The conservative solution consisted of an electric power system similar to those already long used in

T180 *Man's wristwatch with quartz movement by Rado, of 1970. It is equipped with a Beta 21 quartzcaliber developed by the Swiss "Centre électroniqie horloger" (CEH).*

large clocks. A concept that went further—essentially followed in the experiments of Hamilton, Lip, Epperlein and Ebauches—retained the mechanical balance with its hairspring as a regulatory organ. An electromagnetic drive system in which the balance serves as the magnetic anchor deals with the necessary energy transfer and intervenes as a regulator when the swing arcs change. The swings of the balance are transmitted mechanically to a pacemaking wheel and sent on to the under-the-dial system in the traditional way. Even in this system important elements of the mechanical wristwatch are missing, but at least its "heart", the mechanical running regulator as a low-frequency oscillator, is retained.

The conception of the Bulova Accutron went one step farther: the hairspring was replaced by a tuning fork. The classic regulator swings far and slowly; the ticking of the watch makes this rhythm clear. But the tuning-fork watch just hums. The humming is caused by the 360 swings per second of a 25 mm. long, electrically stimulated tuning fork and the transfer mechanism for the under-the-dial mechanism that is linked with it.

"The project's weakness was the instability of the tuning fork amplitude and the insufficient functioning security of the switching system," Max Hetzel wrote in 1968 in retrospect. But when, after long experiments, the tuning fork's arc of swing was successfully held constant, a time norm was available that excelled the exactitude of the previous systems. That is why Bulova could guarantee the buyer of the Accutron a maximum deviation of + / – one minute per month.

T181 *Max Hetzel (born 1921). He developed the Accutron electronic tuning-fork watch. The mechanical wristwatch was thereby confronted by a new technology. Even though the tuning-fork watch was soon replaced by the quartz watch, Max Hetzel's technical achievement remains undeniable.*

The difficulties that arose in converting the swinging motion of the tuning fork into a steadily running revolution of the hands have already been noted. In the Accutron this conversion is made by a drive blade, firmly attached to the swinging arm of the tuning fork, that meshes with a switching wheel of 2.4 mm diameter with 300 teeth. This small beryllium-bronze cogwheel revolves one in 5/6 of a second, while in comparison the fastest wheel of the mechanical watch, the escapement wheel, revolves once in six seconds. Aside from the mechanics of transition, the tuning-fork watch has scarcely any similarity to the movement of a mechanical wristwatch.

Technologically and commercially, the tuning-fork watch was soon replaced by the quartz watch. Its basic principle was explained by the Seiko firm in 1981 as follows: "When a quartz crystal is cut at a certain angle and attached to an appropriate power source, it produces constant oscillations. In most watches quartz usually has a frequency of 32,768 Hz. This high frequency is constantly halved by a frequency divider, until a constant rate of one cycle per second is attained. This is the basis of all quartz watches."

Proceeding from that, the oscillations could be used in various ways. In the Quartz-Analog watch they were transmitted to the under-the-dial mechanism by a micro-step-switching motor.

In the digital quartz watch the oscillations are converted via a switching circuit into digits on a fluid-crystal indicator. Quartz wristwatches attain a previously scarcely imaginable degree of precision for time measurement. Whereas the deviations in a mechanical chronometer were expressed in seconds per day, in the quartz watch they become seconds per month. Some day historians will be able to verify more exactly when the end came for the mechanical wristwatch. Was it in 1960, when the Accutron came on the market with its new construction principle, or only in the Seventies, when the fully electronic quartz watch went into mass production? One thing, though, is eternally fascinating: how a threatened technology in its last stage simultaneously brings about its highest achievement. Even if their economic assessment does not disappear, the complicated mechanical wristwatches of the later years will always fascinate the watch lover.

The following firms exhibited their models, fitted with the Beta 21 caliber movement, at the Basel Sample Fair of 1970: Bulova, Credos, Ebel, Eberhard & Co., Elgin, Enicar, Fabre-Leuba, IWC, Jaeger-LeCoultre, Juvenia, Longines, Omega, Patek Philippe, Piaget, Rado, Synchron, Universal, Zenith and Zodiac.

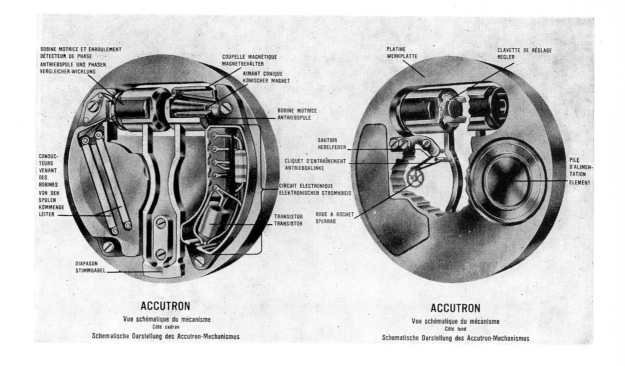

ACCUTRON
Vue schématique du mécanisme
Côté cadran
Schematische Darstellung des Accutron-Mechanismus

ACCUTRON
Vue schématique du mécanisme
Côté fond
Schematische Darstellung des Accutron-Mechanismus

BOBINE MOTRICE ET ENROULEMENT DÉTECTEUR DE PHASE
ANTRIEBSPULE UND PHASEN-VERGLEICHER-WICKLUNG

COUPELLE MAGNÉTIQUE
MAGNETBEHÄLTER

AIMANT CONIQUE
KONISCHER MAGNET

BOBINE MOTRICE
ANTRIEBSPULE

CONDUC-TEURS VENANT DES BOBINES
VON DEN SPULEN KOMMENDE LEITER

CIRCUIT ÉLECTRONIQUE
ELEKTRONISCHER STROMKREIS

TRANSISTOR
TRANSISTOR

DIAPASON
STIMMGABEL

PLATINE
WERKPLATTE

CLAVETTE DE RÉGLAGE
REGLER

SAUTOIR
HEBELFEDER

CLIQUET D'ENTRAÎNEMENT
ANTRIEBSKLINKE

ROUE A ROCHET
SPERRAD

PILE D'ALIMEN-TATION
ELEMENT

T182 *Schematic drawing of the interior of the Accutron. In this drawing, only one cogwheel is still reminiscent of mechanical wristwatch technology.*

T183 *Parts of the Swiss Beta 21 caliber quartz watch, state of the art in 1969. In the Beta 21 the frequency of the quartz is 8192 Hz., which is reduced to 256 Hz. by a frequency divider. A micro-computer transmitted the oscillations to the behind-the-dial mechanism by means of a ratchet. The first wheel has 256 teeth and makes one revolution per second.*

T184 *Longines "Quartz Chron" of 1970, Beta 21 movement.*

T185 *Universal "Uniquartz", 1970, Beta 21 movement.*

T186 *Girard-Perregaux "Elcron" man's wristwatch of 1970. This firm did not use the Beta 21 caliber, but had developed its own quartz movement in cooperation with Thomson C.S.F. of Paris. The quartz frequency was the usual 8192 Hz.*

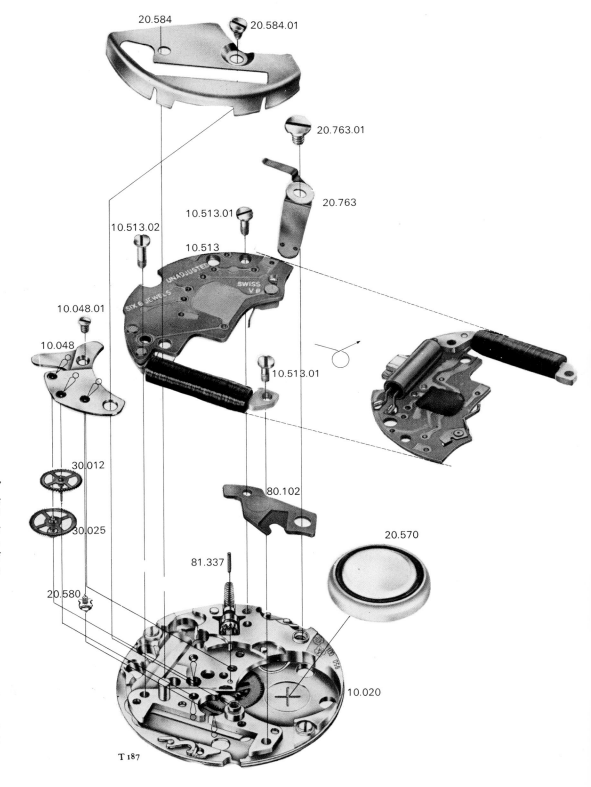

T187 *Exploded view of an ESA-ETA quartz caliber in current production.*

Collecting wristwatches

Originally more or less laughed off, the ranks of wristwatch collectors constantly increased in past years. Meanwhile even established pocket watch collectors have chosen to expand their collections with watches worn on the arm.

At first glance, this is hard for the lover of old watches with lots of tradition to understand. The wristwatch, as one pocket-watch fan put it, is "only a piece of mass production without individual worth."

Surely it is not easy to contradict him, in view of the great quantities of wristwatches that have been made. Here one must refer to personal experience and say that interesting, well-made mechanical wristwatches are rare, not just the products of those watch manufacturers who were active only in price ranges that the ordinary mortal can reach only through great financial sacrifices. These watches, because of their material worth and in part also their idealized value, were usually handled with great care and are still in good condition after many years.

No, particularly good and technically high-valued wristwatches that were made in large series for broad levels of the population and went with their owners into everyday life and work are very rare in good condition, since daily wearing under rough conditions left traces that cannot be over-looked, and the watches became either defective or unpleasant to look at. Many examples, especially if their case was not of precious metal, were simply thrown away.

But watches with gold cases did not fare that much better. What with the massive increases in the price of gold in recent years and the desire to own a modern quartz wristwatch, many cases were sold to be melted down. This explains why, even today, one can still obtain interesting movements relatively often without cases. The making of new cases is a handicraft and thus rarely to be had at any price today. It is worth the price only for truly extraordinary watch movements.

Obtaining collectable watches

Dealers of antiques and old clocks generally shrug their shoulders with boredom if one asks them about wristwatches. Dealing in such objects is much too trivial, and besides, the things are so new! Ever since it became fashionable to wear an old mechanical watch on one's wrist, though, there have been shops that deal in interesting wristwatches. Some auction houses also put them up for sale at times.

Though in former days it was still practical to inquire after collectible mechanical wristwatches in "normal" clock and watch shops, it is hardly worth doing today, for since the appearance of the quartz watch, the interesting items have been cleaned out of the shop and sold off at sometimes considerably lowered prices. This is understandable from the businessman's point of view, since a big stock of goods that will not sell represents a lot of tied-up capital.

There remain the many antique shows and flea markets, at which, with a little luck, one can still make an interesting purchase.

If a collector or enthusiast comes across a desirable item, it will be the external condition that catches one's eye first. A bad outward appearance generally indicates a hard life, and may also suggest that the interior of the watch has had hard times too. In such cases it is well to proceed with caution. Worn places in the finish of gold doublé, chromed or nickel-plated cases are an obvious sign of long wearing. Cases of steel or stainless steel may just get a few scratches, and for this reason they must be looked at more closely.

That is way an experienced collector will always carry his loupe with him on his expeditions, so as to give questionable specimens a closer look.

The dial and hands of a watch should also be given a good look, for they have much to do with the overall impression of a watch.

The interior of a watch must next receive an equally thorough examination—and be in a condition to be examined. Of course, it is usually impossible to open the case on the spot, especially when the watch has a screwed-on bottom. At least one should have a paring knife with one, in order to be able to remove a sprung bottom. An opener for screwed bottoms will also prove to be handy, for with it one can get into a great many watches of that type without scratching the bottom. But in the end there will be watches that resist any attempts to open them, and whose interiors are thus hidden from the buyer's eyes.

If one has managed to persuade the seller to let the watch be opened and has exposed the movement, a first glance should be directed toward the inside of the bottom. It will give evidence about the number of overhaulings and repairs the watch has had, and sometimes of their dates, for watchmakers generally scratch in their repair symbols, in part so as to be able to defend themselves against unjustified complaints. A good look should be given to the heads of the numerous screws. They can tell of frequent loosenings and tightenings, especially if done by careless watchmakers, in the form of damaged slots and heads. Naturally one must also look to see if water has entered and left rust damage. Technical details, such as the right swing, the liveliness of a spring, or the trouble-free winding of an automatic, can only be recognized by the collector who is thoroughly at home with the principles of watches or has acquired a similar knowledge through plenty of experience.

In this respect it might be mentioned that the mere fact that a watch does not run need not be a reason to refuse to buy it, especially if its external condition is good. The non-synthetic oils once used had the tendency to become resinous after a long period of inactivity and stop the watch from running. A gummed-up movement thus can indicate that the watch has not been worn for a long time and will probably come back to life after a thorough cleaning.

One weak point, especially of old and roughly used wristwatches with hand winding, might finally be mentioned: the setting and winding mechanism. Even the layman can tell by feeling whether the stem can be pulled out without difficulty for setting, and how much play there is in it before the hands move. One can also tell by feel (and by listening), after just a few turns of the stem, how the cogwheels mesh with each other when being wound.

Wristwatch collectors and watchmakers

In the end one needs a reliable and thorough watchmaker, and they are not easy to find.

The enthusiast who begins to collect mechanical wristwatches might think that one need only seek out the nearest watch dealer to get a watch repaired.

This notion will soon prove to be deceptive, for many shops nowadays only sell watches and give such services as changing batteries or watchbands. They take watches that need repairs and send them on to a watchmaker in their hire, who never meets the customer face to face.

Personal contact and discussion, though, are very advisable in order to solve the problems of defective watches. Dealers' main interest is usually to sell the customer a new (quartz) watch, because there is more profit in that than in time-consuming repair work.

The argument of diminished profit is all too often heard in this situation.

In any case it is unproblematic and practicable to replace a defective or scratched glass, bad-looking hands, the winding stem or its knob, the mainspring or other such parts. Replacing an unusable shock-absorbing system or a broken bearing jewel should be no great problem for a well-trained watchmaker.

Oxidized, rusted or peeling dials can be restored by specialist firms.

Worn gold doublé, chrome or nickel plating can be restored with the help of a willing galvanizing plant, provided the movement and glass are first removed.

Repairs are more difficult when they require the obtaining, or worse yet the making, of specific replacement parts (such as for a broken balance arbor or damaged hairspring). Here the ability and availability of a capable watchmaker and his machines play a major role.

In principle, one should not take the best watch in one's collection to a watch dealer or watchmaker for repairs on one's first visit. It is best to have a few less valuable pieces repaired first as a test. One can usually tell very soon whether the watchmaker feels any interest, joy and affinity for repairing mechanical watches of bygone years or complex construction.

Wristwatch collectors on their own

The precision, complexity and small size of wristwatch movements generally prevent the layman from making repairs himself. His activities should be limited to the external care of watches.

With the help of silver polish or other suitable polish such as "Mezerna", "Unipol" or "Edel-Bonit", dull or worn surfaces can be made to shine again. And it is justified, not only for esthetic reasons, to rid a watch of traces of perspiration with a "Selvyt" cloth. Finally, the pieces in the collection should be housed so that they do not get scratched by the container or each other.

The mechanical wristwatch enthusiast can contribute much to the building up of a collection through patience and sagacity while searching. What one is going to collect, by what system one proceeds, whether one stresses optics, technology, names, materials, age, rarity or uniqueness, every individual must decide for himself.

This book attempts to unveil the wristwatch to the watch enthusiast through examples in text and illustration.

Joy and increased wisdom come, as a rule, through deep devotion and through collecting itself.

T188 *Swiss wristwatches from the catalog "The Swiss Watch in Switzerland. Zürich State Fair 1939". 1. Universal, chronograph with hour indicator. 2. Rolex Oyster. 3. Roamer. 4. Recta Inclinex. 5. Woman's wristwatch by Longines. 6. Rolex Oyster, steel goad. 7. Recta. 8. Doxa.*

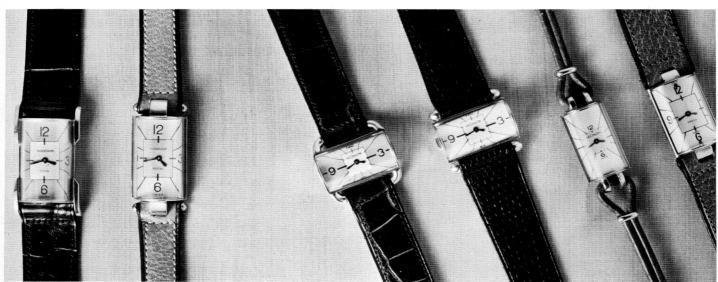

38

126

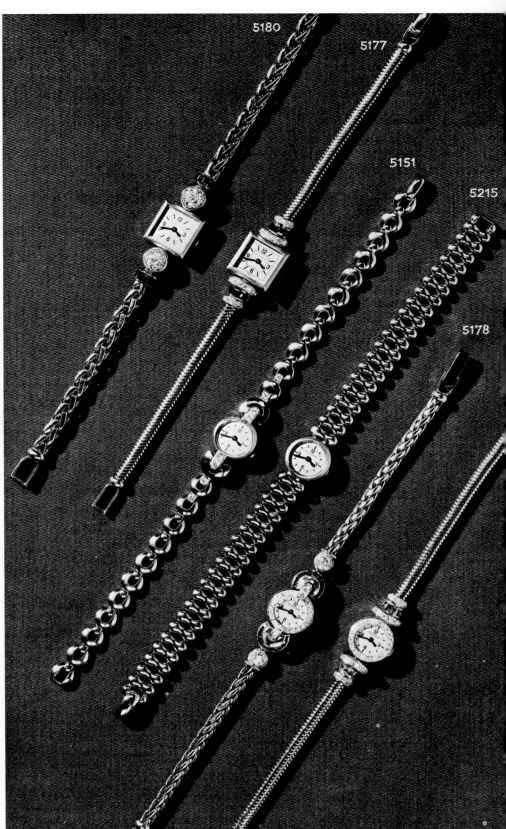

Various women's and men's wristwatches by Jaeger- LeCoultre, 1945.

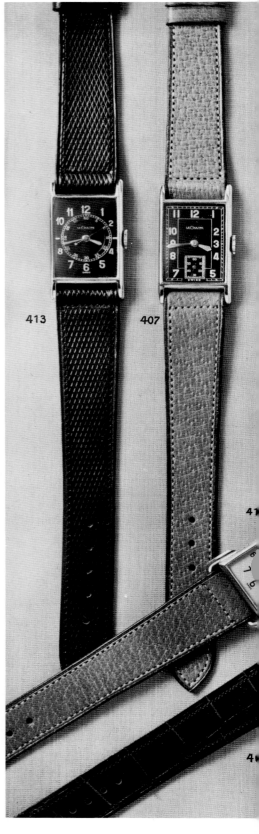

413

407

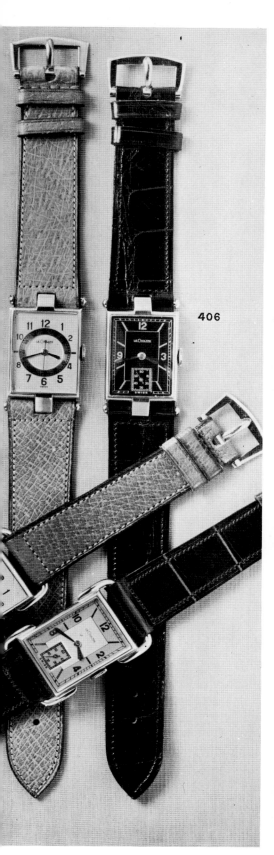

Various women's and men's wristwatches by Jaeger- LeCoultre, 1945.

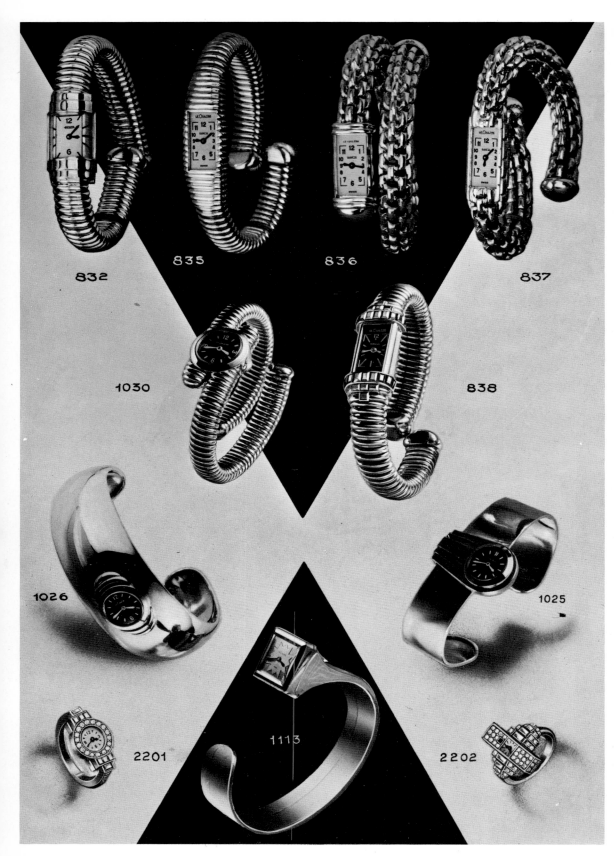

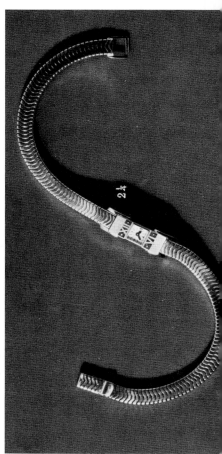

Various women's and men's wristwatches by Jaeger-LeCoultre, 1945.

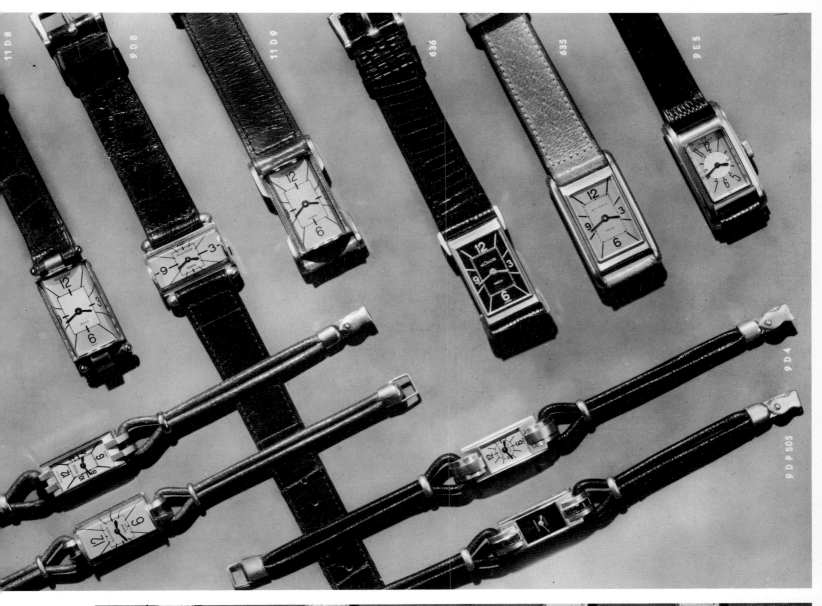

131

Various women's and men's wristwatches by Jaeger- LeCoultre, 1945.

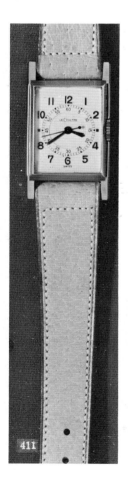

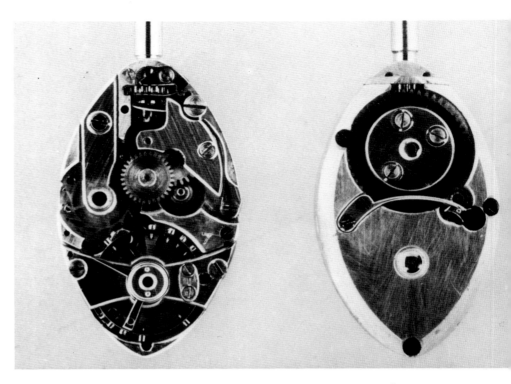

Specially constructed oval wristwatch movement (1923), caliber 7 AJ. 15.00 x 9.00 mm, 4.30 mm high; the movement was built into a case so that the balance was visible through a cutout in the dial (see woman's wristwatch by Cartier, Illustration 58).

Extra-flat movement of 1908, caliber 6-line EB 13.33 x 11 mm, 1.50 mm high.

Movement with minute repetition of 1908, caliber 13-line RMV, diameter 30.50 mm, height 3.25 mm.

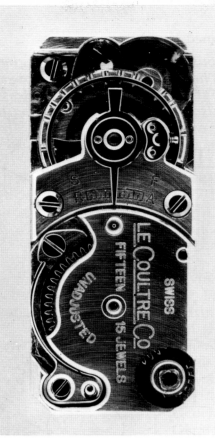

"Duoplan" wristwatch movement of 1932, caliber 9 BF, 20.00 x 8.50 MM, height 3.73 mm; winding and setting are done from the back.

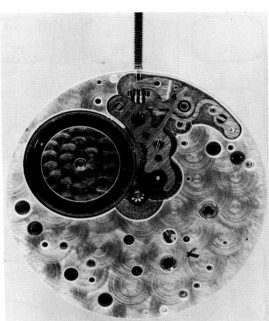

Wristwatch movement, caliber 839, of 1962, which was also built into an engraved case of massive 14-karat gold; diameter 20.80 mm, height 1.85 mm.

Wristwatch movement with automatic winding, and winding indication shown through a cutout in the dial, 1947, caliber 476-12 AD, diameter 29.56 mm, height 6.15 mm.

Lacloche, Paris
Laco-Durowe (Lacher & Co. Deutsche-Uhren-Rohwerke), Pforzheim
Lanco (Langendorf Watch Co.), Langendorf
Landeron, Le Landeron
Lange und Söhne, Glashütte
Jean Lassale, Geneva
Lemania, L'Orient
Leonidas Watch Factory, Saint-Imier
Léon Leroy, Paris
Lip, Besançon
Longines, Saint-Imier
Luxor, Le Locle

Martel Watch Co., Les Ponts-de-Martel
Marvin, Compagnie Des Montres, La Chaux-de-Fonds
Mido, Biel
Mimo, Graef & Co., La Chaux-de-Fonds
Minerva Sport S.A., Villeret
Minerva Watch, Villeret
Moeris Watch, Le Locle
Henry Moser, Le Locle
Movado, La Chaux-de-Fonds, Le Locle
Mulco, La Chaux-de-Fonds

Ollech & Wajs, Zürich
Omega, Biel
Orfina, Grenchen
Oris, Hölstein

Parc, Carouge/Geneva
Para (Paul Raff), Pforzheim
Patek Philippe & Co., Geneva
Perfecta S.A., Porrentruy
Peseux, Peseux
Daniel Perret, Zürich
Le Phare-Sultana S.A., La Chaux-de-Fonds
Piaget, La Côte-aux-Fées-Geneva
Th. Picard Fils, La Chaux-de-Fonds
Pierce, Biel
Plojoux, Geneva
Poljot, Moscow
Porta, Pforzheim
Pronto Watch, L. Maître & Fils, Le Noirmont
Prorubis, Courtemaîche

Record Watch Co., Tramelan, Geneva
Recta, Biel
Revue, Waldenburg
Roamer Watch, Solothurn

Rolex, Geneva
Le Roy & Fils, Paris
Ruhla, Glashütte
Rumanel Watch, Biel

Sauter Frères, Biel
René Schaldenbrand, La Chaux-de-Fonds
A. Schild S.A., Grenchen
Seiko, Tokio
Sickinger, Pforzheim
Silvana S.A., Tramelan
Helmut Sinn, Frankfurt
Smiths, England
Starina, La Chaux-de-Fonds
Theodore B. Starr, New York
Stowa (Walter Storz), Pforzheim, Rheinfelden

Ta-Cy (Tavannes-Cyma Watch), Tavannes
Tavannes Watch, Tavannes
Thiel, Ruhla
Thommen, Waldenburg
Tiffany, New York
Tissot, Le Locle
Tourist Ad. Allemann, Welschenrohr/Solothurn
Tressa, Geneva
Türler, Zürich

Ufag (Uhrenfabrik Ag), Glashütte
Ulysse Nardin, Le Locle
Union Horlogère Alpina, Biel
Unitas, Tramelan
Universal, Geneva
Urofa (Uhren-Rohwerke-Fabrikation), Glashütte

Vacheron & Constantin, Geneva
Valjoux, Les Bioux
Vulcain, La Chaux-de-Fonds

Waltham, Waltham Massachusets/Neuchâtel
Wempe, Hamburg
Werba, Geneva
West End Watch, Schweiz, USA
Wilka Watch, Geneva
Wittnauer Watch, Geneva
Wostok, Moscow
Wyler S.A., La Chaux-de-Fonds
Wyler Watch, Biel

Zenith, Le Locle
Zentra, Ulm
Zodiac, Le Locle

Trade marks

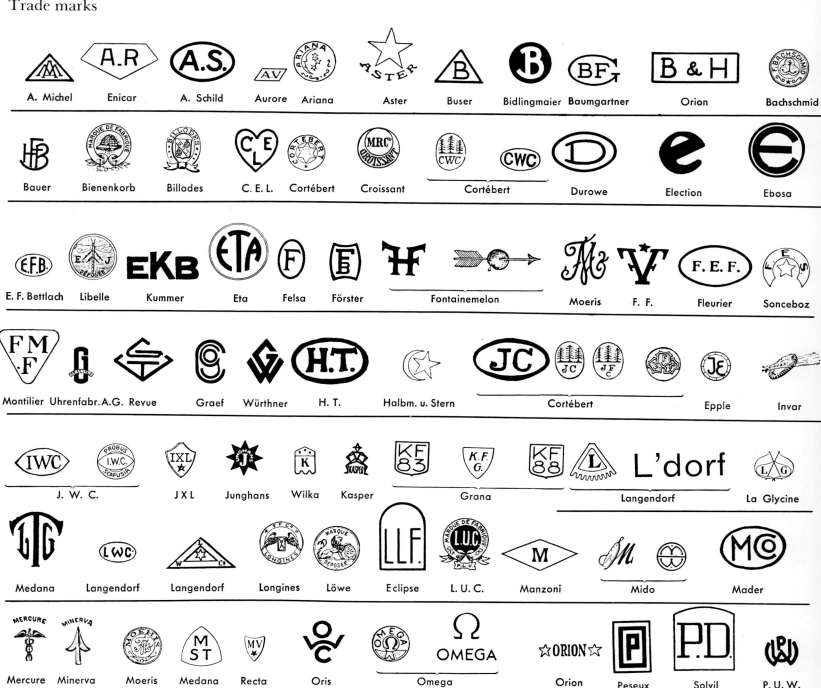

A. Michel	Enicar	A. Schild	Aurore	Ariana	Aster	Buser	Bidlingmaier	Baumgartner	Orion	Bachschmid
Bauer	Bienenkorb	Billodes	C. E. L.	Cortébert	Croissant	Cortébert		Durowe	Election	Ebosa
E. F. Bettlach	Libelle	Kummer	Eta	Felsa	Förster	Fontainemelon		Moeris	F. F.	Fleurier	Sonceboz
Montilier Uhrenfabr. A.G.	Revue	Graef	Würthner	H. T.	Halbm. u. Stern	Cortébert			Epple	Invar
J. W. C.	JXL	Junghans	Wilka	Kasper	Grana		KF88	L'dorf	Langendorf	La Glycine
Medana	Langendorf	Langendorf	Longines	Löwe	Eclipse	L. U. C.	Manzoni	Mido		Mader
Mercure	Minerva	Moeris	Medana	Recta	Oris	Omega		Orion	Peseux	Solvil	P. U. W.
Postala	Minerva	Recta	Rhein	Rosk. Patent	Eterna	S. F. H.	Reconvilier	Ebauches Trust	Unitas
Tavannes	Tavannes	Venus	Vogt	Freya	Cupillard	Wasa	Freco			

Trade marks from the Flume Werksucher, 1938.

The trade marks with lettering are arranged alphabetically, those without lettering are at the end of the chart.

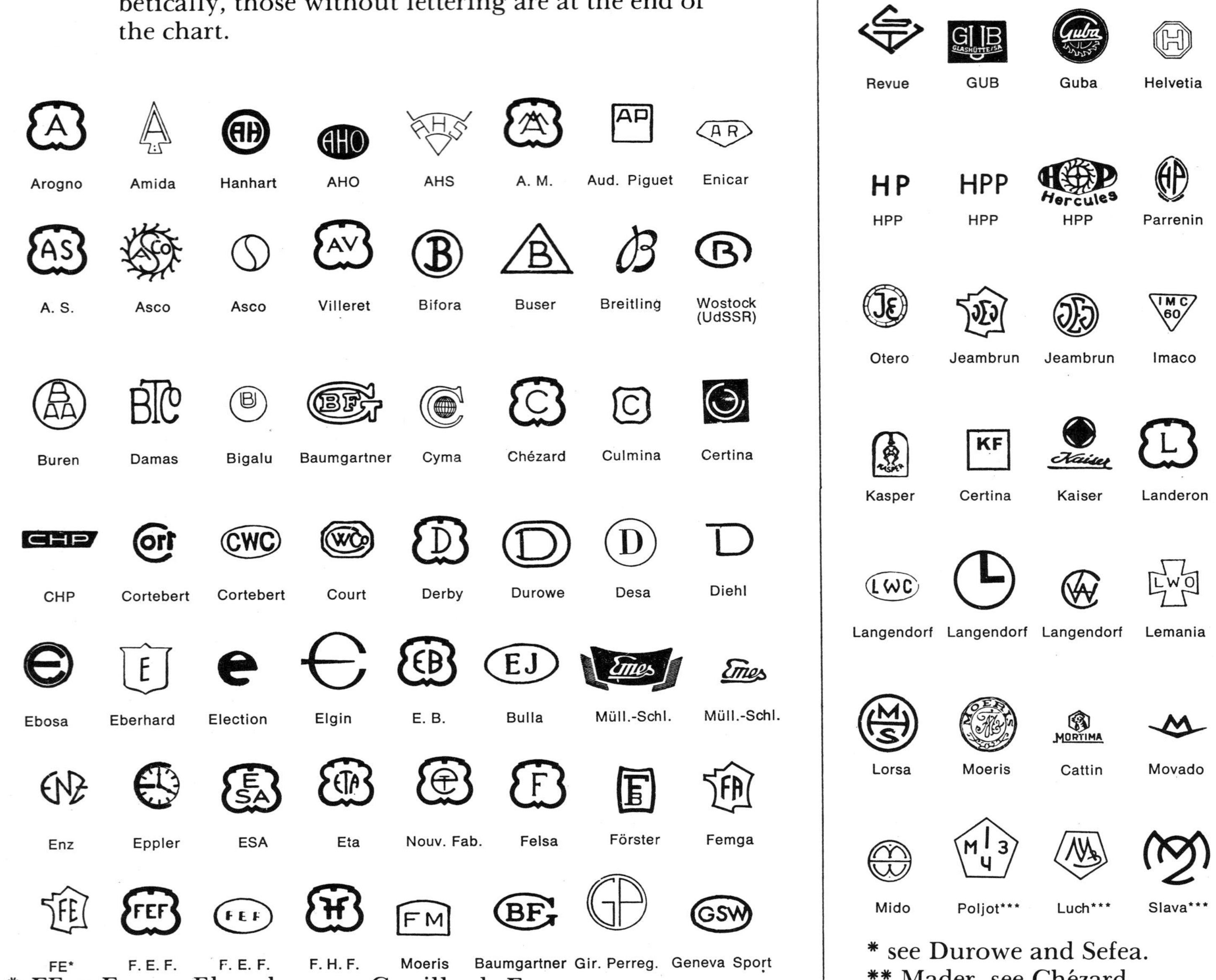

Column 1 (left chart)

 Arogno   Amida   Hanhart   AHO   AHS   A. M.   Aud. Piguet   Enicar

A. S. Asco Asco Villeret Bifora Buser Breitling Wostock (UdSSR)

Buren Damas Bigalu Baumgartner Cyma Chézard Culmina Certina

 CHP   Cortebert   Cortebert   Court   Derby   Durowe   Desa   Diehl

 Ebosa   Eberhard   Election   Elgin   E. B.   Bulla   Müll.-Schl.   Müll.-Schl.

 Enz   Eppler   ESA   Eta   Nouv. Fab.   Felsa   Förster   Femga

FE*   F. E. F.   F. E. F.   F. H. F.   Moeris   Baumgartner   Gir. Perreg.   Geneva Sport

* FE = France Ebauches, see Cupillard, Femga, Jeambrun, Lorsa, TE.

Column 2 (right chart)

 Revue GUB   Guba   Helvetia

H P — HPP HPP  HPP (Hercules)   Parrenin

 Otero   Jeambrun Jeambrun Imaco

Kasper Certina   Kaiser   Landeron

 Langendorf   Langendorf Langendorf   Lemania

 Lorsa   Moeris   Cattin   Movado

Mido Poljot*** Luch*** Slava***

* see Durowe and Sefea.
** Mader, see Chézard.
*** see USSR calibers.

German and Swiss gold and silver stamps

 0,800   0,875
Swiss silver marks

German silver mark

German gold mark

 14 kar. = 0,585   18 kar. = 0,750
Swiss gold marks

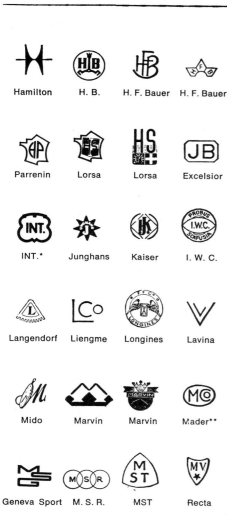

Hamilton · H. B. · H. F. Bauer · H. F. Bauer
Parrenin · Lorsa · Lorsa · Excelsior
INT.* · Junghans · Kaiser · I. W. C.
Langendorf · Liengme · Longines · Lavina
Mido · Marvin · Marvin · Mader**
Geneva Sport · M. S. R. · MST · Recta
Oris · Oris · Osco · Peseux

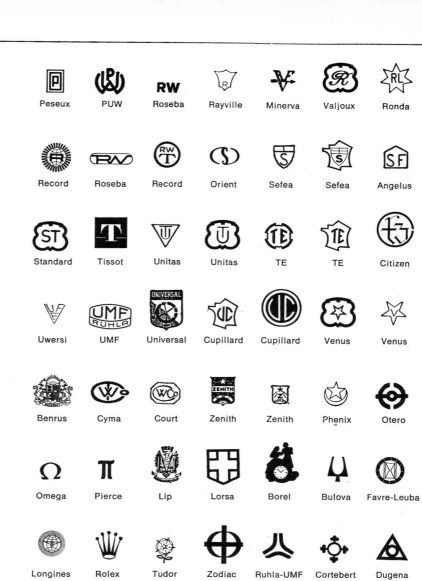

Peseux · PUW · Roseba · Rayville · Minerva · Valjoux · Ronda · Revue
Record · Roseba · Record · Orient · Sefea · Sefea · Angelus · Reconvilier
Standard · Tissot · Unitas · Unitas · TE · TE · Citizen · Universal
Uwersi · UMF · Universal · Cupillard · Cupillard · Venus · Venus · Vulcain
Benrus · Cyma · Court · Zenith · Zenith · Phenix · Otero · Minerva
Omega · Pierce · Lip · Lorsa · Borel · Bulova · Favre-Leuba · Hamilton
Longines · Rolex · Tudor · Zodiac · Ruhla-UMF · Cortebert · Dugena · Ultra
Chaika* · Luch* · Molnia* · Poljot* · Raketa* · Slava* · Wostok* · Zaria*

* see USSR calibers

Conversion Table

lignes	mm	sizes	lignes	mm	sizes	lignes	mm	sizes	lignes	mm	sizes
1‴	2,26		13‴	29,33	0	7‴	15,79		19‴	42,86	16
1/4	2,82		1/4	29,89		1/4	16,35	16/0	1/4	43,43	
1/2	3,38		1/2	30,45		1/2	16,92		1/2	43,99	
3/4	3,95		3/4	31,02		3/4	17,48		3/4	44,55	
2‴	4,51		14‴	31,58		8‴	18,05		20‴	45,12	18
1/4	5,08		1/4	32,15	3	1/4	18,61		1/4	45,68	
1/2	5,64		1/2	32,71		1/2	19,17		1/2	46,25	
3/4	6,20		3/4	33,27		3/4	19,74	12/0	3/4	46,81	
3‴	6,77		15‴	33,84		9‴	20,30		21‴	47,37	21
1/4	7,33		1/4	34,40		1/4	20,87		1/4	47,94	
1/2	7,90		1/2	34,97	6	1/2	21,43		1/2	48,50	
3/4	8,46		·3/4	35,53		3/4	21,99	10/0	3/4	49,07	
4‴	9,02		16‴	36,09		10‴	22,56		22‴	49,63	
1/4	9,59		1/4	36,66	8	1/4	23,12		1/4	50,19	
1/2	10,15		1/2	37,22		1/2	23,69	8/0	1/2	50,76	25
3/4	10,72		3/4	37,79		3/4	24,25		3/4	51,32	
5‴	11,28		17‴	38,35		11‴	24,81		23‴	51,88	
1/4	11,84		1/4	38,91		1/4	25,38	6/0	1/4	52,45	27
1/2	12,41	20/0	1/2	39,48		1/2	25,94		1/2	53,01	
3/4	12,97		3/4	40,04	12	3/4	26,51		3/4	53,58	
6‴	13,53		18‴	40,61		12‴	27,07		24‴	54,14	
1/4	14,10		1/4	41,17		1/4	27,63		1/4	54,71	
1/2	14,66	18/0	1/2	41,73	14	1/2	28,20		1/2	55,27	
3/4	15,23		3/4	42,30		3/4	28,76	2/0	3/4	55,83	31

Bibliography

Aebi, Peter: John Harwood, dem Erfinder der automatischen Armbanduhr gewidmet; in: Neue Uhrmacher-Zeitung (1966) Heft 5, S. 18-20

Bauer, F.: Taschen- und Armbanduhren — Erzeugung und Sondermaschinen für den Werkzeubgau der Gebrüder Thiel GmbH, Ruhla, Thüringen, Leipzig 1938

Béguin, Pierre: Reinhard Straumann (1892-1967). Zum Gedenken; in: Schweizerische Uhrmacher-Zeitung (1969), Heft 10, S. 50-55

Belmont, Henry-L.: Léon Hatot; in: Horlogerie Ancienne Nr. 12 (1982) S. 97-104

Bergler, Georg: die Uhr im Urteil des Verbrauchers; in: Die Uhrmacherkunst (1938) S. 78-80

Berner, G.-H.: La montre-bracelet, autrefois, aujourd'hui; Biel 1945

Bolaffi, Giulio (Hrsg.): Bolaffi Arte presenta Omega, numero speciale monografico; Turin 1979

Boy, Albert: Ubersicht über die Chronographen; in: Die Uhr (1953) S. 11-14

Brinkmann, Hermann: Einführung in die Uhrenlehre; 7. Auflage, Düsseldorf 1979

Brunner, Gisbert L.: Armbanduhren der Fabrikations- und Handelsmarke "Andreas Huber" in München; in: Alte Uhren (1982) Heft 1, S. 43-50

_____ .: Mechanische Armbandchronometer aus der Manufaktur von Junghans in Schramberg; in: Alte Uhren (1982) Heft 4, S. 312-320

_____ .: Die Stundenwinkel-Armbanduhr Typ "Lindbergh" von Longines; in: Alte Uhren (1983) Heft 2, S. 128-131

_____ . und Sinn, H.: Beobachtungsarmbanduhren — ein Vergleich; in Alte Uh-ren (1983) Heft 3, S. 243-246

Centre d'Information de la Montre Française (Hrsg.): Die Französischen Uhrwerke; 2. Auflage, Paris 1974

Chaponnière, H.: Le Chronographe et ses applications; Biel und Besançon 1924

Chapuis, Alfred/Jaquet, Eugène: La Montre Automatique Ancienne 1770-1931; Neuchâtel 1952

Château des Monts, Musée d'Horlogerie (Hrsg.): Horamatic — Montres à remontage automatique de 1770 à 1978; Le Locle o.J.

de Carle, Donald: Complicated Watches and Their Repair; Reprint 1978

_____ .: Watch & Clock Encyclopedia; New York 1977 (Reprint)

Defossez, Léopold: "Accutron", die elektrische Armbanduhr Bulova; in: Schweizer Uhren und Schmuck Journal (1961) S. 79-86

_____ .: die Genauigkeit der Uhr; in: Schweizer Uhren und Schmuck Journal (1961), S. 587-597

Divo Institut (Hrsg.): Gruppenwirtschaftliche Untersuchung der deutschen Uhrenindustrie; Juni 1969 (als Manuskript gedruckt)

Ebauches SA: Die automatische Uhr; Neuchâtel o.J.

Ebauches SA: Les Ebauches, deux siècles d'histoire horlogère; Neuchâtel 1951

Ebauches SA: Répertoire des calibres classés par position tarifaire, grandeur et hauteur; Neuchâtel, 1973

Fischer, A.: Les deux premières montres-bracelet avec indicateur de développement; in: Schweizer Uhrmacher-Zeitung, Juni-Ausgabe, Lausanne 1949

Flume, Rudolf (Hrsg.): Der Flume-Kleinuhr-Schlüssel K 2; Ausgabe 1962/ 63, Berlin und Essen 1963

_____ .: Flume Kleinuhr Schlüssel K 3, Ausgabe 1972, Berlin und Essen 1972

Glaser, Günther: Lexikon der Uhrentechnik; Ulm 1974

Good, Richard: Collecting Wristwatches; in Clocks (March 1980) S. 43-45; (1982) Teil 1, Heft 11, S. 21-24; Teil 2, Heft 12, S. 15-19

Guye, S.: La Montre-Bracelet; in Chapuis, A. (Hrsg.): L'Horlogerie. Une Tradition Helvétique. Neuchâtel 1948, S. 161-185

Harwood, John: Geschichte der automatischen Armbanduhr, erzählt von ihrem Erfinder; in: Schweizerische Uhrmacherzeitung (1951) Heft 11, S. 31-34

Hein, J.: Eine Schweizer Armbanduhr mit abstellbarem Weckwerk und Schutzgitter über dem Glas aus der Ziet zwischen 1914 und 1918; in: Uhren und Schmuck, Heft 1, Berlin (Ost) 1984, S. 22-24

Helwig, Alfred: Von der Taschenuhr zur Armbanduhr; in: Die Uhrmacher-Woche (1930) S. 568f. in Fortsetzung

Herkner, Kurt: Die Glashütter Armbanduhren bis 1945 von A. Lange & Söhne; in: Schriften der Freunde Alter Uhren, Heft XX, Ulm 1981, S. 125-129

_____ .: Urofa- und Tutima-Armbanduhren in: Schriften der Freunde Alter Uhren XXI, o. O. 1982, S. 81-85

_____ .: Glashütte und seine Uhren; Dormagen 1978

Hillmann, Bruno: Die Armbanduhr, ihr Wesen und ihre Behandlung in der Reparatur; Berlin 1925

Hofrichter, Arno: Die Reparatur der kleinen Armbanduhr; in: Die Uhrmacherkunst (1926) S. 62 in Fortsetzungen

Huber, Martin: Kostbare Uhren der Gegenwart — begehrte Antikuhren von morgan; in: Alte Uhren (1981) Heft 3 S. 182-187

Huber, Martin/Banbery Alan: Patek Philippe, Genève; Zürich 1982

Humbert, B.: Die Armband-Weckeruhr; in: Schweizer Uhren und Schmuck Journal (1958), S. 385-397 in Fortsetzungen

_____ .: Moderne Kalender- und Datum-Uhren; in: Schweizerische Uhrmacher Zeitung (1951) Heft 6, S. 49-51 in Fortsetzungen bis 1953

_____ .: Die Schweizer Uhr mit automatischem Aufzug; Lausanne 1956

Jaquet, Eugène/Chapuis, Alfred: Technique and History of the Swiss Watch; London/New York 1970

Jendritzki, Hans: Die Reparatur der Armbanduhr; Halle 1973 (viele Auflagen)

_____ .: Vom Zugfeder-Antrieb; in: Schriften der "Freunde Alter Uhren", Heft 21, Ulm 1982, S. 71-80

Jobin, A.-F.: La Classification Horologie; Genf o.J. (vermutlich 1938)

Journal Suisse d'Horlogerie. Le livre d'or de l'horlogerie, Genève/Neuchâtel o.J. (1927)

Kahlert, Helmut: Die frühen Jahre der Armbanduhr; in: Alte Uhren (1981) Heft 1, S. 27-35

Kocher, Hans: Automatische Uhren; Ulm 1969

Kreuzer, Anton: Die Uhr am Handgelenk; Klagenfurt 1982

_____ .: Die Armbanduhr; Klagenfurt 1983

Kühnhanss, H.: Stoßsicherung im Selbstaufzug; in: Die Uhr (1954) Heft 23, S. 12-14

Lavest, R.: Grundlegende Kenntnisse der Uhrmacherei; 2. Aufl., Biel o.J. (1945)

Lechner, Anton: Laßt den Vata a Ruh', der macht eine ganz kleine Armbanduhr!; in: Süddeutsche Uhrmacherzeitung (1933) 1, S. 12 in Fortsetzung

Lehotzky, Ludwig: Merchanische Uhren; 1. Band, 3. Auflage, Wein-Heidelberg, 1960

Leuthold, Fritz: Von Armbanduhren und ihren Formen; in: Die Uhrmacher-Woche (1928) S. 150-153 in Fortsetzung

Loeske, M.: Die Uhren in den letzten fünfzig Jahren; in: Deutsche Uhrmacher-Zeitung (1926) S. 960-966

Mann, Helmut: Porträt einer Taschenuhr; München 1981

Marti, F.: Gibt es eine Entwicklung in der Technik der Stoßsicherungen?; in: Journal Suisse d'Horlogerie et de Bijouterie (1954) S. 420-422

Martinek, Zdenek/Rehor, Jaroslav: Merchanische Uhren; 3. Auflage, Berlin 1980

Mercier, F.: Horloges et Montres a remontage automatique mécanique; in: Horlogerie Ancienne (1982), Heft 11 Fortsetzungsfolge S. 61-79, Heft 12 Fortsetzungsfolge S. 39-54

Mongrolle, Yves: Les Productions Horlogeres de Cartier; in: ANCAHA, Nr. 31, Sommer 1981, S. 63-67

Neher, F. L.: Ein Jahrhundert Junghans; Schramberg 1961

Parechoc S. A. (Hrsg.): Die Vollsicherung KIF; Hefte 1 und 2, Le Sentier, 1962

Pohl, Helga: Wenn Dein Schatten sechzehn Fuß mißt; Berenice, München/Wien 1955

Schindler, Georg: Entwicklung, heutiger Stand und Reparatur der automatischen Uhr; in: Die Uhr (1964) Heft 18, S. 18-24

Stock, Karl: Die deutschen Armbanduhrkaliber; in: Neue Uhrmacher-Zeitung (1953) S. 28f.

Vogel, Horand M.: Uhren von Patek Philippe; Düsseldorf 1980

Vereinigung Schweizer Juwelen und Edelmetall-Branchen: Schmuck, Edelsteine, Uhren; Thun 1975

Wartmann, E.: Die automatische Uhr; in: Die Uhr (1950) Heft 1, S. 5-9 in Fortsetzungen

Weaver, J. D.: Electrical & Electronic Clocks & Watches; London 1982

Weger, Fritz: Armbanduhr und Uhrarmband; in: Die Uhr (1963) Heft 16, S. 14-23

_____ .: Das regulierende Organ; in: Neue Uhrmacher-Zeitung (1956) Heft 1, S. 10f. in Forts.

Wendorff, Rudolf: Zeit und Kultur. Geschichte des Zeitbewußtseins; in Europa, 2. Aufl., Opladen 1980

o. V.: Deutsche Taschen- und Armbanduhren aus deutschen Rohwerken; in: Deutsche Uhrmacher-Zeitung (1934) S. 85-89

o. V.: Die Kaliber der deutschen Armbanduhrenfabriken; in: Die Uhrmacher-Woche (1939) S. 446ff. in Fortsetzungen

o. V.: offizieller Katalog der Ersatzteile der Schweizer Uhr; 2 Bände, Soleure 1949 (Loseblattsammlung)

o. V.: Ständige Musterausstellung Schmuck — Uhren — Edles Gerät; Industriehaus Pforzheim o.O., o.J. (1956) (enthält Markenzeichen und Kaliberangben der Pforzheimer Uhrenindustrie)

o. V.: Das Uhrwerk in modisch-technischer Entwicklung; in: Die Uhr (1953) Heft 23, S. 15-17

o. V.: Werkzeuge und Arbeitsmethoden für Armbanduhren; in: Deutsche Uhrmacher-Zeitung (1934), S. 321-324

Additional Bibliography for the third edition

Brunner, Gisbert L.: Armbanduhren für besondere Zwecke; in: Alte Uhren (1985) Heft 2, S. 70-72

Brunner, Gisbert L.: Armbanduhren mit "ewigem" Kalender — ein Vergleich; in: Alte Uhren (1985) Heft 4, S. 41-61

Brunner, Gisbert L.: Armbanduhren mit Repetitionsschlagwerk; in: Uhren — Alte und modern Zeitmessung (1986) Heft 2, S. 65-79, und Heft 3, S. 50-58

Brunner, Gisbert L.: Basel 1986; in: Uhren — Alte und modern Zeitmessung (1986) Heft 3, S. 70-73

Brunner, Gisbert L.: Audemars Piguet — Manufacture d'Horlogerie; in: Uhren — Alte und moderne Zeitmessung (1986) Heft 3, S. 9-40

De Carle, Donald: Watch & Clock Encyclopedia; New York 1977

Faber—Castell, Christian von: Die Zeit am Puls; in: Sammeln (1985) Heft 7/8, S. 34-39

Flume GmbH (Hrsg.): Service-Informationen für merchanische Uhrwerke der Ebauches S.A.; Essen und Berlin 1985

Glaser, Günther: Handbuch der Chronometrie und Uhrentechnik, Band II — Mechanische Uhren; Ulm 1981

Habinger, Otto: Tourbillon-Konstruktionen bei Armbanduhren; in: Alte Uhren (1984) Heft 1, S. 32-36

Jagger, Cedric: Some early wrist watches; in: Clocks (1985), Heft 4, S. 21-33

Kreuzer, Anton: Faszinierende Welt der Alten Armbanduhren; Klagenfurt 1985

Lecoultre, François: Komplizierte Taschenuhren; Neuenburg 1985

Meis, Reinhard: IWC-Uhren; Klagenfurt 1985

Mercier, François: Merchanische Uhren mit automatischem Aufzug; in: Alte Uhren (1985) Heft 1, S. 21-32, und Heft 2, S. 27-47

Nadelhoffer, Hans: Cartier, Juwelier der Könige — König der Juweliere; Herrsching 1985

Nadelhoffer, Hans: Cartier—Die Uhr als Juwel; in: Alte Uhren (1985) Heft 2, S. 9-26

Nencini, Franco / Negretti, Giampiero: Ore d'Oro; Mailand 1984

_____ .: Die schönsten Armbanduhren, München 1986

Oppermann, Cristiane: Luxus am Mann — Kapitalanlage am Handgelenk; in:

Manager Magazin (1982) Heft 11, S. 204-208

————.: Mond am Mann — die hohe Zeit der Monduhren; in: Manager Magazin (1986) Heft 1, S. 154-161

Stolberg, Lukas: Lexikon der Taschenuhr; Klagenfurt 1983

Tölke, Hans-F. / King, Jürgen: IWC — International Watch Co., Schaffhausen; Zürich 1986

Träger, Klaus: Alte Armbanduhren; in: Capial (1986) Heft 3, S. 413-419

Zagoory, Jac / Chan, Hilda: A Time to Watch; Hongkong 1985

Periodicals

Allgemeines Journal der Uhrmacherkunst, Halle

Alte Uhren, Wissenschaftliche Instrumente und Automaten, Vierteljahreszeitschrift, Callwey Verlag, München

Deutsche-Uhrmacher-Zeitschrift, Stuttgart-Degerloch

Deutsche Uhrmacher-Zeitung, Berlin

Die Uhrmacherkunst, Leipzig

Die Uhrmacher-Woche, Leipzig

Gold & Silber, Uhren & Schmuck, Leinfelden

Journal Suisse d'horlogerie, Lausanne

Neue Uhrmacher-Zeitung, Ulm Donau

Osterreichisch-Ungarische Uhrmacher-Zeitung, Wien

Revue internationale de l'horlogerie, La Chaux-de-Fonds

Schweizerisches Uhrmacher Journal, Zürich

Schweizerische Uhrmacher-Zeitung, Lausanne

Süddeutsche Uhrmacher-Zeitung, Augsburg

Uhrmacherkunst, Verbandszeitung der Deutschen Uhrmacher, Halle

Illustrations

Unless otherwise noted, the illustrated watches are
equipped with Swiss anchor escapement.

Forerunners of the Wristwatch and early wristwatches to about 1925

1a, b *Gold ornamental watch worn on a cloth band. Oval formed movement, small white dial below the unusually formed decorative balance. Reading the time was a bit difficult with this dial arrangement. Probably from Paris, post-1800. At that time women also wore watches of this kind on rings or as decorative pendants.*

2 *Very early example of a watch firmly attached to the bracelet. Marked "Capt et Freundler, 1813". Spindle movement with chain and fusee, metal dial and Breguet hands. Diameter 29.5 mm. Band and case of gold, enameled and set with rubies. Fine-link band with snake motif.*

3 *Woman's wristwatch in gold enamel with pearls around the glass, circa 1815; white enamel dial with visible four-shank balance below; formed movement with cylinder escapement; case height 33 mm, width 20 mm.*

4 *Early silver band with black enamel work from Egyptian mythology, and watch with visible balance built into it, circa 1820.*

5 *A second variation of the previous wristwatch: the watch is set visibly in a case. The pointed-oval gold watch can also be worn as a pendant. Cylinder movement, small enamel dial above the diamond-studded balance. Cobalt blue gold enamel case as centerpiece of a gold Milan bracelet.*

6 *Gold enamel bracelet with inset gold miniature watch, La Chaux-de-Fonds, circa 1830; engraved silver dial, Breguet hands, diameter of the watch 21 mm; additional chains with gold enamel signet and key.*

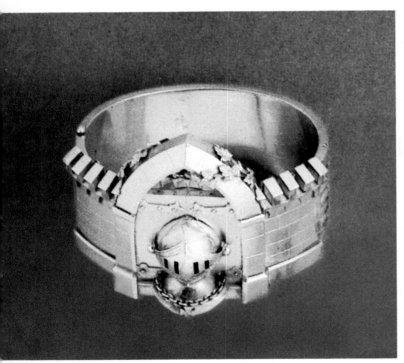

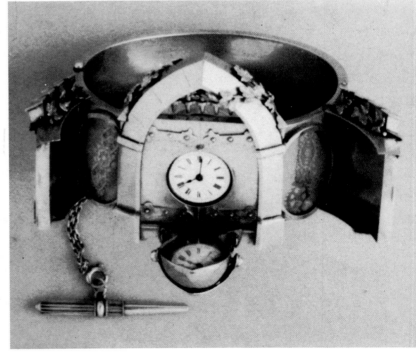

7a, b *Early wristwatch in the form of a castle gate, circa 1850, with oval cylinder movement; the dial is covered by the visor of a knight's helmet, and exposed by opening it to the front; left and right beside the dial, hidden by the openable "sections of the wall", are two picture frames; winding by a gold key attached to a chain.*

8 *It takes some imagination to suspect the presence of a watch in this bracelet. Again it is a woman's small ornamental watch that can also be worn without the bracelet. Enamelwork and pearls heighten the ornamental effect. Doehner, circa 1840/1850.*

9 *Gold enamel bracelet with room inside for the woman's pocket watch shown beside it. Cylinder movement and key winding, diameter 35 mm. The ornamental watch is not visible inside the closed bracelet. On the front is an enamel painting: a girl holds a dog in her right arm, a mirror in her left, reflecting the dog's head. Circa 1840.*

10a-c *Massive ornamental bracelet with watch capsule. A woman's small slim watch with cylinder movement is set in and fastened. Noticeable in this watch-bracelet combination is that the dial axis, from the 6 to the 12, runs in the direction of the band as in modern watches. The watch is not supposed to be an ornament in itself and thus is hidden behind a decorated lid.*

11 Enamel link bracelet with built-in watch. Metal dial with Breguet hands. Winding keyhole on the dial. Here again the spring lid hides the watch. Probably made in Geneva, circa 1850.

12a, b *Gold womens wristwatch in the form of a belt with concealed clock, signed Czapek & Cie, Geneva, 1860; Belt buckles with cut diamonds and black enamel; 8 jewels.*

13 *Golden bracelet with built-in watch by Patek Philippe, 1868, Baguette movement; the dial is hidden under the middle part, which is set with a precious stone.*

14 *Woman's silver ornamental watch, wound by turning the engraved lunette to the left; to set the hands—as seen in the picture—the case rim must be raised; a second glass inside to protect the hands; enamel dial; outer extent of the case 29mm, depth 12mm, round gilded 11-line cylinder movement, held in the case by four screws at the sides; circa 1890.*

15a-c *Gold ornamental wristwatch set with gems, circa 1900; movement by Le Roy & Sohn, Paris, case by Charles Victor de Vernon.*

16a, b *Woman's ornamental gold watch mounted on Milanese band, case set with jewels, decorated enamel dial, 11-line anchor movement with 15 jewels, unusual winding through the lid. Turning a spur gear winds the stem. Swiss, circa 1900.*

17a, b *Gold ornamental wristwatch set with gems, circa 1900, by Frédéric Boucheron, Paris; the movement with number 308 390 probably by Vacheron & Constantin, the case is presumably also from Geneva; it is said that this watch, whose band is inscribed with the French motto, "L'union fait la force", was made for King Leopold II of Belgium (1865-1909).*

18 *Woman's wristwatch in the form of a cherry, Geneva, pre-1900. The golden watch case is enameled dark red, and the two leaves are set with diamonds. The gold bracelet portrays a branch. On the side of the watch is a small push-button; this lets the cherry open, whereby the small enameled dial with Arabic numerals becomes visible. The 15-jewel movement of this watch has anchor escapement, and the balance becomes visible when the bottom of the case is opened. The watch is wound by turning the glass. Diameter of the cherry 22 mm, height 17 mm.*

20 *First wristwatch by Omega, from 1902; 15-line movement, silvered metal case and enamel dial; made by Omega for an English customer, "Edwin J. Vokes, Bath".*

19 *Woman's watch as an ornament, developed on the basis of women's pocket watches, silver case with gold decorations, decorated silver band for wearing on the arm. Round cylinder movement, 10.5 lines, 10 jewels. Push-button hand setting. Swiss, circa 1905.*

21a, b *Man's "Riverside Maximus" wristwatch by Waltham, circa 1907, 19 jewels, four of them set in screwed chatons, bimetallic balance, Breguet hairspring, access for adjusting the regulator, case of 14-karat gold.*

22a, b *Extra-flat watch movement by Jaeger-Le Coultre, 1908, caliber 6" EB, 13.33 x 11 mm, 1.50 mm high.*

23a, b *Woman's gold wristwatch by Charles Frodsham, London, circa 1910; ¾ plate movement, bimetallic balance wheel with gold regulating screws, Breguet hairspring, enamel dial.*

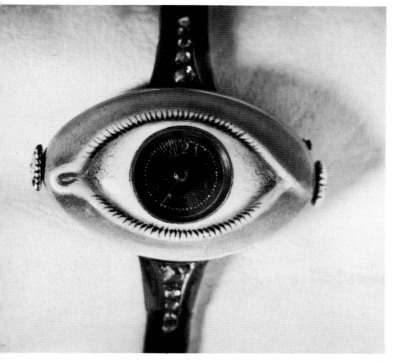
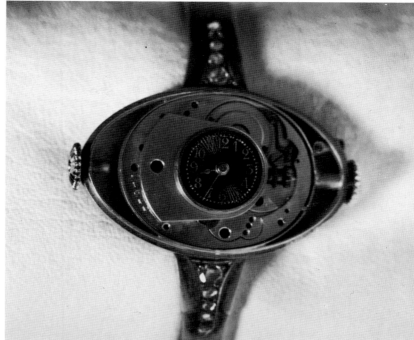

24a, b *Woman's ornamental watch in the form of an eye, small dark blue dial as the pupil, colorful enamel decoration, jewels on the bracelet. Striking movement construction, filling the rounded part of the oval case. Made by Delimorge, circa 1910.*

25 *Wristwatch in plate case by Cartier. This model was created by Cartier in 1904 for Santos-Dumont and can still be found in Cartier's watch assortment under the name "Santos".*

26a, b *Gold woman's "Chronomètre Movado" wristwatch in octagonal form, circa 1910. Winding by the stem knob set in the upper bow. White enamel dial with red 12. 15-jewel anchor movement with three screwed chatons, Geneva band.*

27a-e *"Polyplan" wristwatch by Movado, in gold case, from 1912. This wristwatch is a typical example of many manufacturers' pleasure in experimentation. In the "Polyplan", so the long watch will fit the curve of the wrist, the two end plates are angled downward. 15-jewel anchor escapement, 3 screwed chatons, bimetallic balance, Breguet hairspring.*

28 *Round white-gold wristwatch by Cartier, circa 1912.*

29 *Wristwatch for women by Patek Philippe & Co., number 167,197, sold on November 6, 1912. Case and band of 18-karat gold, engraved, set with diamond roses and rubies, blue steel hands; 10-line movement with anchor escapement, 17 jewels, bimetallic balance.*

30 *Gold enamel decorative wristatch by Vacheron & Constantin, Geneva, made in 1913, 9-line movement, caliber RA 9.*

31a, b *Woman's gold octagonal wristwatch by Patek Philippe, circa 1913; anchor movement, third quality, bimetallic balance, flat hairspring, wolf-toothed winding wheels.*

32 *Ornamental wristwatch by Vacheron & Constantin, Geneva, made in 1914, sold in the USA in 1921; 8-line anchor movement, caliber RA 8, platinum case set with diamond roses, pearls and onyx balls.*

34a, b *Man's round wristwatch with 8-day movement; Swiss, circa 1915; silver case, diameter 36 mm; enamel dial with visible balance; 14-line movement with large barrel.*

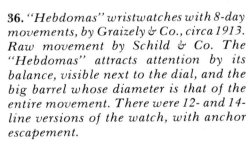

35 *Woman's gold wristwatch by Movado with calendar date seen through a window under the number 6, circa 1914.*

36. *"Hebdomas" wristwatches with 8-day movements, by Graizely & Co., circa 1913. Raw movement by Schild & Co. The "Hebdomas" attracts attention by its balance, visible next to the dial, and the big barrel whose diameter is that of the entire movement. There were 12- and 14-line versions of the watch, with anchor escapement.*

33a, b *Octagonal ornamental wristwatch by Vacheron & Constantin, made in 1915, 8-line movement, caliber RA 8, savonnette case of platinum set with diamonds, onyx and amethyst balls.*

37 *Large 8-day wristwatch, burnished steel case, enamel dial with balance cutout. 13-line anchor movement, 7 jewels, flat hairspring, central barrel with same diameter as the movement. Gintz patent, Swiss, circa 1920.*

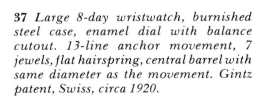

38 *Woman's wristwatch in a form very popular around 1915; case and expansion band of 800 Tula silver; white enamel dial with red number 12. Case diameter 28 mm. Movement 10.5 lines, with anchor escapement, 15 jewels, bimetallic balance; Swiss.*

39 *Woman's wristwatch, circa 1915, case and expansion band of 800 Tula silver, enamel dial with red number 12; case diameter 23.5 mm, cylinder movement, 10.25 lines, hands set by turning the knob while pressing the button under it.*

40a, b *Expansion band with adjustable hooks for fastening a pocket watch, circa 1915. These expansion armbands were made in various forms (steel, doublé, silver, gold) and served to convert the already owned pocket watch to a wristwatch.*

41 *Pearl band with three platinum cases: center for 6-line movement, caliber RA 6, left dial to show the day, right dial for a definite hour, made in 1916 by Vacheron & Constantin, Geneva.*

42a, b *Woman's wristwatch, circa 1915, of Tula silver. Typically for this era, the form of the dial is not the same as the dial opening in the case. Cylinder movement.*

43 *Man's wristwatch, circa 1915, signed "Mobilia" on the movement, engraved anchor movement with 15 jewels, bimettalic balance; case of silver, enamel dial, blue steel hands.*

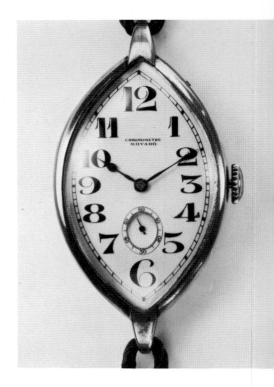

44a, b Woman's "Chronomètre Movado" wristwatch with expansion band, circa 1915. Gilded metal dial with red 12. The movement of this watch is much like that shown in 26b.

45 Pointed oval "Chronomètre Movado" wristwatch, circa 1915.

46 Longish octagonal "Chronomètre Movado" wristwatch, circa 1915.

47a, b Man's wristwatch by International Watch Co. (IWC), sold 1916; case of 18-karat gold, 15-jewel anchor movement with 3 screwed chatons, bimetallic balance, Breguet hairspring.

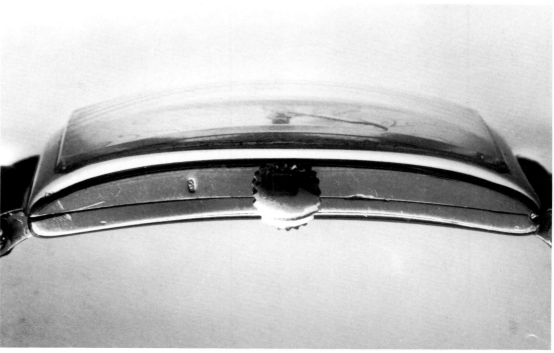

48a, b *Man's large gold wristwatch by Patek Philippe & Co., circa 1918.*

49 Man's wristwatch, "Ingersoll Wrist", 1915 hook anchor movement (compare with #304b).

50 Man's silver wristwatch in half-savonnette case by Waltham Watch, circa 1918, case diameter 35 mm; the movement corresponds to that on page 10, lower left.

51 *Silver woman's watch, octagonal case, enamel dial, red 12, blue steel hands, 10½-line cylinder movement, 6 jewels. Swiss, 1918.*

52 *Woman's wristwatch with link band, plated, circa 1915, with cylinder movement.*

53a, b *Man's gold wristwatch by Henry Moser, circa 1920. White enamel dial with eccentric second hand by the 9. Small pocket-watch movement built into a wristwatch case. Breguet hands, set via the stem plus the button by the 2. Anchor movement, 15 jewels, bimetallic balance, flat hairspring.*

54a, b *Man's wristwatch with centrally located second hand, Swiss, circa 1920, 10.5-line cylinder movement with ¾ plate, hand-setting button by the 4, metal case.*

55a, b *Man's wristwatch with 8-day movement (maker unknown) in 800 silver case, 15-jewel anchor movement with bimetallic balance and flat hairspring; the watch was probably made around 1920. White enamel dial, blue steel hands.*

56a, b *Man's Swiss wristwatch with Roskoph movement, circa 1920. Steel case with 41 mm diameter. Metal dial with yellow luminous numbers, blue steel hands with yellow luminous panels. Setting by stem and button by the 2.*

58a

57a

59a

57a, b *Man's gold wristwatch by Zenith, circa 1920; gilded anchor movement, bimetallic balance, Breguet hairspring, fine regulation.*

58a,b *Man's gold wristwatch by IWC, 1914; 12-line anchor movement, caliber 64, bimetallic balance, Breguet hairspring, three screwed chatons, enamel dial; the movement is screwed into the case back from above; sold to Staufer, Son & Co., London, thus the movelent is also signed "S & Co."*

59a, b *Man's silver wristwatch with black enamel dial, by Rolex, circa 1920; 13-line anchor movement, 15 jewels, bimetallic balance, flat hairspring.*

61a, b *Swiss man's wristwatch, circa 1920, in silver case, 35 mm diameter, white enamel dial with black numerals and red 12. Blue steel pear-shaped hands. Fine nickel-plated anchor movement with 17 jewels, four screwed chatons, bimetallic balance and Breguet hairspring. The regulating indicator can be adjusted with the help of a gooseneck apparatus.*

60 *Man's gold wristwatch by Vacheron & Constantin, 1923; caliber RA 9-94 anchor movement.*

62a, b *Man's gold watch with elegant bow attachments, blue steel hands, small second hand. 11.5-line anchor movement, 15 jewels, flat hairspring. Brand: Borel Fils et Cie, circa 1925.*

63a, b *Woman's gold watch, 12-sided English case. Silver dial with pointed arbor, blued Breguet hairspring. 9.75-line anchor movement, 15 stones, bimetallic balance. Rolex, circa 1925.*

64a, b *Woman's silver sport watch, black numbers, blue steel hands, very early central second hand, setting button, 8.75-line anchor movement, 15 jewels, Breguet hairspring, central second outside the power flow. Seller's name on the dial: Beyer, Zürich Switzerland, circa 1930.*

65a, b *Rounded square wristwatch, enamel dial with radium numerals and hands, small second hand, setting button. 10.5-line fine anchor movement with three visibly screwed chatons, Breguet hairspring, first class designation. Made by Beyer, Zürich Switzerland, circa 1925.*

66a, b *Imitation of a Patek-Philippe wristwatch; valuable 17-jewel anchor movement with screwed minute-wheel chaton; large bimetallic balance, Breguet hairspring, bridge, wolf's-tooth winding wheels. The movement is signed but not numbered, and the hairspring block is not bean-shaped, as is customary for Patek-Philippe. The regulating indicator is broken off. Yet the movement is of high value.*

67 *Man's wristwatch with springing digital hour indication through a window by the 12, by Audemars Piguet for E. Gübelin, Lucerne; 10-line caliber 10 GHSM anchor movement (see #69b), 18 jewels, 1925; two-tone yellow and white gold case, 31 x 28 mm.*

68 *Man's rectangular wristwatch with springing hour indication, presumably by C. H. Meylan, circa 1925.*

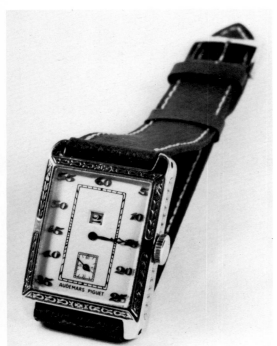

69a, b *Man's rectangular wristwatch with springing digital hour indication, by Audemars Piguet, No. 37 908, ten-line anchor movement, caliber 10 GHSM, 18 jewels, bimetallic balance, Breguet hairspring; the movement of this watch was delivered to "Metric Watch" of New York, Audemars Piguet's American importer, who had a case made in the USA according to Audemars Piguet's original plans, to circumvent the high import duties for finished watches.*

70 *Wristwatch, marked "Tiffany & Co." on the dial, and on the movement "Longines Watch Co.", #3,900,813, 18-karat gold case. Silver dial with luminous Arabic numerals and hands. Silver-plated anchor movement with compensation balance and Breguet hairspring. Circa 1925.*

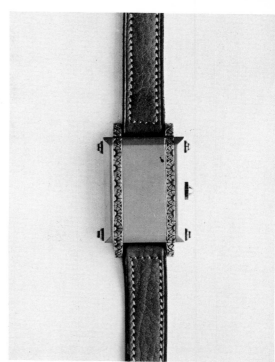

72a, b *Rectangular savonnette wristwatch by Vacheron & Constantin, 1928; caliber 9-94 anchor movement; yellow gold case with white gold decoration.*

71a, b *Man's wristwatch with movable band attachments, by Elgin Watch, USA, 1928; 18-karat white-gold case; 15-jewel anchor movement, 3 screwed chatons, bimetallic balance, Breguet hairspring.*

73a, b *Man's wristwatch in barrel-shaped, lightly arched 14-karat gold case; metal dial with raised Roman numerals, red XII; small second, steel hands; case size 43 x 30 mm; West End Watch Co., circa 1920; round 15-jewel movement, gilded, with compensated balance; size 12½ lines.*

74a, b *Gold barrel-shaped wristwatch by Patek Philippe & Co., 1918; 12-line anchor movement with 18 jewels, bimetallic balance, Breguet hairspring, wolf-toothed winding wheels.*

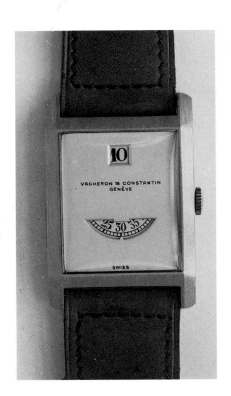

75 *Man's gold barrel-shaped wristwatch by Vacheron & Constantin, 1929; caliber RA 11M anchor movement.*

76 *Man's rectangular wristwatch with digital hour and minute indication, by Vacheron & Constantin, ten-line anchor movement; made 1929, sold in Geneva May 20, 1941.*

77a, b *Man's hand-wound wristwatch by Patek Philippe & Co., circa 1930; made for Greenleaf & Crosby Co., Jacksonville, Florida, USA; 18-jewel bridge movement, bimetallic balance, Breguet hairspring, 8 adjusting points; wolf's-tooth winding wheels; 18-karat gold case.*

81a, b *Man's wristwatch by Longines, Fracillon Ltd., in "Carré cambré" case, circa 1935; movement caliber 10.68 Z, 10 lines, 15 jewels, monometallic balance, selfcompensating flat hairspring, dial with luminous numerals and hands.*

78, 79, 80a, b *Men's wristwatches with 8-day movements, circa 1930, in steel cases approx. 40 x 27 mm; all watches fitted with the 10.5 x 12.75-line formed movement shown; the Swiss anchor movement has 17 jewels and a bimetallic balance; the barrel is of normal size, unlike the "Hebdomas", but the wheel train has two intermediate wheels*

82 *Square art-deco man's watch in silver case, gold numerals and hands. Round anchor movement, 10.5 lines, 15 jewels, flat hairspring. Dial inscribed "Chronometre P.G.M." Movement inscribed "Starina", circa 1932.*

83a, b *"Direct-Time" by Mido, with visible second hand; 7.75 x 11-line formed movement, 15 jewels, bimetallic balance, 18-karat gold case, 1932.*

84a, b *Man's digital wristwatch, maker unknown, showing hours, minutes and seconds. 17-jewel formed movement, 8.75 x 12 lines, gold doublé case, circa 1932.*

85a, b, 86a, b *Two wristwatches with digital indiation of hours, minutes and seconds, by Eterna, circa 1932. Round caliber 716 movement, 15 jewels, momometallic balance, selfcompensating flat hairspring; gold doublé case.*

87a, b Man's wristwatch, "Andreas Huber Urania", circa 1935, steel "Carré cambré" case, 32 x 32 mm; movement by IWC, caliber 83, 12 lines, 15 jewels, bimetallic balance, Breguet hairspring; this watch was assembled and sold by the firm of Andreas Huber in Munich.

88a, b Man's wristwatch in imaginative square steel case with concealed band attachments, by Glycine, circa 1935; round anchor movement, 9.75 lines, 18 jewels, monometallic balance, flat hairspring.

89 *"Chronomètre Movado" Wristwatch in silver case with snakeskin cover, circa 1935.*

90 *Man's wristwatch by Wilka Watch, circa 1935, in chromed "carré cambré" case, 28 x 28 mm, this "self regulating" watch has a window at left, under the 1, in which a red dot appears every seven days, signaling the possibility of regulating the watch. Regulation via the button above the stem knob without having to open the watch. For this purpose the button is linked to the regulator via a drive every seven days. 15-jewel anchor movement, 10½ lines, bimetallic balance, Breguet hairspring.*

91a, b *Man's wristwatch by Ulysse Nardin, circa 1935; steel case, 22 x 30 mm, formed movement, 7.75 x 11 lines, raw movement of Eta caliber 735; 17 jewels, monometallic beryllium balance, self-compensating Breguet hairspring, no shock resistance, soft iron capsule for protection from magnetic influences.*

92a, b *Man's wristwatch by Eterna, circa 1935; steel case 21 x 31 mm, caliber 629 movement, nickel-plated brass, 15 jewels, beryllium balance, self-compensating flat hairspring, no shock resistance.*

93 *Man's gold watch decorated case, stem knob with semi-precious stone, rectangular dial, yellow hands. Anchor movement, 7.75 x 11 lines. Seller's name on dial; Beyer, Zürich Swiss, circa 1935.*

94a,b *Man's wristwatch by Record Watch, circa 1935; steel case 24 x 39 mm, formed movement 8.75 x 12 lines, 15 jewels, 3 chatons, beryllium balance, self-compensating flat hairspring, no shock resistance, Geneva stripes.*

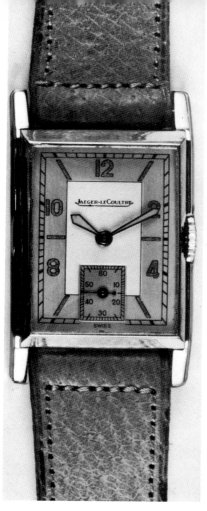

95a, b *Man's wristwatch by Jaeger-LeCoultre, circa 1935; steel case, 22 x 37 mm, formed movement, 7.75 x 11 lines, 15 jewels, beryllium balance, self-compensating flat hairspring, no shock resistance, Geneva stripes.*

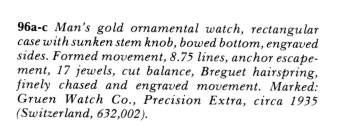

96a-c *Man's gold ornamental watch, rectangular case with sunken stem knob, bowed bottom, engraved sides. Formed movement, 8.75 lines, anchor escapement, 17 jewels, cut balance, Breguet hairspring, finely chased and engraved movement. Marked: Gruen Watch Co., Precision Extra, circa 1935 (Switzerland, 632,002).*

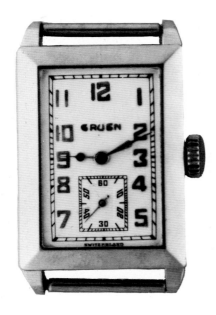

97a, b *Man's rectangular watch in steel case, small second hand, 7.75 x 11-line anchor movement with 15 jewels, unusual construction: the second wheel is mounted in a deep bridge. The minute wheel is bored out to take a central second pivot, but not used. Cut balance, Breguet hairspring; made by Gruen, circa 1935.*

98 *Man's wristwatch in rectangular 18-karat gold case, circa 1930; 10.75-line Swiss anchor movement, marked "Bosch Watch Co.", 15 jewels, two of them set in chatons, bimetallic balance, Breguet hairspring, no shock resistance, winding by the knob below the 6.*

99a, b *Man's wristwatch by Movado, circa 1935, seller's name, Huber, of Munich, on the dial; strongly arched steel case, 41 x 23 mm; integrated stem knob; 15-jewel formed movement, 9 x 13 lines, 4 chatons, 3 of them screwed, Geneva stripes, bimetallic balance, Breguet hairspring.*

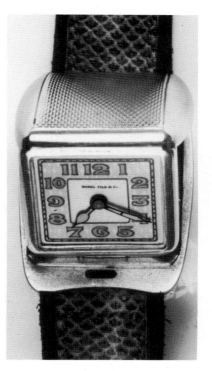

100a, b *Man's ornamental art deco watch in silver case, with black numerals and hands. 10½-line round cylinder movement, neatly made. Ten jewels. Signed "Le Parc" on the dial. Swiss, circa 1932.*

101a, b *Wristwatch by Borel, Fils & Co., circa 1935, in a 14-karat gold case. The round 8.5-line Swiss anchor movement is set in an opening housing. When it is pulled upward by the 6, it takes a standing position. It can also be used as a desk clock when open. Hand winding and setting are both done by a knob on the back of the movement.*

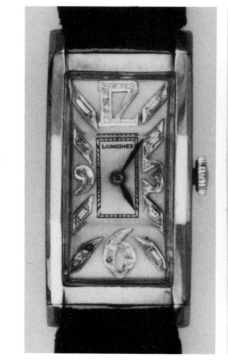

103a, b *Man's rectangular wristwatch by Longines, 18-karat platinum case with elegant diamond-studded numerals, 43 x 20 mm, 8.75 x 11.5-line anchor movement with 17 jewels; early shock resistance developed by Longines, recognizable by the U-shaped clamp on the balance bearing; bimetallic balance, Breguet hairspring.*

102a, b *Man's watch by International Watch, circa 1937; hand-wound formed movement, 8.75 x 12 lines, 15 jewels, 4 chatons, bimetallic balance, Breguet hairspring, Geneva stripes, caliber 87; steel case, 39 x 22 mm.*

104a, b *Early woman's wristwatch with central second hand, by Gruen Watch Co., circa 1935; steel case, "Gruen Gilde" formed movement with 15 jewels, central second with drive outside the power flow, bimetallic balance, Breguet hairspring, 4 adjusting points.*

Duo-Dial

In the years around and after 1930, rectangular wristwatches with a two-part dial came onto the market; the lower part of the dial was reserved for the second indicator and allowed an exact reading of the seconds. In America these were also called "Doctors'" or "Nurses' Watches", wristwatches for professions in which an easy reading of the seconds was useful, for example, in taking the pulse. Generally one must distinguish between these watches with Baguette movements (for example, by Rolex or Gruen), with normal formed movements (for example, 8.75 x 11 lines, by Lorie Watch, among others), or with round movements. Duo-Dial wristwatches differ from wristwatches with normal dials only through their modified dial arrangements. (see #105-13, 276-277).

105a-c *Rolex Prince Chronometer, circa 1935; 18-karat yellow and white gold case; Baguette movement of "Observatory" quality, 6 points of adjustment, 15 jewels, monometallic balance, self-compensating Breguet hairspring.*

106 *Rolex Prince, circa 1930, in an 18-karat yellow and white gold case, 42 x 22 mm. Digital hour indication through a window at 60 minutes. The hour indicator jumps one position farther at the end of each hour. Baguette movement, 7.5 lines, nickel-plated, 15 jewels, lateral anchor (in all Rolex Prince watches): the anchor fork is set at a right angle to the pallets.*

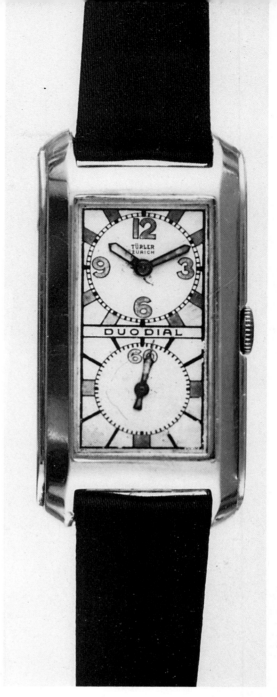

107 *Duo-Dial wristwatch, circa 1930, assembled by Türler, Zürich, in an 18-karat gold case. 15-jewel Baguette movement, bimetallic balance, Breguet hairspring.*

108a, b *Rolex Prince, circa 1930. The movement is that shown in illustration 105 but has 17 jewels.*

109a, b *"Tecno" Duo-Dial wristwatch, circa 1930, by Alpina Gruen in a "Staybrite" stainless steel case. Baguette movement, caliber 877 S, 15 jewels, lateral anchor, monometallic balance, self-compensating Breguet hairspring.*

110 *Duo-Dial wristwatch, circa 1940, in steel case, unidentified; 15-stone Swiss anchor movement, adjusted at 3 points.*

111 *Rolex Prince with seller's name: "Beyer", on the dial; circa 1945; 14-karat gold case, 46 x 19 mm, "Losagne" hands. Baguette movement, 7.5 lines, nickel plated, 17 jewels, Glucidur balance, Breguet hairspring, gooseneck fine regulating, adjusted at 7 points.*

112a, b *Man's gold rectangular Duo-Dial wristwatch by Longines, circa 1935, 17-jewel forled movement with Geneva stripes, bimetallic balance, Breguet hairspring, shock resistance.*

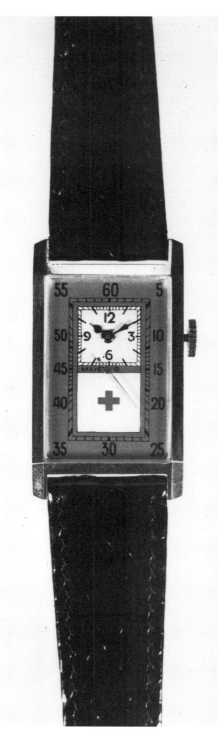

114a, b *Man's wristwatch by Omega (S.A. Louis Brandt & Frère) circa 1935; round steel case, 33 mm diameter, 11.75-line gilded movement with 15 jewels, four of them in screwed chatons, bimetallic balance, Breguet hairspring, no shock resistance.*

113 *Silver wristwatch for medical corpsmen, World War I; round anchor movement with small second, which led, through its being built into the upper part of the case, to watches with centrally located second hand.*

115a, b *German man's wristwatch, circa 1935, presumably made by Sickinger; chromed metal case, round cylinder movement, caliber 24 OE, gilded, 6 jewels.*

116a, b *Man's rectangular watch in 14-karat gold case, small second, Swiss. Formed movement, 7.75 x 11'', 16 jewels, flat hairspring. Signed "Lange, Glashütte/SA", circa 1939.*

117a, b *Man's wristwatch, marked "Andreas Huber Urania", circa 1940; steel case, 39 x 22 mm, 8.75 x 12-line formed movement, marked "International Watch", Schaffhausen, 15 jewels, 4 of them set in chatons, bimetallic balance, Breguet hairspring.*

118a, b *Man's wristwatch in rectangular steel case, by Paul Raff (Para), circa 1940; the watch has the so-called "space utilizing movement", caliber 58, 9 x 12 lines, by Urofa (Uhren-Rohwerk-Fabrikation, of Glashütte); 15 jewels, monometallic screw balance, flat hairspring, no shock resistance, gilded movement.*

From left to right:

119 *Square gold enamel watch, Touchon & Co., Cartier, circa 1940; 18-karat case, 27 mm side length; the blue Roman numerals are enameled.*

120 *Square savonnette wristwatch, signed "Cartier", circa 1935, anchor movement; 18-karat gold case, 30 mm side length.*

121 *Man's wristwatch with automatic winding and eternal calendar, by Patek Philippe & Co., circa 1972; 37-jewel anchor movemernt, caliber 27-460 Q; 18-karat gold case, 39 mm diameter; seller's name "Tiffany & Co." on the dial.*

122 *Man's wristwatch with chronograph and "eternal" calendar by Patek, Philippe & Co., circa 1965, 23-jewel nickel anchor movement; gold case, 35 mm diameter.*

123 *Man's wristwatch with automatic winding and "eternal" calendar, by Patek Philippe & Cc., circa 1970; anchor movement, 37 jewels, caliber 27-460 Q, 18-karat gold case, 39 mm diameter.*

124 *Skeletal wristwatch by Patek Philippe & Co., circa 1978, 18-karat gold case, 27 mm diameter.*

125 *Man's wristwatch with automatic winding, calendar and moon phase indication, signed "Rolex Oyster Perpetual, officially certified chronometer", circa 1953; 18-karat oyster gold case with gold Pesident band; case diameter 37 mm.*

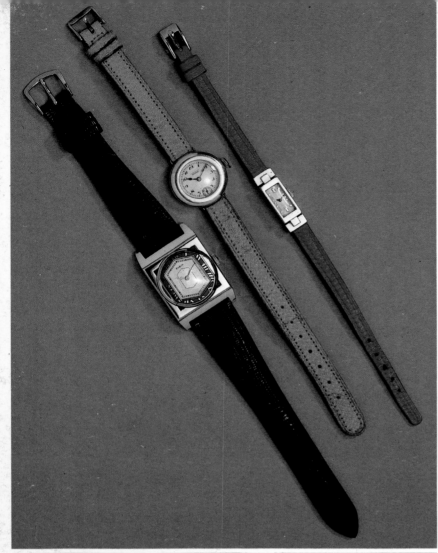

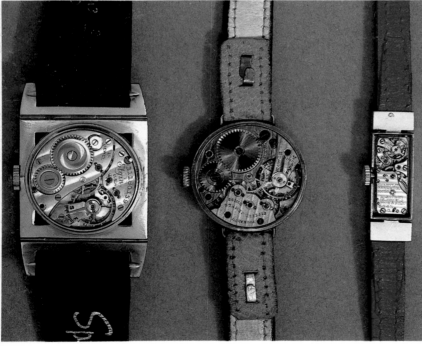

126-129 *From left to right:*
126 *Man's wristwatch by Elgin, 1928.*
127 *Woman's wristwatch by Movado, circa 1915.*
128 *Woman's gold wristwatch, C.H. Meylan, Brassus, 18-jewel baguette movement, 2⅝ x 5 lines, bimetallic balance, flat hairspring, case dimensions 8.1 x 27 mm (at the attachments).*

129 *Early wristwatch, signed Capt et Freundler, 1813.*

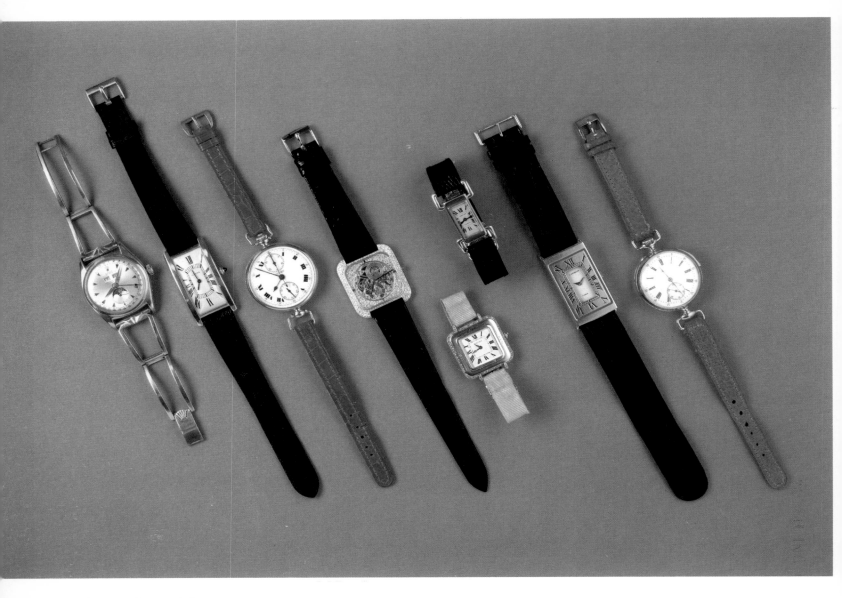

130-137 *From left to right:*

130 *Man's gold wristwatch with automatic winding, calendar and moon phase indication, signed "Rolex Oyster Perpetual". circa 1953, case diameter 40 mm.*

131 *Man's wristwatch, circa 1925, signed "Cartier", 18-jewel round anchor movement by European Watch & Clock Co., arched 18-karat white gold case.*

132 *Man's wristwatch with chronograph and 30-minute indicator, signed "Ulysse Nardin", circa 1910, round 18-karat gold case, 39 mm diameter.*

133 *Man's wristwatch with skeletal movement by Vacheron & Constantin, circa 1970, 17-jewel anchor movement; square white gold case set with diamonds, side length 33 mm.*

134 *Woman's wristwatch, signed "Cartier France". circa 1911, round nickel anchor movement by Jaeger-Le Coultre; 18-karat white gold case set with diamonds, side length 30 mm.*

135 *Woman's wristwatch, signed "Cartier France", circa 1935, movement by Jaeger-Le Coultre with winding and hand setting from the back; 18-karat gold case, 41 mm long.*

136 *Man's rectangular wristwatch in 18-karat half-savonnette case, signed "Cartier", circa 1930, 43 mm long.*

137 *Early man's wristwatch with minute repetition, signed "L. Brandt & Frères", circa 1910, anchor movement, bimetallic balance; striking control by a button near the 3, winding crown near the 12; 18-karat gold case, 36 mm diameter.*

138a, b *Man's wristwatch by Rolex, circa 1940; long barrel-shaped gold case, made for seller Sam Lyon Jr.; 8 x 12-line formed movement, caliber 360, 15 jewels, monometallic balance, self-compensating hairspring, no shock resistance.*

139a, b *Man's wristwatch in steel case, marked "Meridiano", circa 1940; on this watch the seconds are shown by a disc over the 6; Swiss anchor movement, 8.75 x 12 lines, 15 jewels, without shock resistance, monometallic screw balance, flat hairspring.*

140a, b *Elegant man's watch, doublé case, arched glass. Round anchor movement, 10.5 lines, 17 jewels, flat hairspring. Roamer, circa 1940.*

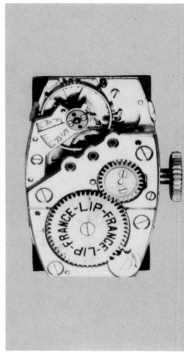

142a, b *Man's wristwatch by LIP, circa 1945, steel case; formed movement, 7.75 x 11 lines, fitted with a soft iron capsule for protection against magnetic effects, 15 jewels, anchor with fork in 90-degree angle to the pallet, monometallic screw balance, self-compensating Breguet hairspring.*

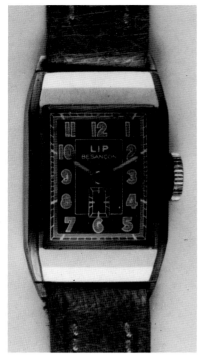

141 *Man's wristwatch by Patek Philippe & Co., circa 1940; rectangular arched case of 18-karat gold, 36 x 24 mm, formed movement, caliber 9-line-90, 18 jewels, monometallic balance, self-compensating Breguet hairspring; fine regulation.*

143a, b *Square gold watch, central second outside the power flow; anchor movement, 11.5 lines, 15 jewels, flat hairspring, shock resistance. Cyma, circa 1945.*

144a-c *Rectangular steel watch with unusual dial markings, two rotating discs with balls instead of hands. 7.75 x 11-line anchor movement, 15 jewels, three fine adjusting points, flat hairspring. Melik-Mido, circa 1945.*

145a, b *Man's square wristwatch by Silvana, circa 1945; steel case 32 x 32 mm; 15-jewel formed movement with Geneva stripes, monometallic screw balance, flat hairspring, no shock resistance; with a total height of 5 mm, a very flat watch in its time.*

146a, b *Man's square gold watch, round anchor movement, 10.5 lines, 16 jewels, central second outside the power flow, flat hairspring. Made by Cortèbert, circa 1945. Dial inscribed "anti-magnetic" and "Beyer, Zürich".*

147 *Man's silver wristwatch with winding crown at the 12, signed "Tristan", 8.75-line gilded anchor movement by Urofa, Glashütte, circa 1945.*

148, 149a, b *Man's barrel-shaped wristwatches by Thiel, in chrome-nickel cases, circa 1940; pillar movement, 7.75 x 11 lines, hook anchor escapement, stripes on the rear of the plate.*

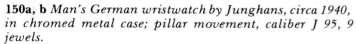

150a, b *Man's German wristwatch by Junghans, circa 1940, in chromed metal case; pillar movement, caliber J 95, 9 jewels.*

151 *Barrel-shaped sport watch, small second hand, luminous dial, chrome-nickel case with steel bottom. Round ahcnor movement, 10.5 lines, 15 jewels, flat hairspring. Trade mark "Zentra", circa 1940.*

152a, b *Man's wristwatch in chrome-nickel case, circa 1940; maker not known; 7.75 x 11-line anchor movement with 15 jewels, monometallic screw balance, flat hairspring, no shock resistance.*

153a, b *Wristwatch in chrome-nickel case with moving band attachments, circa 1940; formed movement with Swiss anchor escapement and 15 jewels, 6.75 x 11 lines, Eta, caliber 765, monometallic screw balance, flat hairspring.*

154a, b *Wristwatch by Stowa, circa 1940, in steel case, 35 mm diameter, gilded formed movement, 8.75 x 12 lines, by the Pforzheimer Uhren Rohwerke GmbH (PUW), caliber 500, 15 jewels, monometallic screw balance, self-compensating hairspring.*

155a, b *Man's wristwatch by Tavannes Watch, circa 1940; steel case, 32 mm diameter; 11.5-line movement without shock resistance, 15 jewels, monometallic screw balance, self-compensating flat hairspring, Geneva stripes.*

156a, b *Zenith man's wristwatch, in 18-karat gold case, circa 1940, presumably made for the American market; 31 mm diameter; 15-jewel anchor movement, 11.25 lines, bimetallic balance, Breguet hairspring, without shock resistance, engraving on the back of the movement surface.*

157a, b *Man's wristwatch by Record Watch Co., circa 1940, round steel case, 30 mm diameter; 9.75-line anchor movement, caliber 160, 15 jewels, three of them set in chatons, no shock resistance, monometallic screw balance, self-compensating flat hairspring, Geneva stripes on the back of the movement.*

158a, b *Man's wristwatch by Longines, circa 1940, steel case, 17-jewel movement with screwed minute wheel chaton, monometallic screw balance, self-compensating Breguet hairspring; interesting fine regulating mechanism for the regulator indicator, no shock resistance.*

159a, b *Man's wristwatch by Vacheron & Constantin, circa 1940, in round gold case, 32 mm diameter, 15-jewel movement, bimetallic balance, Breguet hairspring, shock resistance.*

160a, b *Man's wristwatch in military style, assembled by Andreas Huber, circa 1945; steel case, 34 mm diameter, 9.5-line movement, presumably made by Tavannes Watch Co., 17 jewels, five of them set in chatons, Incabloc shock resistance, monometallic screw balance, self-compensating flat hairspring.*

161a, b *Man's wristwatch by IWC, circa 1945; steel case, 31 mm diameter; 12-line movement, caliber 83, 15 jewels, 3 of them set in chatons, no shock resistance, monometallic screw balance, self-compensating Breguet hairspring, Geneva stripes.*

162a, b *Man's wristwatch, marked "TA-CY" (Tavannes-Cyma Watch), circa 1945; 10.5-line anchor movement, 15 jewels, four of them set in chatons, monometallic screw balance, self-compensating flat hairspring, no shock resistance.*

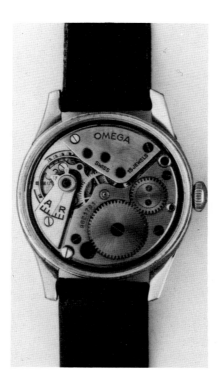

163a, b *Man's wristwatch in 14-karat gold case by Omega, circa 1945, movement caliber 30 T2, 15 jewels, bimetallic screw balance, Brgeuet hairspring, no shock resistance.*

164 *Man's wristwatch by Patek Philippe & Co., 1948; 18-jewel anchor movement, caliber 12''' 120, monometallic screw balance, self-compensating Breguet hairspring, gooseneck fine regulation; red gold case, 34 mm diameter.*

165a, b *Man's gold wristwatch by Patek Philippe & Co., No. 99045; woman's wristwatch movement, circa 1896 (formerly built into a steel pocket watch case), built into a gold wristwatch case by Patek Philippe in 1950; nickel bridged movement with Geneva stripes, fine regulation, wolf's-tooth winding wheels.*

166 *Man's rectangular wristwatch by Patek Philippe, No. 2456, circa 1950, caliber 9'''-90 (see page 56).*

167 *Model with ten-line round anchor movement, circa 1950.*

168-169 *Models with caliber 9'''-90 from the Forties.*

170 *Man's wristwatch by Patek Philippe & Co., circa 1950; square 18-karat gold case, round movement, caliber 10-line/200, 18 jewels, monometallic balance, self-compensating Breguet hairspring, gooseneck fine regulation.*

171a, b *Man's square wristwatch, "Rolex Precision", circa 1950; 14-karat gold case, 17-jewel movement with monometallic "Superbalance" wheel, self-compensating Breguet hairspring, shock resistance.*

172 *Elegant gold watch "Gruen Curvex" original case form with two pairs of arches, black dial, small second hand, 14-karat formed movement (9 x 10 lines), anchor escapement, 17 jewels, unadjusted, Breguet hairspring. Case engraved: "Cased and Timed in USA by the Gruen Watch Co."*

173 *Man's platinum-diamond wristwatch with white gold band, marked "Audemars Piguet". Rhodin platinum case, the sides of the glass decorated with diamond baguettes, white gold stem. Silvered dial with diamond baguettes and set diamonds instead of numerals, white gold hands. 18-jewel anchor movement.*

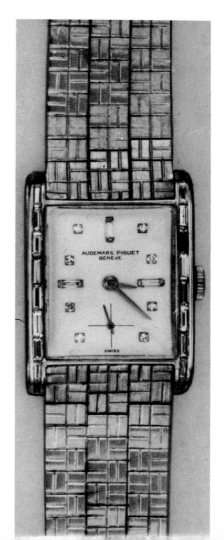

175a, b *Man's wristwatch in transparent acrylic case, marked "Zentra Sola", circa 1950. 15-jewel anchor movement, 8.75 x 12 lines, Incabloc shock resistance, monometallic screw balance, self-compensating flat hairspring. The case (24 x 41 mm) is made of four acrylic parts screwed together.*

174 *Man's wristwatch in rectangular gold case, Tuchon & Co., #330,119, with seller's name "Tiffany & Co." on the dial.*

176a, b *Man's wristwatch by Walter Storz, circa 1950; 15-jewel anchor movement, no shock resistance, monometallic screw balance, flat hairspring.*

177a, b *Man's wristwatch, Junghans "Meister" circa 1960; doublé case, 34 mm diameter; 17-jewel anchor movement, caliber 84/S 3, 11 lines, direct central second, monometallic ring balance, self-compensating flat hairspring, gooseneck fine regulation.*

178a, b *Man's wristwatch in 18-karat gold case by Universal, circa 1950; 12-line anchor movement, caliber 263, 15 jewels, no shock resistance, monometallic screw balance, self-compensating flat hairspring.*

179a, b *Man's wristwatch, marked "Glashütter Tradition Dr. Kurtz", circa 1950; steel case, 31 mm diameter, hand-wound movement with anchor escapement, 10.75 lines, 17 jewels, "Super-Shock-Resist" system, beryllium balance, Breguet hairspring, indirect central second (Dr. Kurtz was originally director of UFAG and Urofa, Glashütte after World War II he tried to build up watch production in Pforzheim.)*

180a, b *Man's wristwatch in watertight oyster case, steel with gold cap, marked "Tudor", made by Rolex, circa 1950; 17-jewel anchor movement, "Shock-Resist" system, indirect central second, monometallic screw balance, self-compensating flat hairspring.*

181a, b *Man's wristwatch by Eterna, with seller's signature "Beyer-Zürich" circa 1950; 12-line anchor movement, caliber 520, 15 jewels, Eterna shock resistance, monometallic screw balance, self-compensating flat hairspring, indirect central second.*

182a, b *Cortébert "Sport" man's wristwatch, circa 1950, with seller's signature "Beyer-Zürich", anchor movement, caliber 677 S, 12 lines, 16 jewels, monometallic screw balance, self-compensating flat hairspring, indirect central second, Incabloc shock resistance.*

183a, b *Man's wristwatch for the American market by Wittnauer Watch, circa 1950; doublé case, 32 mm diameter; 17-jewel anchor movement, caliber 10 FL, no shock resistance, monometallic screw balance, flat hairspring.*

184a, b *Man's wristwatch, "Lord Elgin", USA, circa 1950; Elgin caliber 688, 21 jewels, screwed anchor wheel chaton, Incabloc shock resistance, monometallic screw balance, self-compensating hairspring.*

185a, b, 186 *Men's wristwatches by Universal, circa 1950; in 14-karat gold case; Universal caliber 262 movement, 15 jewels, without shock resistance, monometallic screw balance, self-compensating flat hairspring.*

187a, b *Cortébert "Sport" man's wristwatch, 1952; steel case, 33 mm diameter, anchor movement, caliber 689, 15 jewels, Incabloc shock resistance, "Spirofix" regulation for the hairspring.*

188a, b *Man's wristwatch by Patek Philippe & Co., 1952; #2456, caliber 9'''-90, Gyromax balance, self-compensating Breguet hairspring, gooseneck fine regulation, 18 jewels, 1952; yellow gold case, 23 x 39 mm.*

189a, b, 190 *Men's wristwatches by Eterna, circa 1953; 35 mm diameter, 13-line anchor movement, caliber 1117, 17 jewels, three of them set in chatons, Eterna shock resistance, monometallic screw balance, self-compensating flat hairspring, direct central second.*

191a, b *Man's wristwatch by Piaget, circa 1955; 18-karat gold case, 34 mm diameter; 10½ line anchor movement, 17 jewels, Incabloc shock resistance, monometallic screw balance, self-compensating flat hairspring.*

192a, b *Round plated wristwatch, signed "Zenith Pilot"; 12-line anchor movement, caliber 120, with balance stopping apparatus, 18 jewels, monometallic screw balance, self-compensating flat hairspring, Incabloc shock resistance, circa 1955.*

193a, b *Man's wristwatch by Wyler Watch, circa 1955; steel case with bayonet bottom closing, 31 mm diameter, anchor movement, caliber E 1081, 17 jewels, Incaflex shock resistance (balance wheel sprung by long elastic balance shanks), direct central second.*

194 *Man's wristwatch in 18-karat gold case by Piaget, circa 1956; 10.5-line anchor movement, 17 jewels, Incabloc shock resistance, direct central second.*

195a, b *Cyma "Triplex" man's wristwatch, 1952; steel case, 33 mm diameter; 10.5-line anchor movement, caliber 459, 17 jewels, "Cymaflex" shock resistance, indirect central second, monometallic screw balance, self-compensating flat hairspring.*

196a, b *Man's wristwatch with calendar, by Alpina, circa 1958; doublé case, 34 mm diameter; 17-jewel movement, caliber 394 R CS, Incabloc shock resistance, indirect central second.*

198a, b *Man's round watch in metal case with stainless steel bottom, champagne dial with radium points and hands. Pillar movement, 10.5 lines, with hook anchor escapement, 4 jewels, by Kienzle, circa 1955.*

197 *Man's square watch, luminous dial, chromed case with steel bottom. Round pillar movement, 10.5 lines, hook anchor, 4 jewels, by Kienzle, circa 1956.*

199a, b *Woman's simple sport watch, chromed case, luminous hands. Round hook anchor movement, 8.75 lines, without jewels. Dial inscription: "Ancre", circa 1950.*

200a, b *Man's wristwatch by Certina, Kurth Frères, circa 1953; doublé case, 33 mm diameter, anchor movement, caliber 324, 12 lines, 16 jewels, Incabloc shock resistance, indirect central second, monometallic screw balance, self-compensating flat hairspring.*

201a, b *Man's wristwatch by IWC, March 1959; steel case, 34 mm diameter, 10-line anchor movement, caliber 401, 19,800 half-swings per hour, 17 jewels, Incabloc shock resistance, indirect central second, monometallic screw balance, self-compensating Breguet hairspring, gooseneck fine regulation, Geneva stripes.*

202a, b *Man's wristwatch by Vacheron & Constantin, circa 1960; 18-karat gold case, 9.25-line anchor movement, caliber 1003 (same as Audemars Piguet caliber 2003), 17 jewels, no shock resistance, monometallic screw balance, self-compensating flat hairspring, movement height 1.64 mm.*

203 *Man's wristwatch, "ruhla", from the German Democratic Republic, circa 1970; hook anchor movement without jewels, balance arbor mounted in seed bearings, no shock resistance.*

204a, b *Woman's sport watch in metal case with steel bottom, round anchor movement J 80, 10.5 lines, 15 jewels, flat hairspring, by Junghans, circa 1950.*

205a, b *Woman's wristwatch by Kienzle, circa 1968; chromed case, 8-line pillar movement with anchor escapement, caliber 059 b 25, 17 jewels, shock resistance, direct central second.*

206a, b *Man's round wristwatch, black dial with luminous numerals. Chromed case. Kienzle hook anchor movement of 12 lines (051) without jewels, rocker winding. Kienzle, circa 1950.*

207a, b *Woman's sport watch in chromed barrel case, 8.75-line anchor movement, 15 jewels, flat hairspring. Made by Ankra, 184, circa 1940.*

208a, b *Man's wristwatch, marked "Shanghai", presumably circa 1960; movement with Swiss anchor escapement (presumably imitation of a Swiss AS caliber), 17 jewels, no shock resistance, indirect central second.*

209a, b *Man's wristwatch, marked "Tourist", circa 1960; in steel case, 34 mm diameter, "Wehrmacht" movement, 13-line AS caliber 1130, 17 jewels, Incabloc shock resistance, gooseneck fine regulation, monometallic screw balance, self-compensating flat hairspring, watch also existed as Tourist "President".*

210a, b *Man's wristwatch by Jaeger-LeCoultre, circa 1965; 18-karat gold case and gold band; 15-jewel anchor movement with Geneva stripes, monometallic ring balance, self-compensating flat hairspring, "Kif-Flector" shock resistance, combined "Kif-Duofix" anchor wheel pivot bearing system.*

211a, b *Man's wristwatch with calendar, marked on the dial "Ankra", circa 1970; anchor movement, presumably made in Switzerland, with two mainsprings that are wound simultaneously, 21 jewels, monometallic ring balance, flat hairspring, shock resistance; the movement may have been built into this case and fitted with the dial shown, since the 17 jewels noted on the dial do not equal the 21 of the movement.*

212 *Man's wristwatch from the Zenith-Movado "Museum Collection", made from 1959 on; the design was honored by the inclusion of the watch in the permanent display of the New York Museum of Modern Art; the watch was also produced with various movement calibers.*

213a-c *Man's wristwatch by Jean Lassale, made since 1978; 18-karat gold case with glass bottom allowing view of movement; anchor movement caliber 1200; 9 lines, 9 jewels and 14 miniature ball bearings, 21,600 half-swings per hour; this is the flattest mechanical movement ever built; 1.20 mm high. The movement has only one plate, with the wheels mounted in flying ball bearings developed by the manufacturer.*

214a, b *Woman's fashion watch, signed Old England on the dial; barrel-shaped steel case with stiff link band, Jura Watch Co., post-1970; round hook anchor movement with one stone, size 8½ lines, shock resistance, Ebauches Bettlach caliber 8350-67.*

From left to right:
215-218 *"Nostalgic" wristwatches in present production, in the styles of the Thirties and Forties, signed "Numa Jeannin"; various models with different movement calibers.*

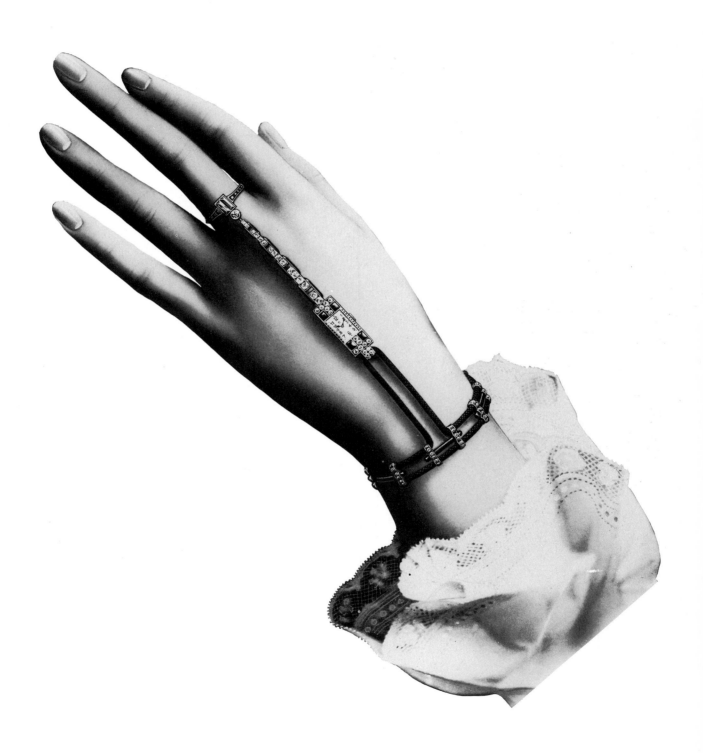

219 *Woman's baguette-form wristwatch, to be worn along with a ring; Omega, circa 1915.*

221a, b *Rectangular wristwatch "Patria", circa 1920, in gold case. Metal dial with stamped numerals, 1-12 black and 13-24 red. Swiss anchor movement with 15 jewels.*

220 *Woman's wristwatch by Cartier, circa 1920; platinum case, 1.3 cm wide, set with diamonds; silver painted dial with black Roman numerals, blue steel hands. The Baguette movement was wound by the stem over the 12.*

222a, b *Woman's gold wristwatch by Plojoux, circa 1920, case measures 19 x 23 mm. Gold painted metal dial with blue numerals and hands. Anchor movement with 17 jewels, 8.25 lines, bimetallic balance, Breguet hairspring, Geneva stripes.*

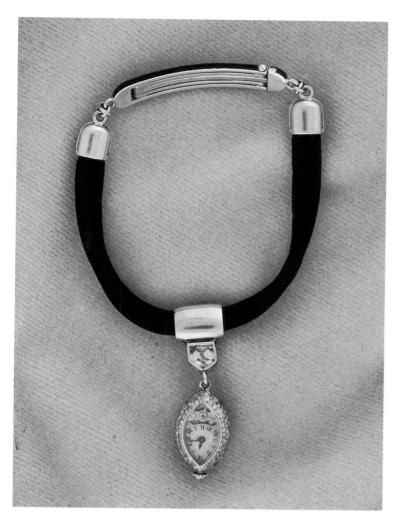

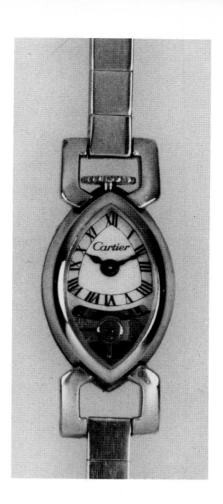

223 *Woman's bracelet watch by Cartier, 1925, movement presumably by Jaeger-LeCoultre.*

224 *Woman's miniature wristwatch, signed by Cartier, circa 1925; navette-formed case of 18-karat gold, base screwed on the sides, 11 x 17 mm; white silvered dial with black Roman numerals, under the 6 the balance is visible; pointed oval movement by Jaeger-LeCoultre .*

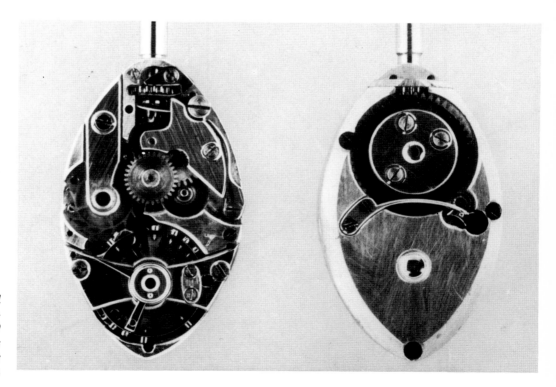

225a, b *Specially constructed oval wristwatch movement by Jaeger-LeCoultre (1923), caliber 7AJ, 15 x 9 mm, 4.3 mm high; the movement was built into a case so that the balance wheel was visible through a cutout in the dial.*

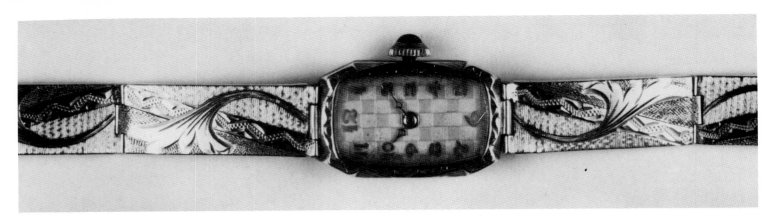

226 *Woman's wristwatch, Germany, circa 1925, in 14-karat gold case with engraved gold band. Gold-painted dial with gold raised numerals, gold hands. Cylinder formed movement with 8 jewels.*

227 *Woman's wristwatch, white gold, set with pearls and diamonds, Cartier, 1923.*

228 *Woman's round sport watch in plaque case with movable attachments, circa 1925; black numerals on enameled dial, Breguet hands; eccentric second; signed Central Watch Co. A Quality.*

229 *Woman's white gold ornamental watch, 18 karats, decorated with eight sapphires and sixteen diamonds; black numerals on silver dial; round movement with 17 jewels, size 8¾ lines; cut screw balance with steel hairspring, three adjustments; signed on the plate Eigeldinger, Switzerland, circa 1925.*

230 *Ornamental watch in 18-karat yellow gold case, art deco, engraved and enameled top and side portions of the case; metal dial with black numerals and hands; signed Flor on the dial; oval 5¼ line anchor movement with 15 jewels, cut screw balance, steel hairspring. Switzerland, circa 1925.*

231 *Woman's wristwatch made of Tula silver (800), 26 x 29 mm, circa 1925; gilded cylinder movement, 10.5 lines, 8 jewels; gold painted dial, blue steel hands.*

232 *Woman's parallelogram-formed wristwatch in gold case with enameled decorations at the sides. Silver painted metal dial with black stamped numerals, blue steel Breguet hands. Round movement with Swiss anchor escapement.*

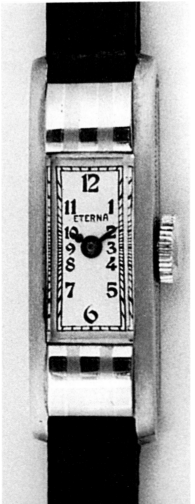

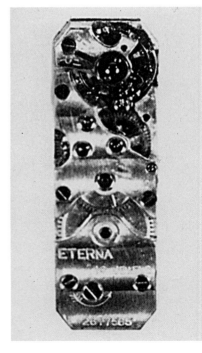

233 *Woman's octagonal wristwatch in silver case, enameled brown with floral decorations; Vitalis Watch Co., Swiss, circa 1925, blue steel hands; 9-line cylinder movement.*

234a, b *Woman's wristwatch by Eterna, 1929, in a yellow and white gold case. Baguette movement, caliber 610, 2.75 lines, 17 jewels, bimetallic balance, Geneva stripes.*

224

235a, b *Woman's gold wristwatch, circa 1930, set with rubies and diamonds, Baguette movement, which at the push of a button springs sideways out of a round housing.*

236a, b *Woman's octagonal wristwatch, unsigned, gilded hook anchor movement with ¾ plate, metal case, circa 1930.*

237a, b *Woman's wristwatch with hook anchor escapement., signed "Favoris Watch Co.", circa 1930; the movement has a foliot instead of a balance wheel; no jewels, plated case.*

238a, b *Woman's gold watch, octagonal, with separating link band, metal dial with blued Breguet hands. 8.75-line anchor movement, 16 jewels; Swiss, circa 1930.*

239 *Woman's gold watch with slim expansion band and safety chain. Black numerals, gold Breguet hands. Round anchor movement, 8.75 lines, 15 jewels. IWC, circa 1930.*

240a-c *Woman's two-faced watch with analog and digital dials, chromed case, black numerals and hands, Baguette anchor movement, 4.25 lines, 15 jewels, digital mechanism mounted on a plate under the customary movement, dial inscription: "Mimorex", Swiss made, circa 1930.*

241a-b *Woman's oval art-deco watch, Tula silver case with rep band, black numerals and hands. Oval anchor movement, 16 jewels, flat hairspring. Swiss, circa 1930.*

242a, b *Art-deco gold watch made to fit the arm, with enamel decoration, octagonal dial, Baguette anchor movement, 15 jewels, flat hairspring, adjusted at two points. Made in Switzerland; seller's name: "Beyer, Zürich" 1935.*

243 *Man's barrel-shaped decorated watch, silver case, yellow metal dial with gold hands, small second hand. 10.5-line anchor movement, 11 jewels, flat hairspring. Swiss movement, German case, circa 1932.*

227

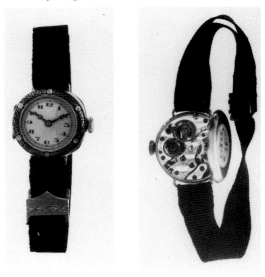

244a, b *Woman's rounded watch of Tula silver with stripes, white dial with blue Breguet hands, 8.75-line fine anchor movement with 16 jewels, cut-through balance and Breguet hairspring. IWC, circa 1932.*

On movement: "Mido", 2 adj. (adjusted in two places).

Maker's name: Beyer, Zürich.

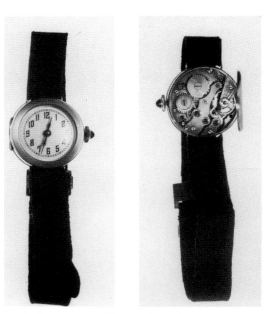

248a, b *Woman's rectangular doublé watch with silver dial and raised yellow numerals, elegant lines, 5.25-line anchor movement with 15 jewels, flat hairspring. Zentra brand name, circa 1938.*

Stem knob decorated with semiprecious stone.

249 *Woman's rectangular wristatch by Eterna, circa 1940.*

250 *Woman's rectangular wristwatch, signed "Zentra", with water-resistant case, circa 1940.*

251a, b *Woman's wristwatch by Andreas Huber, circa 1940, steel case, 26 mm (over attachments) x 14 mm; anchor movement, 5.5 x 6.5 lines, marked "Mimo", caliber 59, Swiss made, 15 jewels, monometallic balance, flat hairspring, finely regulated.*

252a, b *Woman's wristwatch assembled by Andreas Huber, circa 1940, round steel case, 21 mm diameter, 8.75-line Swiss anchor movement, marked "Mimo", caliber 81, 15 jewels, monometallic screw balance, flat hairspring; the character of a bridged movement is only pretended in this one, since the mounts for the anchor and second wheels can be removed only along with the minute wheel bridge. The slots are for optical reasons.*

229

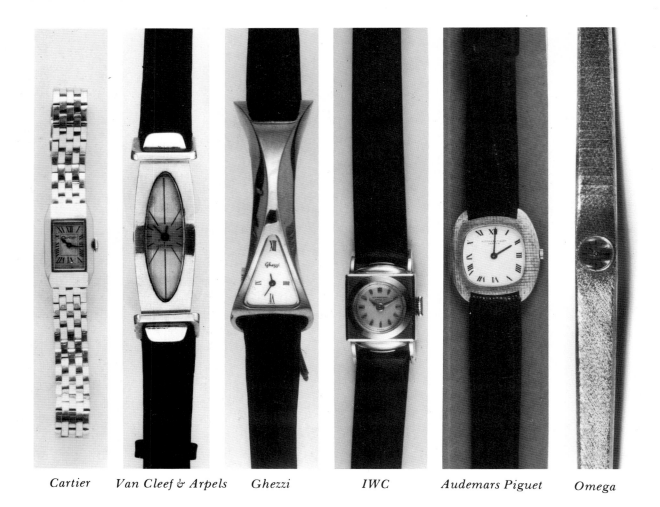

| Cartier | Van Cleef & Arpels | Ghezzi | IWC | Audemars Piguet | Omega |

253-260, 262-265 *Various women's wristwatches of Swiss origin, from the Thirties to present production.*

261a, b *"Duoplan" wristwatch movement from 1932, caliber 9 BF, 20 x 8.5 mm, 3.73 mm high; winding and hand setting from the back.*

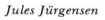 Jules Jürgensen   Patek Philippe

Movado

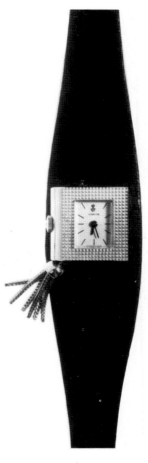

Rolex

Gübelin

Corum

266 *Extremely narrow platinum ornamental watch, marked Cartier. Decorative band set with gems, 2.25-line, Baguette movement, rectangular dial, circa 1935.*

267 *Woman's wristwatch, marked "Breguet", #2308; oval white gold case with glass ringed by gems; silver dial with lapis lazuli center.*

268 *Ornamental gold watch with caterpillar band, square dial, 2.25-line formed movement with anchor escapement, 15 jewels, Swiss, circa 1940.*

269 *Woman's wristwatch in red gold case by Patek Philippe & Co., circa 1945.*

270 *Woman's snake-formed wristwatch, signed "Anker", circa 1960; plated, 17-jewel anchor movement.*

Upper row, from left to right:
271 Gold "Duoplan" wristwatch by Jaeger–Le Coultre, with crown on the back of the case; 17 x 36 mm.

272 Man's gold Duo-Dial wristwatch by Longines; 19 x 33 mm.

273 Man's gold wristwatch in a newly recreated "tank" case by Baume & Mercier, 23 x 31 mm, circa 1970.

274 Rectangular wristwatch in white gold case by Piaget; dial set with four diamonds; 23 x 28 mm.

Lower row, from left to right:
275 Gold "Duoplan" wristwatch by Jaeger–Le Coultre, circa 1930. The crown is on the back of the case. 16 x 35 mm.

276 Man's Duo-Dial wristwatch Rolex "Prince", in 9-karat yellow and white gold case, 25 x 41 mm, circa 1930

277 Man's Duo-Dial wristwatch Rolex "Prince", in 9-karat yellow and white gold case, 26 x 42 mm, circa 1929

278 Man's octagonal gold wristwatch by Cartier; 19 x 38 mm, circa 1972. Movement by Jaeger–Le Coultre.

279 Man's wristwatch with automatic winding, chronograph, 30-minute and 12-hour indicators, calendar and moon phase indication, "El Primero" by Zenith. All indicators switch instantly at midnight; the month indicator switches automatically on the 31st. The day and moon phase indicators can be set by buttons in the case rim, the date and month via the crown. Case of 18-karat gold; the watch was also available in a steel case under the name "Espada".

234

Watertight wristwatches, aviators' and observation wristwatches

280 *One of the first four models of a "Rolex Oyster" wristwatch of 1926; patented case with screwed bottom and screwed winding stem.*

281a–d *Woman's sport watch in 18-karat gold case, water-resistant, case capsule is screwed through the edge of the glass after insertion of the movement. The stem, fastened to the movement when inserted, is made watertight by a second screwed-on knob. Radium numerals and hands. Round anchor movement, 8.75 lines, 15 jewels, flat hairspring. Made by "Cyma", with seller's name on the dial: "Beyer Zürich" circa 1932.*

282a, b *Wristwatch in watertight case with screwed crown, circa 1935; signed "Tropical Watch"; the movement can be taken out after unscrewing the lunette.*

284a, b *Man's wristwatch in "Carré cambré" case by Helvetia, General Watch co., circa 1935; firmly sprung-in rear cover makes the watch watertight; 10.5-line anchor movement, caliber 81-26, Geneva stripes, 15 jewels, 3 fine tuning points; this watch is already equipped with the shock resistance patented for Helvetia, recognizable by the three-shank springing of the balance bearing.*

285a, b *Rolex Oyster Imperial Chronometer in steel barrel case; seller's name, Beyer, of Zürich, on the dial; movement like the Rolex "Observatory" below but with indirect central second (second hand is missing).*

283a, b *Man's "Huber Nautica" wristwatch, circa 1935, in patented watertight steel case (barrel form), 28 x 28 mm, anchor movement with central second (outside the power flow), 10.5 lines, movement made by Helvetia; 15 jewels, 3 chatons, Helvetia shock resistance, monometallic balance, selfcompensating flat hairspring.*

286a, b *Man's sport watch, stainless steel, watertight, with screwed bottom. Metal dial, blue steel hands, small second hand. Dial inscribed: West End Watch Co. (Swiss made for the American market), circa 1938.*

287-288 *Typical advertisement from the Thirties by the Swiss watch industry, with clear references to the utility of the thick case.*

289a, b *Diver's watch in pressure-tight screwed steel case; flat glass, screw crown; massive screw lid front and back, additional inner screw lid behind the movement; external diameter 52 mm; signed Longines on dial and movement, circa 1940; gilded round movement with 16 jewels, size 13¾ lines, cut balance with Breguet hairspring, case number H↑S C 28.*

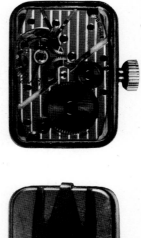

290a, b *Rolex "Oyster Chronometre Centregraph" woman's watertight sport watch in screwed steel case with stem knob screwed onto a housing on the case, radium dial. Round 10.5-line anchor movement, 18 jewels, "Superbalance" wheel. Breguet hairspring. The button by the 2 stops the large second hand independently of the power flow. Resetting to zero via the heart on the second-wheel arbor. Seller's name "Beyer", circa 1938. In the lid: English, French, Swiss, American and German patents.*

291a-c *Man's wristwatch of 1944, in rectangular watertight steel case (22.5 x 41 mm) by BWC; the watertight rectangular watch was very strongly publicized by the manufacturers at that time; caliber 148 formed movement (raw movement by FEF), 7.75 x 11 lines, 15 jewels, anchor escapement, Geneva stripes; for protection against water entering it, the movement was capsuled between the glass and a soft iron shield.*

292a, b *Man's sport watch in screwed stainless steel case, movement in additional capsule, two-color dial with radium numerals, small second hand. 7.75 x 11-line formed movement, anchor escapement, shock resistance. Brand: Cyma "Sport", circa 1940.*

293 *Man's barrel-shaped wristwatch, Rolex "Oyster Chronographe", circa 1940; 14-karat gold barrel case, 10.5-line hand-wound movement, 17 jewels, "Superbalance" wheel, self-compensating hairspring with end curve, fine regulation.*

294 *Woman's sport watch Rolex "Oyster Chronometre", in steel case with steel band, watertight, black numerals. Round anchor movement with eccentric second. Dial bears seller's name, "Beyer". Circa 1940.*

295a, b *Stainless steel diver's watch with rounded glass. In 1960 a special version reached a depth of 10,916 meters on the outside of Jacques Piccard's Bathyscaph, representing a pressure of 1000 kg per square centimeter. Rolex, circa 1945.*

296a, b *Watertight sport watch in stainless steel case, screwed bottom. Metal dial with luminous hands and numerals, small second hand, winding stem with joint, watertight knob with tube housing, 10.5-line Durowe anchor movement with 16 jewels, "anti-magnetic", flat hairspring, Incabloc. Laco brand, 1950.*

297 *Man's wristwatch with built in depth gauge, "bathy 50", by Favre-Leuba, circa 1966; steel case watertight to 50 meters, 40 mm diameter, screwed stem knob; movement and principal additions like those of the "bivouac", though here the membrane box is welded to the perforated rear lid, so no water can enter the movement; the depth gauge goes to 50 meters, the dial includes a decompression scale.*

298 *Wristwatch with decompression indicator by Cornavin Watch, circa 1963; watertight steel case, 42 mm diameter; automatic movement, Felsa caliber 810, 25 jewels, Incabloc shock resistance, winding in both directions of the rotor; seconds and minutes shown by hands, hours through a window.*

299 *Man's wristwatch "Ocean 2000" by IWC, with automatic movement, with date indication, caliber 375, in present production; titanium case and band; the case construction and the 3½ mm thick bombed sapphire glass allow diving depths to 2000 meters.*

300 *Man's wristwatch "Aquatimer" by IWC, circa 1970; first diver's watch by IWC, watertight to 200 meters; 13-line automatic movement, caliber 8541 B, with date indication; the turning ring for diving time can be set by the crown at the 4; stainless steel case with engraved submarine on the back, 37 mm diameter.*

301a-c *Man's wristwatch with automatic winding, Rolex "Sea Dweller", 1970; steel case absolutely watertight to 610 meters; this is the first diver's watch with a helium vent patented by Rolex; it can be seen in the case ring in the middle picture; anchor movement with rotor winding and calendar date.*

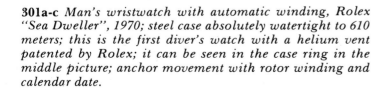

241

302 *Early military watch with openable protective grid, by Girard-Perregaux, circa 1900. This type was supplied to the German Navy until World War I.*

303 *Military wristwatch with protective grid, by Waltham, from World War I times; anchor movement.*

304a-c *"Trench" watch by Robert H. Ingersoll for World War I. On the back of the lid the guarantee of one year's trouble-free running is glued in. Movement with hook anchor escapement, without jewels.*

305a-b *"Trench" or "Soldier" watch by Movado, made for World War I use, 1914-18. To protect the glass and dial, the front is equipped with a grid. Anchor movement with 17 jewels, four screwed chatons, bimetallic balance and Breguet hairspring. The watch is finely regulated at five points.*

306a, b *Round wristwatch with spring lid, on the lid of the case a stamped picture, "General Ulrich Wille" (Swiss), 10.5-line anchor movement, 15 jewels, Breguet hairspring, circa 1918.*

307a-e *Man's wristwatch with alarm and protective grid for the glass, from the 1914-1918 period, by Eterna, presumably made for military use. 15-jewel anchor movement, bimetallic balance, flat hairspring. The power for works and alarm originates from a large barrel; a governor assures power for the works when the alarm is ringing. Alarm time is set by means of a turning glass. The protective lid seen in 307c, with perforations for setting the regulator and turning off the alarm, serves to amplify the sound. Case of silver, 0.875, diameter 36.5 mm, height including grid, 14.5 mm.*

308a, b *Hour-angle wristwatch "Lindbergh" by Longines, for long-distance aviation, developed in cooperation with Charles Lindbergh after 1927 and put on the market in 1932; steel case, 47 mm diameter; because of the clever placing of* *the dials, the Greenwich sun time angle can be read directly; 17-jewel anchor movement, 37 mm diameter, monometallic screw balance, self-compensating flat hairspring, indirect central second.*

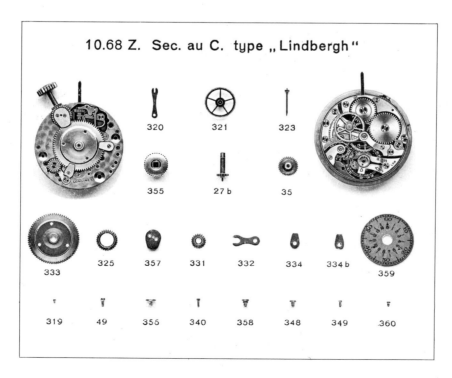

309 *Watch movement, caliber 10.68 Z "Lindbergh", as used in the hour-angle wristwatch shown in #310.*

310 *Smaller type of the Longines "Lindbergh" with a case diameter of 35 mm; aside from this, the watch has the same capabilities as the hour-angle watch shown in #308; ten-line anchor movement, caliber 10.68 Z (see #309), 17 jewels, indirect central second.*

311 *Woman's wristwatch in steel case, marked on the dial: "Longines Weems", patented production for the USA, circa 1950; the outer glass can be locked via the knob by the 2; 10-line Swiss anchor movement by Longines, compensated balance, Breguet hairspring.*

Movements of four observation wristwatches for aviators. The watches were worn over the uniform and had a diameter of 55 mm; built during World War II. All observation watches have in common a balance-stopping apparatus.

312a, b *Aviator's wristwatch, circa 1940, marked "Lanco" (Langendorf Watch Co.); nickel-plated steel case, 41 mm diameter, rimmed turning glass with luminous triangle for setting to, for example, departure time; prominent stem knob, to allow winding with gloves on; 15-line anchor movement with 15 jewels, caliber 2, monometallic screw balance, self-compensating flat hairspring.*

246

313a, b *B-movement type A, Lange & Sons, caliber 47.I. (The movements were made and adjusted during World War II by various German firms, such as Huber of Munich, Felsing of Berlin, Schieron of Stuttgart, Schätzle und Tschudin of Pforzheim or Wempe of Hamburg); 17 jewels, nickel steel balance of 20 mm diameter, Breguet hairspring with inner end curve, bearing jewels set in chatons, gooseneck fine regulation, indirect central second hand, no shock resistance.*

314a, b *B-movement by International Watch Co. (IWC), built in an additional anti-magnetic inner case. 18-line movement with bimetallic balance and Breguet hairspring, gooseneck fine regulation, no shock resistance, indirect central second; IWC built 1200 of these observation wrist-watches.*

315a, b *B-movement by Laco-Durowe (Lacher & Co.-Deutsche Uhren Rohwerke); gilded 22-jewel anchor movement of 22 lines, with large (22 mm diameter) cut Guillaume balance, Breguet hairspring, simple regulating indicator without fine regulation, no shock resistance, indirect central second (outside the power flow).*

316a, b *B-watch by Stowa (Walter Storz); nickel-plated 18-line anchor movement (Unitas caliber) with cut Guillaume balance, Breguet hairspring, gooseneck fine regulation, indirect central second, 20 jewels, no shock resistance, Geneva stripes.*

317a-c *Aviator's watch by Wempe, Hamburg, circa 1935, No. 434, nickel case, diameter 55 mm, gilded caliber 31 anchor movement by Thommen, Waldenburg, with bimetallic balance, Breguet hairspring, fine regulation.*

318 *Observation wristwatch for aviators, with doubled central second, "Deutsche Uhrenfabrikation Glashütte" gilded ¾-plate movement, anchor escapement, gold anchor, bimetallic balance, Breguet hairspring, gooseneck fine regulation. The small inner dial is divided into six 60-degree sections. One of the central second hands can be started and stopped by the button by the 2.*

319, 320 *Observation wristwatches by Vacheron & Constantin from 1936, caliber 20"-11, sold in Germany; steel case. #320 has a chronograph hand controlled by the button near the 4.*

321a, b *IWC military watch in watertight steel case. Round IWC movement, 11.5 lines, 15 jewels, cut balance and Breguet hairspring, circa 1942.*

322a, b *Military wristwatch by IWC, "Mark XI", 1951 (the watch has been supplied to the Luftwaffe by IWC from 1948 to the present); steel case with additional soft iron inner case for protection from magnetic effects, diameter 36 mm; 12-line movement, caliber 89, 17 jewels, 4 chatons, Incabloc shock resistance, indirect central second, monometallic screw balance, Breguet hairspring, balance-stopping mechanism for exact time setting; before delivery, every Mark XI is tested by IWC for 648 hours under extreme conditions.*

323a, b *German Army Watch, clear luminous dial, central sedond, watertight screwed steel case. 11.5-line anchor movement, 17 jewels, movable hairspring stud (piton mobile), shock resistance. Hamilton brand, circa 1942.*

324a, b *Military wristwatch by Smiths of England, made in 1968 for the RAF; steel case, 35 mm diameter, gilded 11.75-line movement with Swiss anchor escapement, "Kif Flector", shock resistance, 17 jewels, monometallic ring balance, self-compensating flat hairspring, indirect central second, balance-stopping mechanism for setting the watch exactly to the second.*

Upper row, from left to right:
325 Wristwatch with platinum case, signed "Boucheron", Paris; 17 x 30 mm.

326 Gold wristwatch with gold band, signed "Cartier", circa 1936.

327 Man's Duo-Dial wristwatch Rolex "Prince", in 9-karat yellow and white goldcase, circa 1933 (see also #105-113, 276, 277).

328 Man's flat wristwatch in gold case, by Vacheron & Constantin; 22 x 30 mm.

Lower row, from left to right:
329 Man's wristwatch with automatic winding, calendar and moon phase indication, Rolex "Precision", in steel case, 38 mm diameter.

330 Gold wristwatch by Cartier, 20 x 28 mm, circa 1976.

331 New White gold and enamel wristwatch with hexagonal dial cutout, by Cartier, movement by Jaeger-Le Coultre; 23 x 30 mm, circa 1976.

332 Man's gold wristwatch with automatic winding, date indication and alarm, "Memovox", by Jaeger-Le Coultre

Wristwatches with automatic winding from 1922 to the present

349a, b *Wristwatch with automatic winding, by Léon Leroy, from 1922. The movement is built into a then-modern pointed-oval case. Leroy was presumably the first manufacturer of automatic wristwatches, but only a few examples of these watches were prepared. Because of the case's form, the swinging weight had very little freedom of movement, and it seems unlikely that the watch could have been wound sufficiently by normal arm movement. Since the watch was also too sensitive for daily use, Leroy did not plan for series production.*

350 *Prototype wristwatch with automatic winding, made by hand in 1922 by John Harwood. Harwood used a flat lead weight fastened to a sheet metal attachment as a swinging mass. He built it, fitted with an appropriate wheel train, into a 13-line round movement by Blancpain, Villeret (Switzerland). Harwood had to equip the case with a specially milled-out area in which the swinging weight could move. As Harwood held the view that the winding/setting stem was the cause of much disturbance and dust in wristwatches, he did away with the stem and closed its hole in the case. For that reason this first prototype had no hand-setting mechanism. Harwood constructed one only later. On the basis of this prototype Harwood developed his automatic winding, which could be put, movement and all, in a case of normal size. Which material should be used for the swinging mass was the problem: lead was heavy enough, but unsuitable because of its material characteristics; brass had good material qualities but a too-low specific weight. Only the idea of mounting the swinging mass in the center of the watch and thereby making it bigger allowed it to be made of brass.*

254

351 *The first series-production automatic wristwatch of the Harwood type, made 1926-1931. The watch came in gold, silver and doublé cases. The hands are set by turning the glass. A red dot under the 6 shows, after the hands are set, that*

power flow between movement and hands has been re-established. 15-jewel anchor movement, 10.5 lines, bimetallic balance, height about 6.5 mm.

352a, b *"Rolls" wristwatch with automatic winding. The watch's name derives from the fact that the movement, mounted on balls, can roll back and forth lengthwise in the case and so winds the watch. The balls are in two grooves running along the sides. This automatic winding system was*

invented by Léon Hatot of Paris and patented in 1930. The manufacture of this 3.75-, 5.5- and 8.75-line movement was done by the Blancpain firm. The "Rolls" in a man's version; 17-jewel anchor movement, bimetallic balance, Geneva stripes.

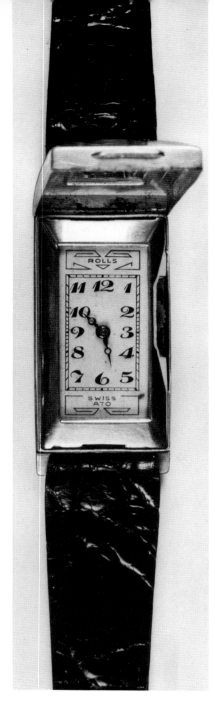

353a-e *The "Rolls" as a woman's wristwatch, 1931. Gold doublé case. Manufactured by Blancpain. The upper case lifts so the watch can be set. The setting knob is mounted horizontally at the right, near the 2. The cutouts above and below are needed so the movement can roll without the knob hitting anything. To set the hands, one pushes the knob toward the dial, it meshes with the setting wheel and thus moves the hands. A look at the 5.5-line movement with 17 jewels, bimetallic balance and flat hairspring. At the top of the cutout in the frame a lever, connecting the frame with the movement, is visible. With every motion of the movement, the visible cogwheel is turned farther. The click in the upper left corner stops it from unwinding. Springs on the short sides of the movement protect it against too-vigorous arm motions. In the thin slits between frame and movement the balls are visible. The movement of the "Rolls" when covered: the cap's only job is to add its weight to the swinging mass. The slit in the covering allows adjustment of the regulator.*

354a-d *Glycine watch with automatic winding. This caliber 20 was developed by Eugène Meylan on the basis of an 8.75-line movement and patented in 1931. The watch, which follows the principle, developed by Harwood, of a segmented swinging mass in the center of the movement, was meant to replace watches with "roll winding" such as the Rolls. The new feature of this movement was that the automatic winding and the actual movement could be completely separated from each other with ease without affecting the working of the movement. This separation was intended to make repair simpler. In the Glycine the automatic winding mechanism (swinging weight, mounting, reduction drive) was attached to a steel ring. The movement was set into this from the front, which in itself connected it to the automatic winding mechanism. The motion of the swinging weight is limited by shock springs, and the winding works in only one direction. The Glycine's hands are set via the stem; it is wound only by the swinging weight.*

355a-e *In 1931 the "La Champagne" watch factory of Louis Müller & Co. patented a watch with "roll winding", which came on the market under the name of "Wig-Wag". As with the Rolls, the movement is mounted in a rolling chamber. The back-and forth lengthwise motion of the movement activates the automatic winding. The energy is transmitted to the mainspring by a jointed parallelogram lever. The jointed levers are mounted elastically, so as to function as shock absorbers too. When the glass, which fits over a glass rim, is lifted, the hand-setting knob can be seen to the right, by the 3.*

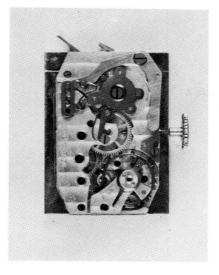

356a-d *"Autorist" wristwatch with automatic winding; 1931/32. The idea for this system came from John Harwood; the invention was manufactured by A. Schild S.A. as caliber 796. The automatic winding works by opening and closing one's hand, thus changing the circumference of the wrist. To carry this energy to the mainspring, the lower band attachments and the bar linking them were made movable. A lever mechanism makes the energy of motion wind the mainspring. The 6.75-line formed movement has 15 jewels. For this winding system to work, the band can scarcely be elastic, nor can the watch be at all loose on the wrist.*

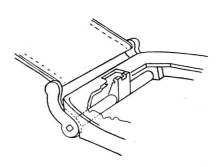

357a, b *Woman's version of the "Autorist" marked "Universe selfwinding". Case of 925 silver, 17 x 33.5 mm (measured over the attachments). This "Universe selfwinding" was also available as a man's watch in a silver case.*

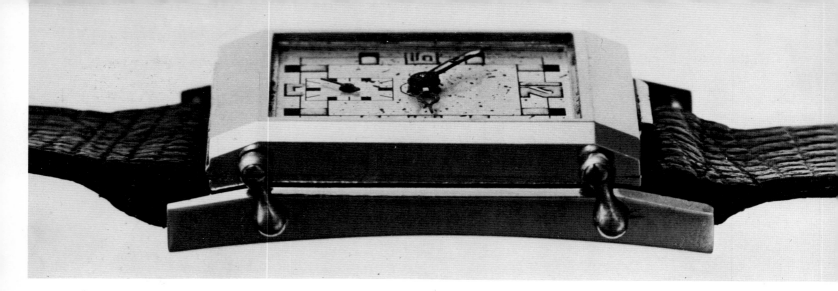

358a-c *Wristwatch with automatic winding, which also works by the rolling principle. The system was patented in 1933 for the Bulova watch. Unlike the "Wig-Wag", the movement does not roll inside the case, but rather the whole upper case, with the movement, rolls on the lower case. Power transmission is effected by levers under the axes of the external parallelogram levers.*

359a, b *Rolex Oyster Perpetual of 1931. This, the first watertight automatic wristwatch, worked on the principle of unlimited rotor turning. Winding this caliber NA 620, though, takes place in only one rotor direction. The automatic winding mechanism is formed as a unit and attached to a 9.75-line movement. As a result, this wristwatch has the disadvantage of being 7.52 mm high, making this Rolex one of the thickest of all wristwatches. The movement is fitted with a "Super Balance" wheel and 18 jewels. Because of the screwed-on winding mechanism, even when the bottom cover is removed nothing of the movement can be seen.*

360a, b, 361 *"Perpetual" wristwatch with automatic winding, sold circa 1935 by the Perpetual Self Winding Watch Co. of New York, manufactured by Frey & Co. Ltd. in Biel. In the Perpetual, the automatic winding works on a pendulum principle. The swinging weight is attached to a formed movement and moves back and forth across it. The energy is transmitted by a ratchet wheel. The anchor movement has 15 jewels and a bimetallic balance. The stem, used only to set the watch, is on the left side of the case.*

362 *Rolex caliber NA 620 (see also #359a, b).*

363a-c *Wristwatch with automatic winding, patented in 1931 for the Wyler S.A. watch factory. As with the "Autorist", the Wyler automatic uses changes in the circumference of the wrist to wind the mainspring. But this automatic watch's case has a fixed and a movable bottom. A spur attached to the movable bottom projects through a hole near the ratchet wheel to transmit the energy to the movement. A lever mechanism with ratchet and click carries the movement of the bottom to the barrel. The 8.75 x 11-line anchor movement has 17 jewels, five chatons and a bimetallic balance with flat hairspring. The hands are set by a knob in the base. The watch also appeared under the name "Mimimatik".*

364a, b *Man's wristwatch with automatic winding, marked "Rodana Automatic", made by Joba Watch, 1941; steel case. 30 mm diameter, 11.25-line movement, AS (A. Schild) caliber 1049, developed 1938, 17 jewels, Incabloc shock resistance, winding by an asymmetrical swinging pendulum; the energy of one direction is transferred via a ratchet to a centrally mounted wheel of the reduction drive.*

365a, b *Man's wristwatch with automatic winding by Eterna, circa 1940; steel case, 31 mm diameter; 17-jewel movement, caliber 834, 12 lines, Eterna shock resistance; automatic winding in one direction of the asymmetrical swinging weight, limited by screw springs.*

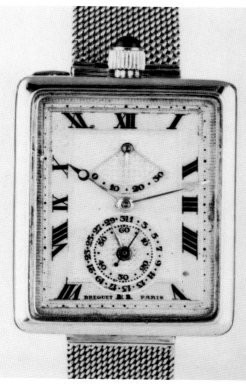

366a, b *Man's wristwatch with automatic winding by Pierce, post-1941; watertight steel case, 30 mm diameter; bottom and thickening are attached with 4 screws; 17-jewel anchor movement with monometallic screw balance, self-compensating flat hairspring and Incabloc shock resistance; winding by a circular weight mass which can move back and forth in the case, guided by two metal pins; a toothed staff carries the up-and-down motions to a diagonally toothed wheel.*

367a, b *Man's wristwatch with automatic winding, marked on the dial "Comint", circa 1943; steel case, 34 mm diameter, 11.25-line anchor movement with 15 jewels, Felsa caliber 279, Incabloc shock resistance, monometallic screw balance, flat hairspring; automatic winding via an asymmetrical swinging pendulum, buffered by two screw springs.*

368a, b *Rectangular platinum wristwatch with automatic winding, marked "Breguet", #2926, of 1933; the watch was sold then to Sir Percival David for 8500 Francs; special silver dial with Roman numerals, under the 12 a quadrant scale showing the running reserve up to 30 hours, over the 6 an inner dial showing the seconds with an outer dial showing the date, each with a hand; gilded 9-line anchor movement with raised oscillating winding mechanism, bimetallic balance, Breguet hairspring.*

369 *Man's wristwatch with automatic winding and winding indicator by Oris, circa 1958; steel case, 35 mm diameter; 12-line anchor movement, presumably caliber 605, 17 jewels, "Kif Trior" shock resistance, automatic winding by unlimited rotor, winding indicator to 36 hours by a hand under the 12.*

370a, b *Man's wristwatch with automatic winding and winding indicator by Jaeger-LeCoultre, 1953; 14-line anchor movement, caliber 497, no possibility of hand winding; when the mainspring is fully wound, the swinging pendulum is blocked, "Kif Protechoc" shock resistance; setting via a knob on the back of the watch, balance stopped by a spring during setting; winding indicator to 40 hours shown by a hand near the 9.*

371a, b *Man's wristwatch with automatic winding and winding indicator, "RotoGraph", by Paul Buhré, circa 1956; 17-jewel anchor movement, AS caliber 1382, 11.5 lines, Incablock shock resistance, winding in both directions of unlimited rotor; winding indicator to 36 hours by a hand under the 12.*

372 *Man's wristwatch with automatic winding and winding indicator to 36 hours by Zodiac, circa 1956; 11.5-line "Autographic" caliber, winding in both directions of the unlimited rotor; winding indicator hand over the 6.*

373a, b *Man's wristwatch with automatic winding and winding indicator, by Junghans, airca 1953; 22-jewel anchor movement, 10.5 lines, Junghans caliber 80/12, automatic winding in both directions of unlimited rotor; winding indicator to 36 hours shown through window over the 6.*

374a, b *Man's wristwatch with automatic winding and winding indicator to 36 hours, by Omega, from 1948 on; steel case, 35 mm diameter, anchor movement caliber 351, 17 jewels, Incablock shock resistance, indirect central second; automatic winding in one direction of the limited swinging pendulum; winding indicator in center of dial.*

375a, b *Man's wristwatch with automatic winding and winding indicator by Jaeger-LeCoultre, introduced 1948; steel case, 33 mm diameter, 13-line anchor movement, caliber 481, "Superchoc" shock resistance; automatic winding in one direction of a limited swinging pendulum, digital winding indicator in a window under the 12.*

376a, b *Wristwatch movement by Jaeger-Le Coultre, with automatic winding and winding indication with the help of a disc showing through a dialcutout, 1947, caliber 476-12 AD, diameter 29.56 mm, height 6.15 mm.*

377a, b *Man's wristwatch with automatic winding by the Union Horlogère Alpina, circa 1950; steel case, 33 mm diameter, 12.5-line red-gilded movement, caliber 582/P 82, automatic winding by an asymmetrical swinging pendulum limited by screw springs; power transmission by ratchets; monometallic screw balance, self-compensating flat hairspring, Incabloc shock resistance.*

378a, b *Man's wristwatch with automatic winding in 18-karat gold case by Longines, circa 1950; 13-line movement, caliber 22 AS (made since 1945), 17 jewels, winding in both directions, rotor not limited, movement 6.5 mm high.*

379a, b *Man's wristwatch with automatic winding, marked "Mido Multifort Super Automatic", circa 1950; steel case, 31 mm diameter, 10.5-line movement, caliber 917, 17 jewels, monometallic screw balance, self-compensating hairspring, automatic winding in one direction of the asymmetrical swinging weight, energy transmission via a ratchet.*

380 *Man's square watertight wristwatch with automatic winding by Cyma, circa 1953; 11½-line movement, caliber R 420 (see also #381b).*

381a, b *Man's wristwatch with automatic winding by Cyma, 1952; steel case with screwed bottom, 34 mm diameter, 11.5-line movement, caliber R 420, developed 1943, 17 jewels, 4 of them set in chatons, "Cymaflex" shock resistance, indirect central second, automatic winding via asymmetrical swinging pendulum, limited by spring buffers.*

382a, b *Man's wristwatch with automatic winding, Longines "Conquest", made since 1952, 11.25-line movement, caliber 19, 19 jewels, monometallic screw balance, self-compensating flat hairspring, "Trishock" shock resistance, indirect central second; rotor winding in both directions.*

383a, b *Man's wristwatch with automatic winding, Omega "Seamaster", circa 1955. Steel case, 34 mm diameter, 20-jewel anchor movement, caliber 470, fine regulation; the rotor winds the mainspring in both directions.*

384a, b *Man's wristwatch with automatic winding by Universal, circa 1953; doublé case, 35 mm diameter, 12.5-line movement, caliber 138 SS, 17 jewels, Incabloc shock resistance, monometallic screw balance, self-compensating flat hairspring; automatic winding by a limited asymmetrical swinging pendulum in one direction, power transmission via ratchet mechanism.*

385a, b *Man's wristwatch with automatic winding, marked doxa, circa 1952; 14-karat gold case, 34 mm diameter, 11-line AS caliber 1250, 11 lines, developed 1944, Incabloc shock resistance, monometallic screw balance, self-compensating flat hairspring.*

386a, b *Man's wristwatch with automatic winding, marked "Tudor Oyster-Prince" by Rolex, circa 1953; Oyster steel case, 34 mm diameter, 17-jewel movement, caliber 390, 12.5 lines, monometallic screw balance, self-compensating flat hairspring, "Kif" shock resistance; winding by rotor with unlimited turning.*

387a, b *Man's wristwatch with automatic winding by Ebel, circa 1953; steel case, 33 mm diameter, 12.5-line movement, AS caliber 1298, Incabloc shock resistance, automatic winding via asymmetrical swinging pendulum limited by screw springs, power of one direction transferred via a ratchet system.*

388a, b *Man's wristwatch with automatic winding and calendar by Movado, circa 1953; steel case with screwed bottom, 33 mm diameter, 17-jewel anchor movement, caliber 224A, 12 lines, Incabloc shock resistance, monometallic screw balance, self-compensating Breguet hairspring; asymmetrical swinging pendulum drives the work in one direction via ratchet wheels. Date correction possible by a button in the case rim by the 9.*

389a, b *Man's wristwatch with automatic winding by Cortébert, made since 1955; steel case, 34 mm diameter; anchor movement, "Cortérotor" caliber 700, 11.5 lines, 21 jewels, monometallic screw balance, self-compensating flat hairspring, Incabloc shock resistance; winding in both rotor directions.*

390 *Man's wristwatch with automatic winding by Jaeger-Le Coultre, circa 1955; gold case, dial set with gems, marked "Mysterieuse", time shown by two rotating dials with gems to indicate minutes and hours; 12½-line movement, caliber P 812, 17 jewels, monometallic screw balance, self-compensating flat hairspring, "Kif" shock resistance; winding by swinging pendulum in one direction of the rotor, limited by a screw spring. (see also #370b).*

391a, b *Man's gold wristwatch with "Regulator" dial by Omega, circa 1960; 12-line anchor movement, caliber 491, 19 jewels, monometallic screw balance, self-compensating flat hairspring, gooseneck fine regulation, Incabloc shock resistance.*

392a, b *Woman's automatic watch, Ernest Borel, circa 1955; screwed stainless steel case; champagne-colored metal dial with raised numerals; gilded staff hands with inner luminescence; Fixoflex link band; movement with 17 jewels, 9¾-line rotor (Bidynator) works in two directions; Incabloc shock resistance; monometallic balance with screws; central second.*

393a, b *Man's wristwatch with automatic winding by IWC, circa 1957; steel case, 36.5 mm diameter, 13-line movement, caliber 852, 21 jewels, 19,800 half-swings per hour, monometallic balance, self-compensating Breguet hairspring, power transmission from the rotor via eccentric converters and ratchet system, winding in both directions without rotor limitation, indirect central second.*

395 *Man's wristwatch with automatic winding by Universal, "Polerouter", 1958; steel case, 34 mm diameter; anchor movement, caliber 215, 12.5 lines, 28 jewels, 3 of them set in chatons, Incabloc shock resistance, "Girocap" mounting of the anchor wheel pivot, Geneva stripes, monometallic ring balance, self-compensating flat hairspring; the watch is equipped 'with the planetary rotor first conceived by Universal in 1958, integrated in the movement; with a height of 4.10 mm, this was the flattest automatic wristwatch of its time; winding in both directions. The watch runs 'for 60 hours thanks to a generously proportioned mainspring barrel.*

394a, b *Man's wristwatch with automatic winding by Patek Philippe, made in this form 1953-1960, 12-line caliber 600 AT movement, 30 jewels, Gyromax balance, self-compensating Breguet hairspring, fine regulation, 19,800 half-swings per hour, winding by a massive 18-karat gold rotor in both directions.*

396a, b *Mans' wristwatch with automatic winding by Universal, "Pole-router", circa 1960; steel case, 34 mm diameter; automatic movement caliber 218-9, like caliber 215 in construction, but with fine tuning for the regulator.*

397a, b *Man's wristwatch with automatic winding, Dugena "Super", circa 1960; doublé case, 34 mm diameter; equipped with Buren caliber 1000 A "Super Slender", which is parallel to the Universal caliber 215; 33-jewel anchor movement, 12½ lines, monometallic screw balance, self-compensating flat hairspring, Incabloc shock resistance, indirect central second, height of movement 4.20 mm; automatic winding in both directions of the planetary rotor.*

398 *Wristwatch movement with automatic winding via planetary rotor, by Patek Philippe, patented Sept. 30, 1977; 12 lines, 27 jewels, free-swinging self-compensating flat hairspring, Gyromax with 21,600 half-swings per hour, ball-bearing microrotor of 22-karat gold, winding in one direction; movement height 2.4 mm.*

399a, b *Man's wristwatch with automatic winding, Movado "Kingmatic", circa 1960; watertight steel case, 11.75-line movement, caliber 531, 28 jewels, Incabloc shock resistance, 21,600 half-swings per hour; the weight of the rotor is sprung via the S-shaped extended carrier.*

400 *Man's square wristwatch with automatic winding and central second by Eterna, circa 1960.*

401a, b *Man's wristwatch with automatic winding, Eterna "Centenaire", 1961; 18-karat gold case, 34 mm diameter. Movement caliber 1438 U, 21 jewels, beryllium balance, flat hairspring, eccentric fine regulation.*

402a, b *Man's wristwatch with automatic winding, Revue "Rotor King" (Thommen), circa 1962; 11.5-line anchor movement, caliber 87, 21 jewels, Incabloc shock resistance, noteworthy fine regulation via helical disc; the rotor winds the mainspring in both directions.*

403a, b *Man's wristwatch with automatic winding by Ulysse Nardin, circa 1965; steel case, 35 mm diameter, 25-jewel anchor movement (AS raw movement), monometallic ring balance, self-compensating flat hairspring, Incabloc shock resistance, ball-bearing rotor winding the mainspring in both directions; date indicator springs at midnight.*

404a, b *Man's wristwatch with automatic winding and calendar, by Baume & Mercier, 1965; 18-karat gold case, 34 mm diameter; 11.5-line movement, AS caliber 1700-1, 25 jewels, monometallic ring balance, self-compensating flat hairspring, Incabloc shock resistance; winding in both rotor directions.*

405a, b *Man's wristwatch with automatic winding, "Cyclotron" by Blancpain-Rayville, circa 1965; steel case, 34 mm diameter, 53-jewel anchor movement, caliber Rollmatic R 300, monometallic screw balance, self-compensating flat hairspring, Incabloc shock resistance; the rotor, running externally on ruby bearings, winds the mainspring in both directions.*

406a, b *Man's wristwatch with automatic winding, "spezimatic" by the Glashütter Uhrenbetriebe, East Germany, circa 1965; doublé case, 37 mm diameter, 12.5-line movement with anchor escapement, 25 jewels, caliber 74, shock resistance; winding in both rotor directions.*

407a, b *Man's wristwatch with automatic winding, Longines "Flagship", circa 1965; steel case, 34 mm diameter, 12-line movement, 17 jewels, caliber 340, monometallic ring balance, self-compensating flat hairspring, fine tuning of the regulator by eccentric screw, "Kif Flector" shock resistance; rotor mounted eccentrically in the movement on ball bearings, winds the mainspring in both directions by an internally toothed ring.*

408 *Man's wristwatch with automatic winding, "Ambassador" by Bulova, circa 1968; 18-karat gold shell case, 35 mm diameter; 30-jewel anchor movement with planetary rotor, 12½ lines, monometallic ring balance, self-compensating flat hairspring, fine tuning of the regulator by eccentric screw; automatic winding in both directions of the rotor, which is integrated in the movement.*

409a, b *Man's wristwatch with automatic winding, Poljot "de luxe", USSR, circa 1965; 10.5-line anchor movement, 29 jewels, caliber 2415, shock resistance, direct central second, automatic winding in both rotor directions; the movement is constructed like Tissot calibers such as 783.*

410a, b *Man's wristwatch with automatic winding by Audemars Piguet, 1977. 34 mm diameter, case, dial, hands and band of 18-karat white gold; 12.5-line anchor movement, caliber 2121, 36 jewels, self-compensating free-swinging flat hairspring, screwless ring balance with adjustable inertia, 19,800 halfsprings per hour; the rotor with its outer weight of 21-karat gold winds the mainspring in both directions; the date indication changes instantly; height of the movement including the date disc 3.05 mm.*

411a, b *Certina automatic watch 'Town and Country', circa 1970; square stainless steel case, screwed rear; metal dial with raised two-tone markings and staff hands, central second, date indication near the 3 with springing date change; 27-*

jewel Certina caliber 25-651 movement, size 11½ lines, Incabloc shock resistance, monometallic balance, central rotor, divided winding stem.

412a, b *Man's wristwatch with automatic winding by Longines, built since 1977; anchor movement, caliber 990. 11.5 lines, 25 jewels, two mainspring barrels in series, ball-bearing rotor, movement height 2.95 mm*

413a, b *Man's wristwatch with automatic winding by Jean Lassale, Geneva, made since 1978; caliber 2000, 9 lines, 9 jewels, 18 miniature bearings, 21,600 half-swings per hour, 50-hour winding reserve, height of the movement including the rotor 2.08 mm.*

Wristwatches with chronographs and wrist stop-watches

414 *Automatic version of the Jean Lassale movement, made since 1978; caliber 2000, 9 lines, 9 jewels, 18 ball bearings, 21,600 half-swings per hour, 50 hours' running time; height of movement including rotor 2.08 mm.*

415 *Man's silver wristwatch with chronograph and 30-minute indicator, Swiss, circa 1924, without maker's name; 16-line anchor movement, 17 jewels, bimetallic balance, Breguet hairspring; white enamel dial with luminous numerals; the button under the 6 operates the chronograph. Chronograph wristwatches of this type were made by, among others, the Martel Watch Co.*

416 *Man's wristwatch with chronograph and 30-minute indicator, "Tortue" model by Cartier, developed in 1912; the watch shows dates from 1927.*

417 *Man's gold wristwatch with chronograph and 30-minute indicator, made by Th. Picard Fils, circa 1930; white enamel dial with hectometer and tachometer scale, the button near the 2 operates the chronograph.*

418 *The movement of another wristwatch-chronograph by Th. Picard Fils, in which the chronograph is operated by a button built into the stem knob; 17-jewel anchor movement, setting of the chronograph mechanism via a switching wheel, bimetallic balance, Breguet hairspring.*

419a

421a

420a

422

419b

420b

419a, b Man's wristwatch with chronograph and 30-minute counter, circa 1920, made by Longines for J. W. Benson, London. 13-line anchor movement, caliber 13.33, 18 jewels, bimetallic balance, Breguet hairspring; all steel parts are polished and (angliert).

420a, b Man's wristwatch with chronograph and 30-minute counter, circa 1920; 15-jewel anchor movement, signed "Rose Watch Co.", bimetallic balance, Breguet hairspring; the starting, stopping and zero setting functions of the chronograph are controlled by a button built into the crown by the 12.

421a, b Man's large silver wristwatch with chronograph and 60-minute counter, circa 1920; the 60-minute hand moves counterclockwise; the crown by the 6 is merely (atrappe), the starting, stopping and zero setting functions of the chrono-graph are controlled by a button built into the crown by the 12; anchor movement, bimetallic balance, Breguet hair-spring.

422 Man's wristwatch with chronograph, 30-minute counter and tachometer scale on the dial, circa 1920.

421b

423a, b *Early chronograph by Longines, metal case with setting button. Chronograph operated by pressing the winding stem. 30-minute indicator, tachometer scale. 13-line anchor movement with cut balance and Breguet hairspring. Swiss, circa 1930.*

424 *Man's wristwatch with chronograph and 30-minute indicator in 18-karat gold case, 40 mm diameter, Swiss, circa 1935; enamel dial with tachometer scale, Breguet hands; 16-line gilded anchor movement with 17 jewels, monometallic balance, self-compensating Breguet hairspring.*

425a-c *"Invicta Chrono Sport" chronograph wristwatch, made by Invicta circa 1930. Only 50 examples were produced of this chronograph built onto a normal formed movement without any further changes; it is screwed onto the front of the movement and covered by the dial. The chronograph is activated by the "lever" located above the stem.*

426a, b, 427, 428 *Man's wristwatch with chronograph by Omega, Louis Brandt & Frère, 1932, in three-part nickel case, caliber 28.9 T.1 movement; central chronograph hand and 30-minute counter near the 3; this watch was worn by General Italo Balbo's crew during their long-distance flight from Rome to New York in 1933.*

429a, b *Man's wristwatch with chronograph and 30-minute indicator by Omega, "Tissot" type, circa 1933. steel case, 35 mm diameter; 17-jewel Lemania caliber chronograph movement with switching wheel, monometallic screw balance, self-compensating flat hairspring, no shock resistance; chronograph activated by the button by the 2. (Chronograph hand is missing.)*

430a, b *Man's wristwatch with chronograph and 30-minute indicator, assembled by Andreas Huber, circa 1935; steel case, 32 mm diameter; 13-line movement with switching wheel, caliber 2400-2416 by Hahn, Le Landeron; 17 jewels, mono-metallic screw balance, self-compensating Breguet hairspring, Geneva stripes.*

431a, b *Man's wristwatch with chronograph, 30-minute and 12-hour counters, tacho- and telemeter scales on the dial, by Heuer, circa 1945; 14-line Valjoux caliber 71, monometallic screw balance, self-compensating Breguet hairspring.*

432 *Man's wristwatch with chronograph and 30-minute indicator, marked on the dial "Huber", circa 1935; chronograph movement with switching wheel by Hahn, Le Landeron, caliber 13, monometallic screw balance, self-compensating Breguet hairspring, no shock resistance; button by the 2 for starting, stopping and setting back.*

433a, b *Man's wristwatch with chronograph (without hand) by Fortis, circa 1940; 10.5-line movement by Venus, caliber 103, 15 jewels, monometallic screw balance, flat hairspring; the button in the stem knob starts, stops and resets the chronograph hand.*

434a, b *Man's wristwatch with chronograph and 30-minute indicator, by the Minerva Sport S.A., 1938; dial with tachometer and telemeter scales; case with movable band attachments; chronograph movement with switching wheel by*

Minerva, 17 jewels, monometallic screw balance, self-compensating flat hairspring, no shock resistance; working via button by the 2.

435 *Man's wristwatch with chronograph, marked "Tutima", made by the UFAG (Uhrenfabrik AG), circa 1940; 15-line chronograph movement with 30-minute indicator, additional stoppings possible, 21 jewels, "Shock-Resist" system, monometallic screw balance, self-compensating Breguet hairspring; the caliber 59 represents the highest quality of wristwatch production in Glashütte.*

436a-c *Men's wristwatches with chronograph and 60-minute indicators by Pierce, circa 1942; about 1940 Pierce developed its own chronograph caliber with switching wheel; the 17-jewel movement, which came with one or two buttons, was patented by Pierce; its special features make it stand out from the other chronograph calibers.*

437a, b *Man's wristwatch with chronograph and 30-minute indicator by Silvana, circa 1940; 13-line chronograph movement with cadracture between dial and front plate, caliber Venus 140; the time dial is by the 12, the 30-minute indicator by the 6; chronograph operation by a switching wheel.*

438a, b *Woman's wristwatch with chronograph and 30-minute indicator, marked on the dial "Huber", circa 1945; dial with tachometer scale; 17-jewel anchor movement, 10½-line Valjoux caliber chronograph mechanism controlled by a button integrated in the stem knob (3 functions: starting, stopping, setting to zero), "Shock-Resist" system.*

439, 440 *Woman's wristwatch with chronograph and 30-minute counter by Eterna, circa 1945; patented watertight bowl-shaped case; the bowl is held in the cap by four wormscrews in the band attachments; two-part winding stem, 10.5-line movement with switching wheel, caliber Eterna 702 (basically like the Valjoux caliber 69).*

441a, b *Man's wristwatch with chronograph, marked on the dial "Edo Super", circa 1945; 15-jewel chronograph movement, "Venus" caliber, monometallic screw balance, flat hairspring; central chronograph hand started, stopped and set back by the button by the 2; dial with tachometer and telemeter scales, small second dial by the 6.*

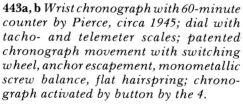

442 *Man's wristwatch with chronograph and 30-minute counter by Rolex, circa 1945; dial with tacho- and telemeter scales; 19-jewel anchor movement, bimetallic balance, anti-magnetic Breguet hairspring.*

443a, b *Wrist chronograph with 60-minute counter by Pierce, circa 1945; dial with tacho- and telemeter scales; patented chronograph movement with switching wheel, anchor escapement, monometallic screw balance, flat hairspring; chronograph activated by button by the 4.*

444a, b *Barrel-shaped wristwatch with chronograph, 45-minute counter, tacho- and telemeter scales, circa 1945, no maker's name; 17-jewel formed movement with switching wheel by Excelsior Park, caliber 42, 27 x 29.4 mm, Geneva stripes, no shock resistance, monometallic screw balance, self-compensating Breguet hairspring, steel case 29 x 31 mm.*

445a, b *Man's wristwatch with chronograph, centrally located 60-minute and 12-hour counter near the 3, by Longines, circa 1945. Longines caliber with polished and (angliert) chronograph levers, monometallic screw balance, self-compensating Breguet hairspring, shock resistance.*

446a, b *Man's wristwatch with chronograph, 30-minute and 12-hour counters, Omega "Seamaster", made from 1946 on; chronograph caliber 321 with switching wheel (raw movement by Lemania), 17 jewels, monometallic screw balance, self-compensating Breguet hairspring.*

447 *Man's wristwatch with chronograph, 30-minute, 12-hour counters and "Memento" dial, "Aero-Compax", by Universal, circa 1950; 14-karat gold case, 36 mm diameter, 17-jewel anchor movement with switching wheel, monometallic screw balance, self-compensating hairspring; the watch has a warning signal by the 12. By using the knob by the 9 one can set it to the time of an event that must not be forgotten.*

449a, b Man's wristwatch with chronograph and 30-minute indicator by Silvana S.A., in doublé case, circa 1950; dial with tachometer and telemeter scales; 17-jewel chronograph movement, 12.5 lines, with switching wheel, caliber Venus 170 (Venus 170 calibers recognizable by the location of the 30-minute indicator by the 12 and the small second dial by the 6).

448a, b Man's wristwatch with chronograph (0 to 60 seconds) by Le Phare, circa 1950; dial with tacho- and telemeter scales; chronograph movement with switching wheel, Venus caliber, monometallic screw balance, self-compensating flat hairspring, no shock resistance; steel case, 33 mm diameter.

450a, b Man's wristwatch with chronograph and 45-minute counter in gold case; back cover hinged; seller's name on the dial "Beyer Zürich"; circa 1950; movement with switching wheel by Angélus, Stolz Frères, caliber 215, 14 lines, 17 jewels, no shock resistance, monometallic screw balance, self-compensating Breguet hairspring.

451a, b *Man's wristwatch with chronograph, 60-minute and 12-hour counters by Movado, circa 1950; 17-jewel movement with switching wheel, Movado's own consruction, 12 lines, caliber M 95, monometallic screw balance, self-compensating Breguet hairspring; steel case, 34 mm diameter, movement protected from magnetic influence by a soft iron capsule.*

452a, b *Man's wristwatch with chronograph and 30-minute counter in square case by Marvin, Compagnie des Montres, circa 1950; 10.5-line chronograph movement with switching wheel, 17 jewels, monometallic screw balance, flat hairspring, no shock absorbing.*

453a, b *Man's wristwatch with chronograph and centrally located 60-minute counter, Mido "Multicenterchrono", circa 1950; 17-jewel anchor movement, 13 lines, caliber 1300, monometaliic screw balance, self-compensating Breguet hairspring, Incabloc shock resistance, dial with tacho- and telemeter scales; steel case.*

454a, b *Man's wristwatch with chronograph, 30-minute and 12-hour counters by Excelsior Park, caliber 40, diameter 31.6 mm, monometallic screw balance, self-compensating Breguet hairspring, Incabloc shock resistance, circa 1960.*

455a, b *Wristwatch with chronograph, pulse and breath counters, by Angelus, circa 1960; the 30-minute indication was left off this watch, though it is included in the Valjoux caliber; for better readability the glass in the sector between the 12 and the 3 is cut as a loupe; 17-jewel anchor movement, monometallic screw balance, self-compensating flat hairspring, steel case.*

460 a, b *Man's wristwatch with chronograph-rattrapante, 30-minute counter and "eternal" calendar with moon phase indication by Patek Philippe, 1955; additional seller's signature: Gübelin, 13-line movement (Valjoux-Ebauche), 25 jewels, monometallic screw balance, self-compensating Breguet hairspring, gooseneck fine regulation.*

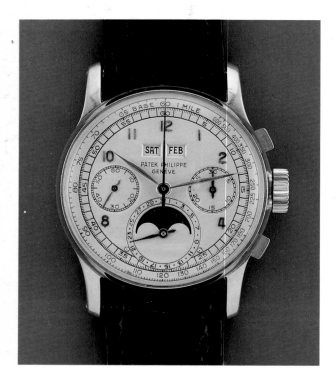

461 *Man's wristwatch with chronograph, 30-minute counter and "eternal" calendar with moon phase indication by Patek Philippe, 1950; reference number 1518, gold case with a diameter of 35 mm, 13-line movement (Valjoux-Ebauche), 23 jewels, monometallic screw balance, self-compensating Breguet hairspring, gooseneck fine regulation.*

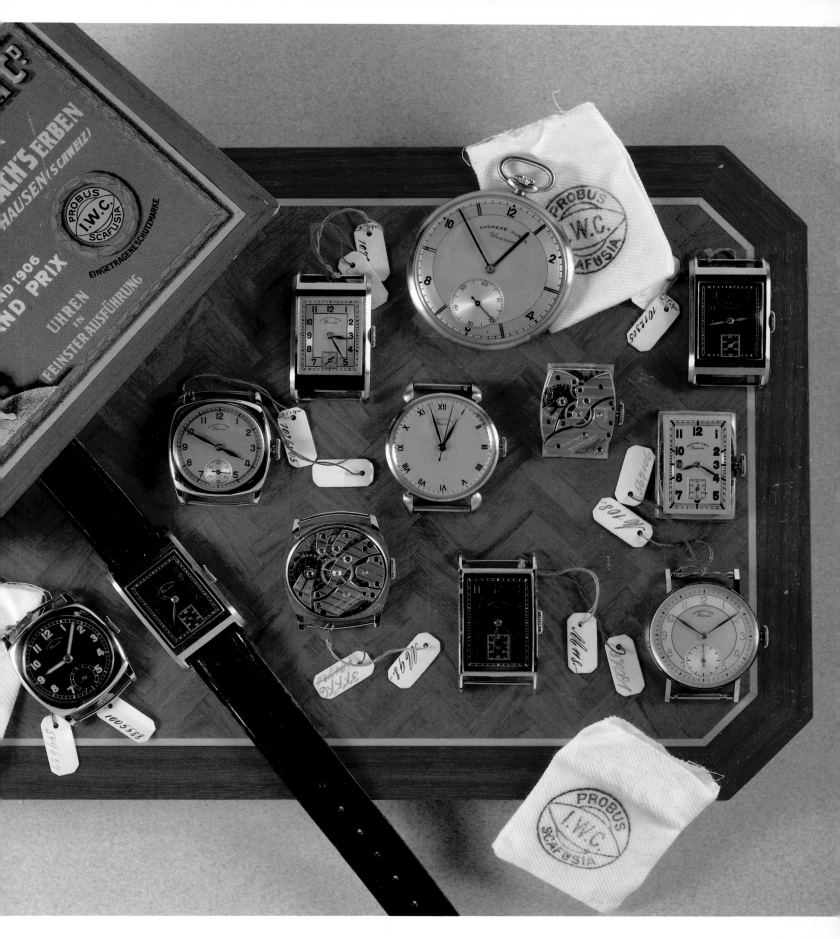

462 *Andreas Huber—Urania brand pocket watch and wristwatches from the Forties. These watches were made by IWC of Schaffhausen for the watch marketing firm of Andreas Huber in Munich, Berlin and Dusseldorf. "Urania" was the additional designation for the best watches sold under the Huber name.*

295

463 *Wristwatch and pendant watch with staff movement by Corum, presently available.*

464a, b *Man's wristwatch with chronograph and 45-minute counter by Jaeger, circa 1955; raw movement with switching wheel by Universal, Geneva, 14 lines, 17 jewels, Incabloc shock resistance, monometallic balance, self-compensating Breguet hairspring, Jaeger caliber 749 D; steel case, 35 mm diameter.*

465a, b *Man's wristwatch with chronograph, digital 15-minute indicator (window by the 3) and 12-hour counter by the 6, by Breitling, circa 1955. Chronograph movement with switching wheel, 17 jewels, monometallic screw balance, self-compensating Breguet hairspring; steel case with turning glass. Venus caliber 178, 14 lines.*

466 *Man's wristwatch with chronograph, 30 minute and 12-hour counters, by LeCoultre, circa 1955; 18-karat gold case, 36 mm diameter; 13-line chronograph movement, self-compensating hairspring, Incabloc shock resistance.*

467a, b *Man's wristwatch with chronograph and 30-minute counter, by Junghans, circa 1955; dial with tacho- and telemeter scales; chronograph movement with switching wheel, 14 lines, Junghans caliber J 88, 19 jewels, monometallic screw balance, self-compensating Breguet hairspring, Junghans shock absorbing.*

468a, b *Wrist chronograph with 45-minute counter by Universal, in gold case, circa 1955; tachometer scale; Universal caliber 289, 10.5 lines, 17 jewels with switching wheel, monometallic screw balance, self-compensating Breguet hairspring, no shock resistance.*

469a, b *Man's wristwatch with chronograph, 30-minute and 12-hour counters, "Speedmaster" by Omega, circa 1960; 17-jewel chronograph movement, caliber 861, monometallic ring balance, self-compensating flat hairspring, Incabloc shock resistance, fine regulation via eccentric screw; no switching wheel for the chronograph; the Omega "Speedmaster professional" was the official watch of the NASA Gemini project astronauts, and was worn on the outside of the space suit during the first 21-minute space walk in 1965.*

471 *The Omega "Speedmaster professional" in the version used by NASA as official wristwatch of the Gemini astronauts, and worn on the outside of the space suit in the first 21-minute space walk in 1965.*

470 *Omega Speedmaster Professional Chronograph on the arm of a NASA astronaut in Apollo space suit (manikin, displayed in the Omega museum, Biel).*

472 *Man's wristwatch with chronograph, 30-minute and 12-hour counters, "Cosmograph Daytona" by Rolex, circa 1960; 12½-line anchor movement, Valjoux caliber 72, 19 jewels, monometallic balance, self-compensating hairspring.*

473 *Man's wristwatch with chronograph, 30-minute and 12-hour counters, "Oyster Chronograph" by Rolex, circa 1960; 18-karat oyster-gold case, 36 mm diameter, dial with tacho- and telemeter scales; 12½-line anchor movement, Valjoux caliber 72; 19 jewels, Glucidur balance. The chronographs were assembled by Heuer for Rolex.*

474 *Man's steel-gold wristwatch with chronograph, 30-minute and 12-hour counters plus complete calendar, signed "Rolex", circa 1950; 13-line Valjoux caliber 723, monometallic screw balance, self-compensating Breguet hairspring, shock resistance, watertight Oyster case.*

475a, b *Man's wristwatch with chronograph and 30-minute counter, with hook anchor movement by Cimier, circa 1960; chronograph and time hands cannot be set to zero by the button, but only started and stopped.*

476a, b *Youth wristwatch with calendar, chronograph and 15-minute counter, "Jacky Ickx Easy-Rider", by Heuer-Leonidas, circa 1975; chronograph movement with hook anchor escapement by Ebauches Bettlach, caliber 8420, 17 jewels. (Note: Jacky Ickx is a Belgian racing driver, who has won the 24 Hours of Le Mans more times than any other driver in history.)*

477 *Man's wristwatch with chronograph, 30-minute counter and date indication via two discs near the 6; 17-jewel Venus caliber with Incabloc shock resistance.*

478a, b *Man's wristwatch with chronograph, 30-minute and 12-hour counters, "Carrera" by Heuer, made since 1963; steel case, 36 mm diameter, 13-line anchor movement, Valjoux caliber 72, 17 jewels, beryllium balance, flat hairspring, Incabloc shock resistance; the Heuer "Carrera" chronograph attracted attention by its functional dial, where reading the stopped counters is not obscured by other divisions of the dial.*

479a, b *Man's gold wristwatch with chronograph and 30-minute counter by Patek Philippe & Co., 1964; 13-line anchor movement, 23 jewels, monometallic screw balance, self-compensating Breguet hairspring, fine regulation, no shock resistance, modified Valjoux caliber 23.*

480a, b *Man's wristwatch with chronograph, 30-minute and 12-hour counters by Zenith, circa 1965; 18-karat gold case, 36 mm diameter, anchor movement, caliber 146H, 14 lines, 17 jewels, monometallic screw balance, self-compensating Breguet hairspring, Incabloc shock resistance; chronograph mechanism controlled by switching wheel.*

481 *Man's wristwatch with chronograph, 45-minute counter and calendar, "Carrera" by Heuer, circa 1965; steel case, 36 mm diameter, 17-jewel chronograph movement without switching wheel, Landeron caliber 189; instead of a permanently running second counter, this watch shows the date by the 9. First chronograph with date indication through a window.*

482. *Man's wristwatch with central chronograph hand and five-minute counter, "Regate" by Aquastar, circa 1965; steel case, 39 mm diameter, anchor movement; Lemania caliber, the window below the 12 shows how many minutes remain until the start of a regatta; the central chronograph hand and the 5-minute counter are returned to their starting positions by the button near the 2.*

483a, b *Man's wristwatch with chronograph, 30-minute and 12- and 24-hour counters, "Autavia" by Heuer, circa 1967; steel case, 36 mm diameter, 13-line chronograph movement with switching wheel, caliber Valjoux 72. 17 jewels, monometallic ring balance, flat hairspring, Incabloc shock resistance; the watch has two hour counters, one revolving once in 24 hours, the other twice.*

485a, b, 486 *Wrist chronographs by Seiko, Japan.*

484 *Man's wristwatch with chronograph, 15-minute counter and date indication, "Skipper" by Heuer, circa 1960; made for sailing use, especially intended for regatta starting.*

487a, b *Man's wristwatch with 60-minute counter, "Superocean" by Breitling, circa 1970; steel case, 38 mm diameter, 17-jewel anchor movement, 14 lines, modified Valjoux 7731 caliber, operating only a central 60-minute chronograph, which is started, stopped and returned to zero by the buttons; the window over the 6 indicates that the chronograph is working properly; case is watertight to 200 meters.*

488a, b *Man's wristwatch with chronograph, 30-minute and 12-hour counters plus 24-hour time dial, "Cosmonaute" by Breitling; circa 1969; Steel case, 40 mm diameter, 17-jewel anchor movement, caliber Valjoux 7736 (no switching wheel), 14 lines, monometallic ring balance, flat hairspring, Incabloc shock resistance.*

489a, b *Men's wristwatches with automatic winding, chronograph with 30-minute and 12-hour counters and calendar by Zenith and Movado, made since 1969; steel cases, 37 mm diameter, 13-line anchor movement, caliber 3019 PHC, 31 jewels, Incabloc shock resistance, fine tuning of the regulator via eccentric screw, balance speed is 36,000 half-swings per hour; this was the first chronograph caliber with automatic winding by a central rotor; it is mounted in ball bearings and winds the mainspring in both directions; height of the movement 6,50 mm.*

490a, b *Man's wristwatch with automatic winding, chronograph with 30-minute and 12-hour counters and date indication, signed "Jaquet-Girard"; the movement is as in #491b, but has an additional 24-hour hand and two turning lunettes operated by the crowns by the 2 and 4, with which times at various locations on earth can be read.*

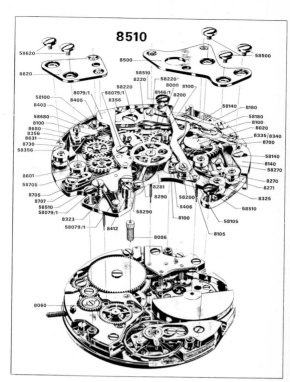

491a, b, c. Men's wristwatches with automatic winding, chronograph with 30-minute and 12-hour counters and calendar by Breitling, made since 1969; steel case, 48 mm diameter, 13.75-line movement built on two levels. The chronograph mechanism is attached to the basic movement with automatic winding via planetary rotor. This caliber 11 has 17 jewels, a monometallic ring balance, self-com-pensating flat hairspring, Incabloc shock resistance and fine tuning for the regulator via eccentric screw. Balance speed 19,800 half-swings per hour, the movement is 7.70 mm high. This chronograph caliber introduced on March 3, 1969, at an international press conference, jointly by Breitling, Hamilton-Büren and Heuer.

492a, b Man's wristwatch in watertight steel case, Omega Speedmaster 125, with automatic winding, chronograph with centrally located 60-minute and 12-hour counters near the 6, date window by the 3 and 24-hour indication by the 9; 13.75-line caliber 1041 anchor movement, central rotor mounted in ball bearings, with winding in both directions, monometallic ring balance, self-compensating flat hair-spring, Incabloc shock resistance, fine regulation via an eccentric screw; the watch was sold with an official chronometer certificate; circa 1975.

305

493a, b *Wristwatch with chronograph, 30-minute and 5-hour counters, signed "Transglobe", 17-jewel anchor movement, monometallic screw balance, self-compensating flat hairspring, Incabloc shock resistance, circa 1970.*

494a, b *Man's rectangular watch with automatic winding, digital hour and minute indication, chronograph with 60-minute counter and date window, signed "Precimax", circa 1975; 11.5-line automatic caliber D.D.K. 1369 by Kelek, La Chaux-de-Fonds, put on the market in 1974; 17 jewels, monometallic ring balance, self-compensating flat hairspring, Incabloc shock resistance, movement 7.6 mm high; the Kelek caliber is the smallest chronograph movement with automatic winding available on the market; the chronograph mechanism was developed by the precision-mechanical firm of Dubois-Depraz in Le Lieu.*

495a, b *Man's wristwatch with automatic winding, chronograph with 30-minute and 12-hour counters, moon-phase and calendar, marked "Aero", current production from remaining parts of the movement developed in 1973; doublé case, 40 mm diameter, 13.25-line anchor movement, caliber Valjoux 7750, 17 jewels, Incabloc shock resistance, balance speed 28,800 half-swings per hour; rotor mounted in ball bearings, winds mainspring in one direction; the movement was originally sold with date and weekday indicators; in the illustrated model the weekday disc was replaced by a moon disc with 59 teeth. Date and moon phase adjustment via the stem when pulled halfway up; balance stopped for exact time setting via the stem when pulled all the way up.*

496 *Man's wristwatch with automatic winding, chronograph, 30-minute and 12-hour counters, date and moon phase indication, signed "A. Rochat", presently in production; Valjoux caliber 7750 movement (see also #495b).*

497 *Man's wristwatch with automatic winding, chronograph, 30-minute and 12-hour counters, day and date indication, by IWC, Schaffhausen, with titanium case and band, presently in production; Valjoux caliber 7750 movement (see also #495b).*

498a, b *Man's gold wristwatch with automatic winding, chronograph, 30-minute and 12-hour counters, date and moon phase indication, signed "Girard-Perregaux", presently in production; engraved Valjoux caliber 7750 movement (see also #495b).*

499a, b *Wristwatch with chronograph, rattrapante, 30-minute and 12-hour counters, No. 46978, made in 1943; 13-line anchor movement, 20 jewels, 8 adjustments, Breguet hairspring, 18-karat gold case, signed "Audemars Piguet, Genève"; sweep hand operated by pressing the crown.*

500 *Man's wristwatch with chronograph, 30-minute counter and sweep hand, signed "Dubey & Schaldenbarnd", circa 1948 (see also #502b).*

501 *Man's wristwatch with chronograph, 30-minute counter and mono-rattrapante, signed "Lowenthal", circa 1945 (see also #503a, b).*

502a, b *Man's wristwatch with chronograph, 30-minute counter and sweep hand, marked "Index Mobile", patented in 1948 by Georges Dubey and René Schaldenbrand; doublé case, 37 mm diameter; simplified sweep-hand construction, in which the two chronograph indicators are linked by a hairspring (visible on the front). The sweep hand is stopped by the button in the stem knob, but only as long as the finger holds the button down. Wheel released, the sweep hand springs to the position of the actual chronograph indicator. Constructed on a 17-jewel Landeron caliber.*

503a, b *Man's wristwatch with chronograph, 30-minute counter and Mono-Rattrapante (see p. 96) by Recta, circa 1945; steel case, 36 mm diameter; chronograph movement with switching wheel, 14-line Valjoux caliber, 17 jewels,* *monometallic screw balance, self-compensating Breguet hairspring, no shock resistance. The sweep-hand mechanism is controlled by the upper button.*

504a, b *Man's wristwatch with chronograph, sweep hand, 30-minute and 12-hour counters, marked "Certina EA", circa 1950; 14-line anchor movement, Venus caliber 185, 20 jewels, no shock resistance, monometallic screw balance, self-compensating Breguet hairspring; steel case, 37 mm diameter; sweep-hand operation by a button in the stem knob.*

505a, b *Man's wristwatch with chronograph, 30-minute counter and sweep hand (Rattrapante), marked "Butex", Buttes Watch, circa 1950; 18-karat gold case, 14.5-line anchor movement, 23 jewels, monometallic screw balance, self-compensating Breguet hairspring, no shock resistance, the sweep-hand mechanism is built onto the Landeron chronograph caliber 39 and controlled by the button near the 10.*

506a, b *Man's wristwatch with chronograph, 30-minute counter and sweep hand by G. Capt, circa 1950; 18-karat gold case; Valjoux caliber, monometallic screw balance, self-compensating Breguet hairspring, no shock resistance, control of the chronograph by the button in the stem knob and of the sweep hand by the button near the 4.*

507a, b *Man's wristwatch with chronograph, sweep hand and 45-minute counter, marked "Breitling Duograph", circa 1950; 14-line anchor movement, Venus caliber 190, 20 jewels, no shock resistance; monometallic screw balance, self-compensating Breguet hairspring, gooseneck fine tuning of the regulator, steel case, 36 mm diameter; the stem knob also serves as the button for the sweep hand.*

508a, b *Man's wristwatch with chronograph, 30-minute counter and sweep hand by Patek Philippe, sold 1938; 18-karat gold case; 13-line anchor movement, 25 jewels, monometallic screw balance, self-compensating Breguet hairspring, no shock resistance; the movement is basically a Valjoux raw movement; sweep-hand control via the button in the stem knob.*

509 *Man's wristwatch with chronograph, 30-minute counter and sweep hand, by Patek Philippe, 1938; the movement is basically like that in #508b.*

510 *Man's wristwatch with chronograph, 30-minute hand and sweep hand, signed "ARBU", Rumanel Watch, circa 1950; 18-karat gold case, 35 mm diameter. 17-jewel chronograph movement, monometallic balance, self-compensating hairspring.*

511a, b *Man's wristwatch with independent central second hand by Longines, circa 1945; patented chronograph movement without switching wheel, monometallic screw balance, self-compensating Breguet hairspring, starting, stopping and returning the central chronograph hand by means of the button by the 2.*

512a, b *Man's wristwatch with balance-stopping mechanism by Omega, circa 1948; 17-jewel anchor movement with indirect central second, Incabloc shock resistance, monometallic screw balance, self-compensating Breguet hairspring; the balance wheel can be stopped by using the button by the 8.*

513a, b *Wristwatch with independent central second hand, signed on the dial "Stop", circa 1945; a simple chronograph with starting, stopping and setting-back mechanism set onto a "Helvetia" movement. Central chronograph hand is started and stopped by the button by the 8; setting back to zero by the button by the 2.*

514a, b *Man's wristwatch with independent central second hand, signed on the dial "ZentRa", circa 1953; steel case with 35 mm diameter; 12-line Eta movement, caliber 1168, 17 jewels, 4 of them set in chatons, monometallic screw balance, self-compensating flat hairspring; the central second and chronograph hand runs permanently; for timing it can be set at 0 with the button by the two, and held there by holding the button; the lower button stops the second hand as long as the button is pressed.*

515 *Man's wristwatch with 60-minute counter, for keeping track of parking times, for example, marked "Daniel Perret Minu-Stop", circa 1968; 17-jewel anchor movement, the disc in the upper dial cutout turns steadily but can be set to zero by using the button near the 2; doublé case, 34 mm diameter.*

516 *Man's wristwatch with independent second hand, signed "Chrono Stop", Swiss, circa 1960; dial with tacho- and telemeter scales; 17-jewel anchor movement, the central second hand runs constantly, can be set at 0 by the upper button and held by the lower one as long as the latter is pushed in.*

517a, b *Large wrist stopwatch, "cronografo a ritorno" (chronograph with zero setting) for air travel. Central 30-second sweep hand, and 15-minute counter near the knob. The arrow seen here by the 5 can be set by turning the glass. Anchor movement, stopping and counting operations via the switching wheel. Using the stopping function stops the balance ring. Steel case.*

518a-c *Man's wristwatch by Henry Moser, circa 1920. Henry Moser was, among other things, a supplier of Carl Fabergé in St. Petersburg. Weekday indication (window) and date shown by a central hand pointing to the outermost dial. Swiss anchor movement, 15 jewels, bimetallic balance, Breguet hairspring. Silver case. (see also #T32).*

519 *Man's wristwatch with calendar, circa 1920, anchor movement, 15 jewels, bimetallic balance, Breguet hairspring, 925 silver case, diameter 34 mm.*

520a, b *Calendar watch made for the English market, in 9-karat gold case; metal dial with four additional dials, date above, weekday to the left, month to the right, second below. Three push buttons at upper left and on right side to set the calendar indications; burnished hour hand (cathedral style) is probably original; circa 1925. Signed Everest Watch Co. on the plate, 15 jewels, two adjustments. Balance with screws and flat hairspring. Movement size 12½ lines.*

521a-c *Wristwatch by Patek Philippe & Co., #97975, with "eternal" calendar, moon phase indicator and 18-karat gold case; white enamel dial; date indicator centrally located; production began Sept. 14, 1898 (woman's pocket watch); converted to a wristwatch in 1925; sold October 13, 1927.*

521b *Under-the-dial view, calendar mechanics and enameled panel for the moon-phase indicator.*

521c *12-line movement with anchor escapement, 20 jewels, Breguet hairspring and compensated balance.*

522 Man's rectangular yellow and white gold wristwatch with date indication by Vacheron & Constantin; caliber 9-line PC movement, made in 1929, sold to England on August 27, 1937.

523 Man's barrel-shaped wristwatch with day, date and moon-phase indication by Vacheron & Constantin, made in 1929, sold in Geneva on July 16, 1937; caliber 10/11-line movement, 18-karat yellow gold case.

524 Man's rectangular gold wristwatch with complete calendar and moon phase indication by Vacheron & Constantin, made in 1919 (in movement and functions this watch corresponds to that by Audemars Piguet shown in #525).

525 Man's gold wristwatch with calendar and moon phase indicators by Audemars Piguet, made 1926, sold 1931; 9.75-line movement with 18 jewels, Geneva stripes, bimetallic balance, Breguet hairspring; the month indication switches automatically only after the 31st; in months with 30 or fewer days, switching the month name must be done manually by means of a button in the case wall.

317

526 *Wristwatch with manually changeable calendar, marked on the dial "Vibra", Swiss, circa 1930; chrome-nickel case with band attachments which contain the weekday (above) and date (below) drums; the indicators can be set by using the side wheels; Swiss Roskopf movement with hook anchor escapement.*

527 *Man's barrel-shaped wristwatch with complete non-eternal calendar, by Patek Philippe, circa 1923; 11-line anchor movement, bimetallic balance, Breguet hairspring.*

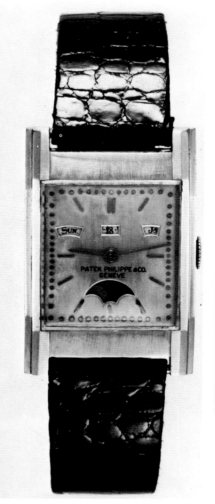

528a, b *Man's wristwatch in rectangular platinum case, by Patek Philippe & Co., #860,182, sold 1938; silver dial with weekday, date, month and moon phase indicated through cutouts. View under the dial shows the calendar mechanism and the enameled moon-phase indicator dial. 7.75 x 11-line barrel-form movement, 18 jewels, Breguet hairspring and bimetallic balance.*

529a, b *Man's wristwatch, circa 1940, in steel case, 22 x 40 mm (over attachments), marked "Hallwatch"; early wristwatch with calendar date showing through a window at the 3, anchor movement, 8.75 x 12 lines, by Mimo, Graef & Co., whose "Mimo-Meter-Patent" name for the calendar mechanism is on the front plate; 15 jewels, shock resistance; watch was presumably prepared for "United Jewelers Inc.", whose name is on the diagonal minute wheel bridge.*

530a, b *Man's wristwatch by Girard-Perregaux, in a steel case; the watch shows the calendar date via two discs visible through windows between the 10 and the 2; 8.75 x 12-line anchor movement, caliber 97 (raw movement by Helvetia, caliber 75-24), 17 jewels, Helvetia shock resistance, circa 1944.*

531a, b *Man's wristwatch, circa 1945, with calendar, marked "Civitas" (Moerïs Watch); steel case, 32 mm diameter, 15-jewel anchor movement, no shock resistance, central date hand, silver dial with orange background for even-numbered days and the 31st., silver background for the uneven numbers.*

532a, b *Man's wristwatch with chronograph, 45-minute counter and calendar (weekday and date) by Angélus, Stolz Frères, this version made from about 1945 on; steel case, 36 mm diameter, 14-line movement, caliber Angélus 217, 17 jewels, monometallic screw balance, self-compensating Breguet hairspring, no shock resistance; chronograph mechanism operated via switching wheel, both calendar functions change automaically, can be corrected via buttons.*

533 *Man's round gold wristwatch with complete calendar (automatic month name switching on the 31st) and moon phase indication by Vacheron & Constantin, circa 1950; 12½-line caliber 495 anchor movement (Le Coultre-Ebauche), monometallic screw balance, self-compensating flat hairspring.*

534 *Man's rectangular gold watch with complete calendar (automatic month name switching on the 31st) and moon phase indication by Vacheron & Constantin, circa 1950; 12.5-line caliber 495 anchor movement (Le Coultre-Ebauche), monometallic screw balance, self-compensating flat hairspring.*

536a, b *Man's wristwatch with chronograph, 30-minute counter and calendar, marked "Butex", Buttes Watch, circa 1950; nickel-plated case, 36 mm diameter; chronograph movement without switching wheel, Landeron caliber, 17 jewels, monometallic screw balance, flat hairspring, no shock resistance; all indicators except the month change automatically (date indication by the 6), correction by turning the glass, by moving a marking on it to the 6, 11 or 1 and moving the glass back and forth, which changes the indicator.*

535 *Man's wristwatch with calendar in watertight 14-karat gold case by Movado, circa 1945; 15-jewel anchor movement, 10 lines, monometallic screw balance, self-compensating Breguet hairspring; automatically changing date and weekday indicators; month indicator manually changeable.*

537 *Man's gold wristwatch with calendar and moon phase indication by Audemars Piguet, circa 1950; case diameter 37 mm; 9-line anchor movement, 18 jewels, Glucidur balance, self-compensating hairspring, Geneva stripes; all indicators change automatically, the month only on the 31st; manual correction by using buttons in case rim.*

538 *Man's wristwatch with complete calendar (date, day, month) and small second hand by Omega, circa 1947; indications are correctable via button in case wall.*

539a, b *Man's wristwatch with calendar, round doublé case, date, weekday and month indicators, central second. The indicators can be corrected by using two buttons. Round 13-line anchor movement, 15 jewels, central second not in the power flow, flat hairspring. "Arsa", A. Reymond S.A., 1948. Cover engraved: Jubile 1898-1948 (43, 952).*

540a, b *Man's wristwatch, marked "Cal-O-Date", circa 1950; nickel-plated round case, 33 mm diameter, 13-line Roskopf movement with hook anchor escapement, marked "Chesterfield Watch Co.", Swiss made, 7 functioning jewels, indirect central second, Geneva stripes; date shown in a window below the 12.*

541a-c *Wristwatch by Patek Philippe & Co., #963,261, with "eternal" calendar and moon phase indicator in 18-karat gold case; silver dial; 1950. View under dial; calendar mechanism, mounted on a separate plate. 12-line movement (caliber 12"-120) with anchor escapement, 18 jewels, Breguet hairspring, fine regulating and compensated balance.*

542 *Man's small wristwatch with date indication by two discs under the 12, signed "Cornavin Datocor", circa 1955, 11.5-line anchor movement, caliber Venus 221, monometallic screw balance, self-compensating flat hairspring, Incabloc shock resistance, direct central second.*

543 *Man's wristwatch with calendar and moon phase indication by Omega, circa 1950; all indicators except the month change automatically; correction via buttons in case rim.*

544a, b *Doublé wristwatch with calendar and moon phase indicators, marked "LeCoultre", circa 1950; 7.75 x 11-line formed movement, caliber 486/AW, 17 jewels, no shock resistance, monometallic screw balance, self-compensating flat hairspring, Geneva stripes; all indications except the month name work automatically, can be corrected by using buttons.*

545a, b, 546, 547 *Three men's wristwatches with calendars, produced in Germany circa 1950-1955, marked "Stowa Parat", "Arctos Parat" and "Anker", Pforzheim; all have an 8.75 x 12-line formed movement, Parat, caliber 42, Swiss anchor escapement, the number of jewels varies from 15 to 21; the date is indicated by a centrally mounted hand.*

548a, b *Man's wristwatch with automatic winding and calendar, anonymous, circa 1950; 12.25-line movement, caliber AS 1315, 17 jewels, winding in one direction of limited swinging pendulum, one power transmission wheel; automatically switching day and date indicators, manually settable month indication.*

549 *Man's wristwatch with calendar by Orfina, circa 1953; doublé case, 36 mm diameter; movement by Eta, caliber 1164, 12 lines, no shock resistance; calendar working like that of the Helvetia wristwatch in #550).*

550 *Man's wristwatch with calendar by Helvetia, circa 1953; doublé case, 35 mm diameter; 13-line Valjoux movement, caliber 90, 17 jewels, Incabloc shock resistance, indirect central second, automatically changing date and weekday, month indicator manually changed via button, all indicators can be corrected by pushing the button.*

551 *Man's wristwatch with calendar, marked "Pierpont", Sauter Frères, circa 1955; doublé case, 35 mm diameter; 11.5-line anchor movement, FHF caliber 205, 15 jewels, Incabloc shock resistance, patented date, weekday and month indication; by using the knob by the 10, a day and date setting for a whole month can be set in advance, so that the outer ring with the dates is set for the first day of that month. The central hand springs one position further per day. The month must be changed manually.*

552a, b *Woman's wristwatch with calendar and moon phase indication, marked on the dial "Valruz", assembled by Henri Duvoisin & Cie., circa 1955; doublé case, 30 mm diameter, 10.5-line anchor movement, Valjoux caliber 89, marked Cornavin Watch, Geneva, 17 jewels, Incabloc shock resistance, indirect central second, automatically changing weekday, date and moon phase indication, manually settable month indicator; all fdunctions correctable via buttons.*

553a, b Man's wristwatch with chronograph, 30-minute and 12-hour counters, date and moon phase indicators by Mulco, circa 1955; 13-line chronograph movement, Venus caliber 186, 17 jewels, monometallic screw balance, self-compensating Breguet hairspring, no shock resistance; automatic date and moon phase changing, indication by the 12, correctable via buttons.

554a, b Man's wristwatch with chronograph, 30-minute counter, calendar and moon phase indicator, marked "Moeris", Moeris Watch, circa 1958; 18-karat gold case, 36 mm diameter; chronograph movement without switching wheel, Landeron caliber 185, 13.75 lines, 17 jewels, Incabloc shock resistance, monometallic balance, self-compensating flat hairspring; all indicators except the month change automatically, manually correctable via buttons.

555a, b Man's wristwatch with chronograph, 30-minute and 12-hour counters, complete calendar (without independent switching of month names) and moon phase indication, "Tri-Compax" by Universal, circa 1950; 15-line caliber 287 anchor movement, 17 jewels, monometallic screw balance, self-compensating Breguet hairspring.

556 *Man's plated wristwatch with date and day indication (moving sun under the 12) by Cornavin Watch, circa 1952. Ten-line red-gilded anchor movement, 17 jewels, mono-metallic screw balance, self-compensating flat hairspring, Incabloc shock resistance; case diameter 33 mm.*

557 *Man's wristwatch with astronomical indicators (calendar and moon phases) by Lemania, circa 1960; 18-karat gold case, 35 mm diameter, 17-jewel anchor movement, Incabloc shock resistance; date, weekday and moon phase are changed automatically; month must be changed manually.*

558a, b *Man's wristwatch with automatic winding and calendar, "Speed Date" by Pronto Watch, L. Maître & Fils, 1964; watertight "Compressor" doublé case,, 35 mm diameter, 11½-line automatic movement, Eta caliber 2472, 25 jewels, Incabloc shock resistance, date indicator springs at midnight; the knob by the 2 sets the outer ring of the dial so that one can read a whole month's calendar at a glance. To help in setting, the weekdays of January 1, 1964 through 1973, are engraved on the back of the case.*

559 *Man's wristwatch with automatic winding, weekday and date indication by Wittnauer, 1971; steel case, 40 mm diameter; 17-jewel Japanese automatic movement with rotor mounted in ball bearings; One can determine the weekday of every date from 1971 to 2015 by bringing the year and the month into agreement through use of the knob by the 4; the date and weekday can be read in the upper window: for example, January 4, 11, 18 and 25, 1987 are Sundays. In 1972 Tressa made a similar watch with automatic AS caliber.*

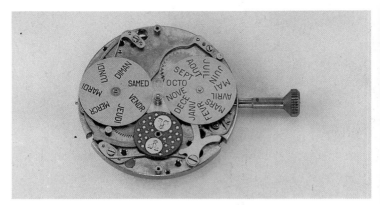

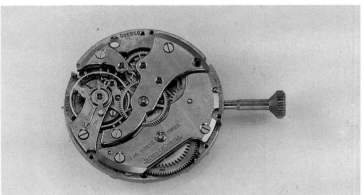

560a-c *Man's wristwatch with calendar and moon phase indicator by Jaeger LeCoultre, created in 1945, assembled in 1982 out of spare parts; 18-karat gold case; hand-wound, all indicators change automatically, the month only on the 31st, manual correction possible via buttons.*

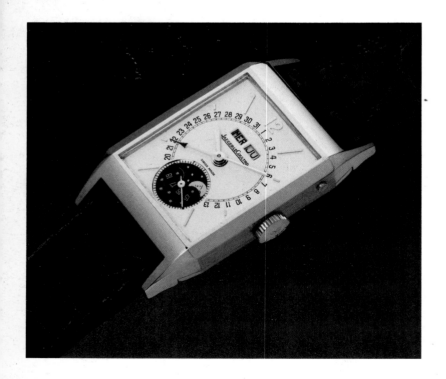

561a-c *Man's rectangular wristwatch with complete calendar (automatic switching of the month indication on the 31st) by Jaeger-Le Coultre, presently in production (the movement is that shown in #544b).*

Pages 330-331

563-572 *Men's wristwatches from various eras.*

Upper row, from left to right:

563 *Man's silver wristwatch with date indication, circa 1920*

564 *Man's gold wristwatch by IWC, made in 1914.*

565 *Silver half-savonnette wristwatch by Waltham, USA, circa 1918.*

566 *Man's gold wristwatch with quarter repetition, signed "Dent au Brassus".*

567 *Man's gold wristwatch by Revue, circa 1950.*

568 *Man's gold wristwatch with automatic winding and winding indicator "Futurematic" by Jaeger-Le Coultre, 1953.*

Center left:

569 *Man's rectangular watertight wristwatch by Jaeger-Le Coultre, circa 1940.*

Below, from left to right:

570 *Gold French spindle watch, 18th Century.*

571 *Man's gold duo-dial wristwatch by Longines.*

572 *Man's gold rectangular wristwatch by Jaeger-Le Coultre, circa 1945.*

562 *Man's gold wristwatch with automatic winding and astrolabe by Ulysse Nardin, presently in production; 11½-line caliber ETA 2892 anchor movement, central rotor in ball bearings, winding in both directions.*

563 to 572
Captions on page 328.

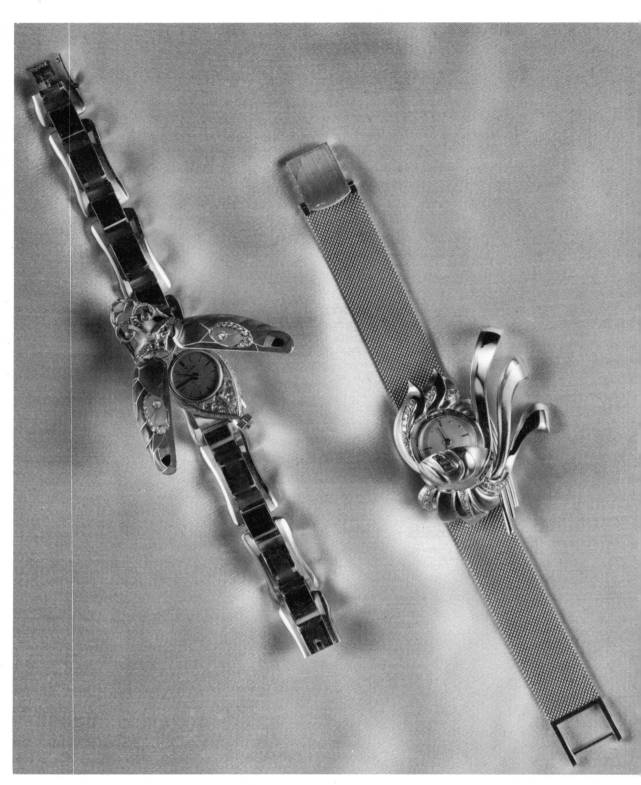

573 Woman's wristwatch of platinum and gold, enameled and set with gems, signed "Lacloche Fréres", Paris, circa 1910.

574 Women's wristwatches by Rolex, circa 1934; left; gold enamel workin the form of a beetle; right: imaginative decorative watch in red gold.

575a-d *Man's wristwatch with automatic winding and "eternal" calendar, marked "Breguet", 1976; indication system follows prototypes by Abraham Louis Breguet; 35-jewel Swiss anchor movement with eccentric rotor (as in Piguet caliber P70), which winds the mainspring in one direction.*

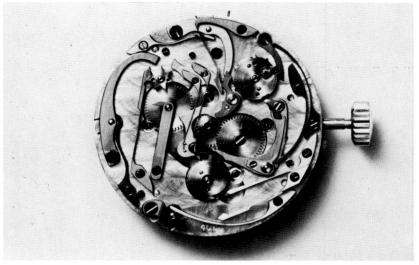

576a-c *Wristwatch by Patek Philippe & Co., #869,406 with "eternal calendar", moon phase indicator, chronograph and 30-minute counter, in 18-karat gold case; silver dial; 1981. View under the dial; calendar mechanism mounted on a separate plate. 13-line movement with anchor escapement, 23 jewels, Breguet hairspring (self-compensating), fine regulation and monometallic balance.*

577a-c *Wristwatch #1,491,199 with "eternal" calendar, leap-year cycle and moon phase indication, central second hand, and18-karat gold case by Patek Philippe, automatic movement (caliber 1-350), 28 mm diameter, height 3.5 mm, anchor escapement, 25 jewels, free-swinging self-compensating Breguet hairspring, Gyromax balance (21,600 half-swings per hour) and shock resistance; 18-karat gold rotor mounted in ball bearings; winding in only one direction. Under-the-dial view: calendar mechanism, mounted on a separate plate; leap year indicator disc at right center of the dial.*

578a, b *Man's wristwatch with automatic winding and "eternal" calendar by Audemars Piguet, present production, 12½-line anchor movement, caliber 2121/1, 36 jewels,, self-compensating flat hairspring, monometallic ring balance, "Kif-Elastor" shock resistance, the rotor with 21-karat gold outer weight winds the mainspring in both directions.*

579 *Man's wristwatch with automatic winding, eternal calendar and moon phase indication by Gérard Genta, currently in production; 12.25-line anchor movement, 34 jewels, overall height 4½ mm.*

580a-c *Wristwatch #1,119,137 with "eternal" calendar and 18-karat gold case by Patek Philippe, silver dial; sold on May 22, 1970. Automatic movement (caliber 27-460 Q), 27 mm diameter, anchor escapement, 37 jewels, free-swinging self-compensating Breguet hairspring, Gyromax balance (19,800 half-swings per hour) and shock resistance; rotor of 18-karat gold, mounted in ball bearings; winding in both directions.*

Under-the-dial view: calendar mechanism, mounted on a separate plate.

581a, b *Man's wristwatch with eternal calendar, leap year and moon phase indication by Vacheron & Constantin, presently in production; 12½-line anchor movement with automatic winding (Ebauche by Le Coultre), overall height 4.05 mm (much like the Audemars Piguet movement in #578b).*

582a-c *Man's wristwatch with automatic winding, eternal calendar, moon phase, leap year and additional 24-hour indications by Patek Philippe, first offerd in 1985; caliber 240 movement, overall height 3.75 mm, 27 jewels, free-swinging flat hairspring, Gyromax balance, 22-karat gold micro-rotor winding in one direction.*

583a, b *Man's wristwatch with automatic winding and eternal calendar, "Louis Brandt" by Omega, made since 1985; 24-jewel anchor movement, Piguet caliber 65/11, diameter 25 mm, overall height 4.65 mm, 18-karat gold rotor winding in both directions.*

584a-c *Man's wristwatch in watertight steel case with glass bottom by Kelek, La Chaux-de-Fonds; automatic winding, eternal calendar with leap year and moon phase indication; anchor movement with 21 jewels, caliber ETA 2892/2, diameter 25.76 mm, central rotor in ball bearings, winding in both directions; produced since 1985.*

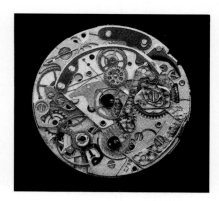

585a-f *Man's wristwatch with automatic winding, chronograph with 30-minute and 12-hour counters plus eternal calendar with year and moon phase indication, "Da Vinci" by IWC, produced since 1985; 36-jewel anchor movement, caliber Valjoux 7750, diameter 30 mm, overall height 8.5 mm (see also #495b).*

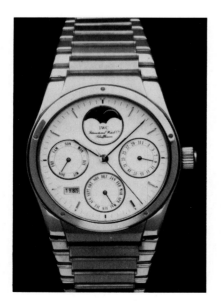

586 *Man's wristwatch with automatic winding, eternal calendar with year and moon phase indication, "Ingenieur" by IWC, produced since 1985; 12½-line anchor movement with 22 jewels, IWC caliber 375-7, corresponds to the ETA caliber 2892/2 (see also #584b), overall height 5mm.*

587 *Drawing of the movement of #586.*

588 *Man's wristwatch with automatic winding, chronograph with 30-minute and 12-hour counters, eternal calendar with leap year and moon phase indication by Ebel, put on the market in 1984; 17-jewel chronograph caliber Zenith 3019 PHC, diameter 31 mm, overall height 8.1 mm, fast swinger with 36,000 half swings per hour.*

 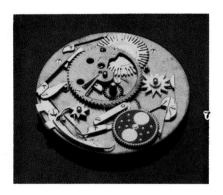

589a, b *Man's wristwatch with automatic winding, eternal calendar with retrograde date and moon phase indication by Chopard, put on the market in 1983; anchor movement, Piguet caliber, diameter 30 mm, overall height 4 mm, 35 jewels, massive gold rotor, Glucydur balance, self-compensating flay hairspring.*

590 *Man's wristwatch with automatic winding, eternal calendar and leap year indication by Chopard, produced since 1984.*

Wrist chronometers and wristwatches with tourbillon

591a, b *Man's wristwatch with automatic winding, eternal calendar and moon phase indication by Blancpain, 1984; 23-jewel anchor movement, Piguet caliber 6511, diameter 27.4 mm, overall height 4.6 mm, Glucydur balance, self-compensating flat hairspring, Incabloc shock resistance.*

592 *Rolex "Oyster Perpetual" chronometer in a barrel-shaped 14-karat gold case, diameter 33 mm; 18-jewel movement, automatic winding via central rotor, 9.75 lines, monometallic balance, self-compensating hairspring.*

593a, b *Rolex "Observatory" chronometer wristwatch in Oyster steel barrel case, 30 x 30 mm, 10.5 lines, nickel-plated anchor movement, "Superbalance" wheel, 18 jewels, 5 chatons, self-compensating Breguet hairspring; six fine adjusting points.*

594a, b *Man's gold wrist chronometer by Omega, circa 1945; 17-jewel anchor movement, cut balance, Breguet hairspring, no shock resistance, fine regulation.*

595a, b *Man's gold wristwatch "Chronometré Royal" by Vacheron & Constantin, circa 1952; 18-jewel anchor movement, caliber P 1007/83 (Le Coultre-Ebauche), mono-metallic screw balance, self-compensating Breguet hair-spring, gooseneck fine regulation, balance-stopping by pulling the crown, Parechoc shock resistance.*

596 *Man's wristwatch, "Chronometre Royal", by Vacheron & Constantin, circa 1965; anchor movement with central second, which can be stopped for accurate setting by pulling the stem; 18-karat gold case, diameter 37 mm.*

597a, b *Wrist chronometer by Omega, circa 1945; 15-jewel anchor movement, cut balance ring, Breguet hairspring, no shock resistance.*

598a, b *Man's wristwatch movement in a chronometer testing case for the observatory, by Ulysse Nardin, 17-jewel anchor movement, bimetallic balance, Breguet hairspring, no shock resistance; the cap jewel of the balance arbor pivot is visible through the cutout in the dial.*

599a, b *Man's wrist chronometer by Omega, 1946; caliber 30 T2 anchor movement (diameter 30 mm), slit screw balance, Breguet hairspring; the movement includes a springing central second hand in additional to the usual small second; 35 mm diameter steel case.*

600a, b *Movement of a wrist chronometer with automatic winding by Zenith, circa 1950, caliber 133.8, 13 lines, 20 jewels, monometallic screw balance, self-compensating flat hairspring, Incabloc shock resistance, winding in one direction of the swinging pendulum.*

601a, b *Wrist chronometer by Junghans, circa 1954, steel case, 34 mm diameter, anchor movement, caliber J 82/I, 12½ lines, 17 jewels, indirect central second, monometallic screw balance, self-compensating flat hairspring, fine regulation, Junghans shock resistance, balance-stopping mechanism for exact setting of the watch.*

602a, b *Wrist chronometer by Laco, circa 1955; 14-karat gold case, 34 mm diameter; anchor movement, caliber Durowe 630, 12 lines, 21 jewels, monometallic screw balance, self-compensating flat hairspring, "Duro-Swing" shock resistance, gooseneck fine regulation, balance-stopping mechanism.*

603a, b *circa 1956, doublé case, 35 mm diameter, anchor movement, caliber J 85, 11 lines, 17 jewels, direct central second, monometallic ring balance with regulating screws on both shanks, self-compensating flat hairspring, gooseneck fine regulation, Junghans shock resistance, balance-stopping mechanism.*

604a, b *Wrist chronometer with automatic winding, Omega "Constellation", 1965 (movement built since 1959); steel case with gold top, 34 mm diameter; anchor movement, caliber 551, 12.5 lines, 24 jewels, Incabloc shock resistance, monometallic ring balance, self-compensating flat hairspring; automatic winding in both directions of the rotor.*

605a, b *Man's gold wristwatch with automatic winding and springing date indication, "Chronometré Royal" by Vacheron & Constantin, circa 1960; 13-line caliber 2072 anchor movement, overall height 6.3 mm, rotor with 18-karat gold outer segment, winding in both directions, indirect central second, 29 jewels, monometallic screw balance, self-compensating Breguet hairspring, gooseneck fine regulation, Kif-Flector shock resistance (this movement was also used in automatic watches by Audemars Piguet at the same time, with Ebauche by Le Coultre).*

606a, b *Zenith 2000 man's wristwatch, circa 1960; steel case, 35 mm diameter, 13-line movement, caliber 135, 19 jewels, Incabloc shock resistance, monometallic screw balance with diameter almost that of the movement radius, self-compensating Breguet hairspring, fine regulation via worm gear, Geneva stripes.*

607 *Wrist chronometer with automatic winding, "Oyster Perpetual Date Submariner" by Rolex, 1970; steel case, watertight to 200 meters; anchor movement, 12.5 lines, 26 jewels, rotor winding in both directions, "Kif Flector" shock resistance.*

608 *Wrist chronometer with automatic winding, "Oyster Perpetual" by Rolex, circa 1960; anchor movement, automatic winding by rotor in both directions.*

609 *Movement with automatic winding by Rolex, caliber 1570, 25 jewels, 12.5 lines, monometallic screw balance, self-compensating Breguet hairspring, "Kif Flector" shock resistance; 19,800 half-swings per hour, winding in both directions of the rotor; this caliber was #1575 with calendar date and #1575 GMT with two hands for 12- and 24-hour indication.*

610a, b *Circa 1961, steel case, 34 mm diameter; anchor movement with automatic winding by rotor in two directions, caliber J 83, 12.5 lines, 28 jewels, monometallic ring balance with regulating screws on both shanks, self-compensating flat hairspring, fine regulation, balance-stopping mechanism.*

611a, b *circa 1963, doublé case, 35 mm diameter, anchor movement, caliber J 85.10, 11 lines, 17 jewels, direct central second, monometallic ring balance, self-compensating flat hairspring, gooseneck fine regulation, Junghans shock resistance, balance-stopping mechanism.*

612a, b *Wrist chronometer, "unima" by Bifora, circa 1965; doublé case, 34 mm diameter, anchor movement, caliber 120, 12.5 lines, 18 jewels, monometallic screw balance, self-compensating flat hairspring, Incabloc shock resistance, indirect central second, balance-stopping mechanism, gooseneck fine regulation.*

613a, b *Man's wristwatch, "Wostok Precision Class", USSR, circa 1965; doublé case, 35 mm diameter, 13-line movement, basically like that of Zenith caliber 135 (see #409a, b), 22 jewels, monometallic screw balance, Breguet hairspring, shock resistance.*

614a, b *Wrist chronometer with automatic winding, Eterna "Centenaire", circa 1956; steel case, 34 mm diameter; 21-jewel anchor movement, ball bearing rotor mounting, rotor winds the mainspring in both directions, shock resistance, beryllium balance, flat hairspring, gooseneck fine regulation.*

615 *Man's wrist chronometer, "Gyromatic" by Girard-Perregaux, circa 1968; steel case and band, 39-jewel anchor movement with automatic winding in both rotor directions, monometallic ring balance, self-compensating flat hairspring, 36,000 half-swings per hour, Incabloc shock resistance, patented fine regulation.*

616a, b *Japanese wrist chronometer by Seiko, "KS HI-BEAT", presumably circa 1970; anchor movement, 25 jewels, caliber 4502 A, monometallic ring balance, flat hairspring, fine regulation, fast swinging, shock resistance, calendar date.*

617a, b *Wrist chronometer by Ulysse Nardin, circa 1975; automatic winding, 25-jewel anchor movement (by Eta), caliber NB 11 QU, fast swinging (36,000 half-swings per hour), monometallic balance, self-compensating flat hairspring, "Incabloc" shock resistance, ballbearing rotor mounting, rotor winds the mainspring in both directions; steel case with 36 mm diameter.*

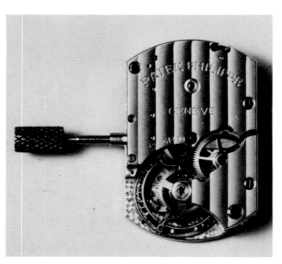

618a-c *Patek Philippe wristwatch, #861,490 in 18-karat gold case; case, dial and hands date from 1980; caliber 34 T (34.4 x 22.2 mm) wristwatch movement by Patek Philippe with Tourbillon (one revolution in 50 seconds), 23 jewels, "Duofix" shock resistance for balance and cage; free-swinging Breguet hairspring with inner end curve, Guillaume balance with 21,600 half-swings per hour; this movement was made in 1956/57, the winding indicator shows 57 hours. Tourbillon made by A. Bornand in finished condition.*

619a-d *Man's wristwatch in 18-karat gold case (35 mm diameter) with 7-minute Tourbillon, marked "Omega", circa 1948, made by Jean-Pierre Matthey-Claudet, Evilard near Biel, and Omega Watch from construction plans by Marcel Vuilleumier, director of the watchmaking school in La Vallée de Joux; the watches (only ten were produced) were regulated by Gottlob Itt, who submitted them to the Kew-Teddington Observatory for testing in the early Fifties. The case has a glass bottom through which the movement can be seen. Under the perforated balance bridge the turning frame can be seen, in which are the bimetallic balance, Breguet hairspring, anchor, anchor wheel and second wheel. The regulator can be noted on a shank of the cage.*

620a, b *Man's rectangular wristwatch with one-minute anchor Tourbillon, built on a 7.75 x 11-line "normal" formed movement by LIP, circa 1948 (see #142b). The mechanics of the turning frame can be seen on the dial side; it has a diameter of 11.5 mm and serves as a second hand. Presumably this was an experimental piece of which only one was made.*

622a-d *Man's flat wristwatch with automatic winding and one-minute tourbillon by Audemars Piguet, in present production, first put on the market in 1986; 18-karat gold case, the bottom of which is also the plate, overall height 4.8mm; 32-jewel movement, turning frame diameter 7.2mm, height 2.5mm; anchor escapement, no shock resistance;*

621a, b *Man's wristwatch (unique) with 1-minute tourbillon, produced in 1985 by Andreas Weber of Glashütte.*

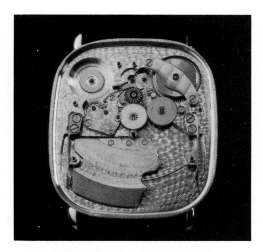

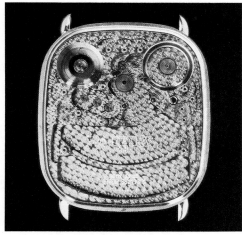

winding by a swinging pendulum of a platinum-iridium alloy, no means of hand winding; the crown on the back of the case is only for hand setting; gold dial, reminiscent of Egyptian mythology in its relief portrayal; the turning frame is visible at upper left, and near the 6 is an opening through which the swinging pendulum can be seen.

623 *Man's wristwatch with 5-minute repetition, signed "Jules Jürgensen" on the dial, movement and case, completed 1906; 12½-line anchor movement, 31 jewels, bimetallic balance, barrel-shaped 18-karat gold case with chasing.*

624, 625 *Wristwatches with minute repetition, signed "Gübelin" on the dial, movements by Audemars Piguet, made in 1906, sold in 1908; 18-karat gold case, 28 x 28 mm.*

626 *Man's wristwatch with minute repetition, by Patek Philippe, No, 138 147, barrel-shaped platinum-gold case, 12-line anchor movement, first quality, 22 jewels; begun May 5, 1908, built into a woman's savonnette pocket-watch case on April 24, 1909, changed to a wristwatch on September 15, 1925, and sold to Tiffany on October 12, 1926 for 2730 Swiss francs.*

627a-c *Wristwatch with minute repetition, signed "Le Roy et Fils, Paris", hallmarked 1912; striking activated by a button near the 6; probably a rebuilt woman's pocket watch, Le Coultre-Ebauche, diameter 32 mm.*

628 *Man's wristwatch with minute repetition, by Patek Philippe, No. 174 191, from 1915. To stress the high cost of such a small movement with minute repetition at that time, it must be noted that in July 1930 an 11-line V. Piguet Ebauche with minute repetition cost 750 Swiss francs, a 17-line Ebauche, on the other hand, cost only 350 Swiss francs. The repetition added an extra 400 Swiss francs to the 11-line movement, and 264 Swiss francs to the 17-line type. The first-quality escapement for the 11-line movement cost 180 Swiss francs, for the 17-line type 136.*

629a, b *Woman's wristwatch with 5-minute repetition, by Patek Philippe, No. 174,603, 1915; 10-line anchor movement with 29 jewels, bimetallic balance, platinum case, 27 mm diameter, with plaited platinum band.*

630a, b *Wristwatch with minute repetition, by Audemars Piguet, No. 12824, made in 1909, sold in 1925 to Metric Watch of New York, then the U.S. importer of AP; 11½-line anchor movement, caliber SMV, 29 jewels, bimetallic balance, flat hairspring, barrel-shaped platinum case, diameter 30 mm.*

631a, b *Wristwatch with minute repetition by T. Moser, 53/rose gold case, enameled dial with recessed second numbered 5 to 60, burnished pear-shaped hands, gilded 13-line Swiss bridge movement with compensated balance, extended anchor wheel and equalizing anchor, four bearings, 26 rubies, 2 tone springs, 1915.*

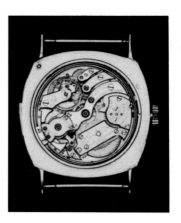

633 *Man's wristwatch with minute repetition, by Jules Jürgensen, No. 17,357, circa 1920; 29-jewel bridge anchor movement, bimetallic balance, pillow-shaped 18-karat gold case, 30 x 30 mm.*

632a, b *Woman's wristwatch with minute repetition, circa 1920, signed "Golay, Fils & Stahl, Geneva"; 8.75-line anchor movement with 32 jewels, bimetallic balance, Breguet hairspring, 18-karat gold case, 26 mm diameter.*

634 *Man's wristwatch with minute repetition, signed "Henry Moser", Locle; 18-karat gold case, 36 mm diameter, hallmarked 1922.*

635a-c *Woman's wristwatch with minute repetition, by Henry Capt, Geneva; cord band, 8½-line anchor movement, Breguet hairspring, bimetallic balance.*

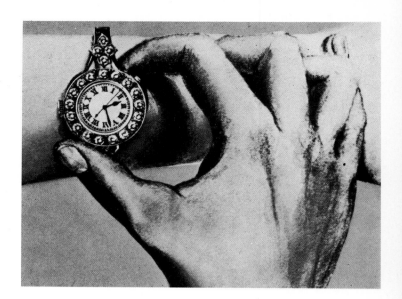

637 *Woman's wristwatch with minute repetition and central second hand, by Audemars Piguet, circa 1920; 10-line anchor movement with 23 mm diameter.*

636 *Woman's wristwatch with minute repetition, by Audemars Piguet; 8-line anchor movement /= 18.05 mm diameter.*

638a, b *Man's large wristwatch with minute repetition, by Audemars Piguet; 14½-line 30-jewel anchor movement, 18-karat yellow gold case, 38 mm diameter.*

639a, b *Man's wristwatch with minute repetition by Cartier, #22,302, of 1925; 18-karat gold barrel case, 39 x 32 mm, 11-line rhodinate anchor movement by "European Watch and Clock Inc.", France; 28 jewels, bimetallic balance, Breguet hairspring, striking shutoff via the button by the 9.*

640a-c *Square wristwatch with minute repetition, signed "Gübelin" on dial and movement; 9.75-line anchor movement (Le Coultre-Ebauche), movement 3 mm high, circa 1925; 29 jewels, bimetallic balance, Breguet hairspring, square platinum case.*

641 *Man's wristwatch with minute repetition, by Minerva Watch, circa 1925; 18-karat gold case; 12-line anchor movement with 17 jewels, bimetallic balance; striking shut off via button in case edge by the 9.*

642 *Man's wristwatch with minute repetition, by Patek Philippe, No. 198,212; barrel-shaped platinum case, 11-line anchor movement, first quality, 28 jewels; begun July 7, 1928, sold March 2, 1929 for 7700 Swiss francs.*

643 *Man's wristwatch with minute repetition, by Patek Philippe, No. 198,306; barrel-shaped platinum case, 11-line anchor movement, first quality, 28 jewels; begun October 30, 1929, sold February 10, 1931 for 5300 Swiss francs.*

644a-c *Man's wristwatch with minute repetition by Cartier, Paris, circa 1930; 11-line anchor movement (Ebauche Le Coultre, see #670a), 29 jewels; platinum case, 35 mm diameter, self-setting buttons, overall case height 8 mm; guilloched silver dial in Breguet style, Breguet hands.*

646a, b *Wristwatch with minute repetition, by Audemars Piguet, No. 41670, begun 1930 and sold 1955; 8.75-line anchor movement with 29 jewels, 18-karat yellow gold case, 30 mm diameter.*

645a, b *Small square wristwatch with minute repetition, by Audemars Piguet, circa 1930; 8.75-line anchor movement, 29 jewels, bimetallic balance and Breguet hairspring, platinum case, 26 x 26 mm.*

647a, b *Man's gold pillow-shaped wristwatch with minute repetition, by Vacheron & Constantin, finished 1940, sold 1946; 31-jewel anchor movement (Le·Coultre-Ebauche), bimetallic balance and Breguet hairspring, wolf's-tooth winding wheels, 3-part white gold case, 32 x 32 mm.*

648a, b *Man's wristwatch with minute repetition by Vacheron & Constantin, No. 341,034, begun 1920, finished 1950; anchor movement (Le Coultre-Ebauche), Breguet hairspring, 18-karat gold case, 36 mm diameter.*

649a, b *Man's gold wristwatch with minute repetition, by Patek Philippe; 29-jewel anchor movement, bimetallic balance, Breguet hairspring, wolf's-tooth winding wheels, case diameter 34 mm.*

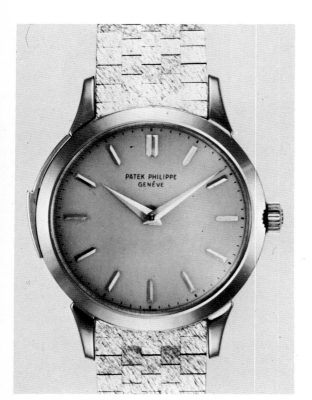
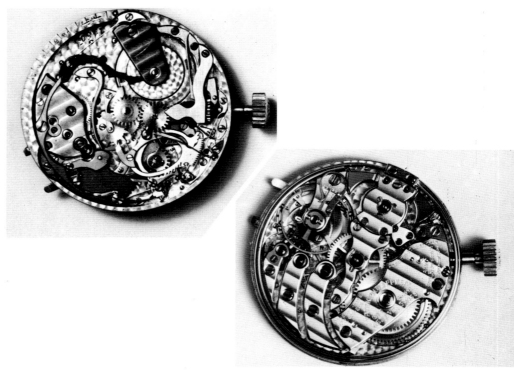

650a-c *Wristwatch by Patek Philippe, #861,491 with minute repetition striking apparatus, in 18-karat gold case; gilded dial; striking activated by the lever on the left rim of the case; 1959. View under the dial; striking mechanism is seen. 12-line movement with anchor escapement, 18 jewels (11 bearing jewels in the striking mechanism), Breguet hairspring, gooseneck fine regulation and compensated balance.*

651a, b *Man's wristwatch with minute repetition, signed "Piaget", No. 12,862, 12-line anchor movement, 30 jewels, bimetallic balance, Breguet hairspring.*

652a-c *Wristwatch with minute repetition, signed "Gübelin" on the dial, unsigned 10½-line anchor movement with Geneva stamp; movement probably made circa 1900-1910, as indicated by construction (Le Coultre-Ebauche); later (1968) set in a yellow gold case with Milanese gold band.*

361

653a, b *Automatic wristwatch with minute repetition, by Gérald Genta, movement with central rotor, flat hairspring; striking activated by a button near the 9; watertight case with glass bottom.*

654a-c *Man's wristwatch with minute repetition, by Vacheron & Constantin, Geneva, movement from 1920, finished 1950 (one of six examples made in 1950 with minute repetition); 29-jewel anchor movement, 11 lines, No, 501,903, flat hairspring, bimetallic balance, Geneva stripes.*

655a-c *Man's wristwatch with minute repitition by Blancpain, developed in 1985 and marketed in 1986; 9-line anchor movement, height 3.2mm, traditional construction of the movement and striking apparatus, monometallic screw balance, self-compensating flat hairspring, small second by the 6; case with concealed lever near the 9 for activating the striking.*

656a-c *Man's square wristwatch with quarter repetition, Driva Repeater, circa 1930, steel case, formed movement, one hammer on one tone spring.*

657a-c Man's wristwatch with automatic winding and quarter striking, marked on dial and case "Angelus Tinkler", 1957/58. Steel case, 37 mm diameter, 11.5-line anchor movement with 17 jewels, AS caliber 1580, Incabloc shock resistance, monometallic screw balance, winding in both rotor directions, quarter-hour striking on a sound spring, control via button near the 9.

In 1957/58 a trial series of 100 of these watches was made by Angelus, mainly by hand; the watches were put on sale, mainly in Switzerland and Germany. For series production the Ebauche-Fabrik A. Schild required a minimum order of 10,000 pieces. Since this number seemed too high to the Angelus firm, production never went beyond the trial run.

658a-c Man's wristwatch with five-minute repetition, Felser's, by Le Phare-Sultana S.A., circa 1975; barrel-shaped plated case, diameter 40 mm; the repetition mechanism was built as a model (diameter 36 mm), developed by Dubois-Depraz, on an Eta caliber 2801, the balance of the 17-jewel movement makes 36,000 half-swings per hour; the repetition is activated via the button near the 8.

660 *Wristwatch with minute repetition, moon phase, "eternal" calendar and chronograph; gold barrel-shaped case, circa 1930; seller's signature "Schulz".*

659 *Wristwatch with minute repetition, with retrograde date indication, day indication and small second, by Vacheron & Constantin, circa 1925.*

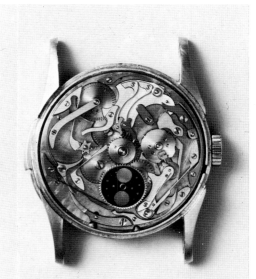

661a-d *Man's wristwatch with minute repetition and eternal calendar by Patek Philippe & Co., 1939, satinized platinum case with 18-karat white gold band; silver dial with raised platinum numerals, date window by the 9, month by the 3, and moon phase indicator by the 6; 11-line anchor movement with 18 jewels for the clockwork and 11 for the striking mechanism, bimetallic balance, flat hairspring, lever to turn off striking in case rim by the 9.*

663 *Wristwatch with minute repetition and "eternal" calendar, with leap year indication, by Gérald Genta, Geneva, presently in production.*

662 *Man's wristwatch with minute repetition and "eternal" calendar, Breguet, 1985; movement No. 4,630, monometallic screw balance, self-compensating Breguet hairspring (see also #684b; view of the movement).*

664a, b *Man's wristwatch by Gérald Genta, presently in production, front and rear views of a skeletal model with moon phase indication, "eternal" calendar and minute repetition controlled by the button near the 8.*

665a-d *Wristwatch with minute repetition, date and moon age indication by Gübelin, Lucerne, 1985-86; Ebauche (30 mm diameter) by Le Coultre, finished by Gübelin; 29 jewels, monometallic screw balance, self-compensating flat hairspring, 19,800 half-swings per hour; date and moon age indications were made and asembled especially for the "Lunea". Correction of the moon age indication is possible only after 120 years via a switching; in the middle of the dial is inset a gold photo of the moon's original topography, based on a NASA relief (16½ mm diameter); yellow gold case set with gems.*

666 *Gold wristwatch with minute repetition, marked on dial and movement with seller's name: Theodore B. Starr, New York. Presumably a rebuilt pocket watch, as suggested by the stem knob by the 12. Swiss nickel anchor movement, compensated balance, Breguet hairspring, fine regulating via gooseneck, bearing jewels held in screwed gold chatons, wolf's-tooth winding wheels; white enameled dial with black numerals; pear-shaped blue steel hands; striking shutoff via button at right near the 3.*

667a, b *Watch movement by Jaeger-Le Coultre with minute repetition, from 1908; caliber 13" RMV, 30.50 mm diameter, 3.25 mm height.*

668a, b *Wristwatch with minute repetition and "eternal" calendar; movement signed "Grandjean" (Le Coultre-Ebauche), circa 1920; "eternal" calendar (newly produced by Svend Andersen, Geneva) with retrograde date indication; case and dial are likewise new.*

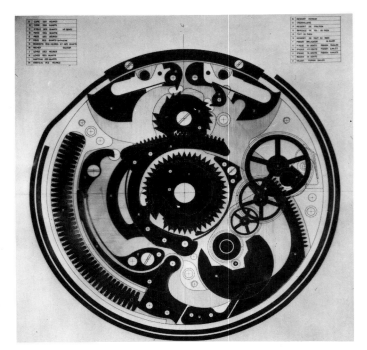

669 *Drawing of a wristwatch prototype with quarter repetition (movement) of 1959; construction from the technology of Vallée de Joux, Le Sentier; it is not known whether the design was ever made into a functioning movement.*

670a-c *Repetition striking apparatus by Le Coultre.*

670a *Under-the-dial view of the 11-line minute repetition apparatus by Le Coultre.*

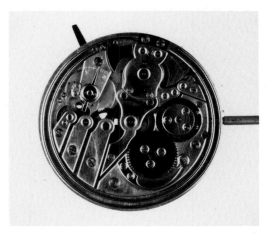

670b *11-line quarter repetition apparatus by Le Coultre.*

671a, b *Man's wristwatch with minute repetition in 18-karat gold case (37 mm diameter), marked "Golay Fils & Stahl Genève" massive gold band; Geneva movement with Swiss anchor escapement, bimetallic balance, Breguet hairspring; striking shutoff via button in left case edge by the 8; enamel dial with black numerals, pear-shaped blue steel hands.*

670c *Under-the-dial view of the 11-line quarter repetition apparatus by Le Coultre, height 2.7 mm.*

672 *Wristwatch with minute repetition and "eternal" calendar, signed "Henry Birks", circa 1920; "eternal" calendar with retrograde date indication, case and dial are newly made, likewise the "eternal" calendar.*

673 *Wristwatch with repetition by Le Roy & Fils; case of gold with gold link band, circa 1910; Repetition turned off by a lever in the edge of the case near the 9.*

674 *Gold wristwatch with minute repetition, made for Tiffany & Co., 27 mm case diameter; presumably rebuilt pocket watch; Swiss nickel-plated anchor movement with fine regulating apparatus; stem knob over the 12; button for shutting off the striking in case edge by the 3; white enamel dial with blue numerals and gold crosses between the numerals.*

675 Man's watch with quarter-hour striking, marked "Ulysses Nardin", circa 1930; 14-karat gold case, 33 mm diameter, metal dial with black Roman numerals, blue steel Breguet hands; nickel anchor movement with compensated balance, striking shut off by a button in the left rim of the case.

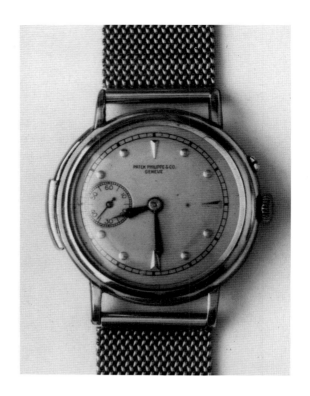

676 Wristwatch in 18-karat gold case with quarter striking, by Patek Philippe & Co., circa 1925; presumably a rebuilt pocket watch, as suggested by the small second dial by the 9; gilded anchor movement, striking shutoff via the button in the case edge by the 9.

677a, b Man's wristwatch with quarter striking, signed from the workshop "Dint au Brassus", 12''' gilded anchor movement by Louis Audemars, wolfs-tooth winding wheel, 29 jewels, Breguet hairspring, two metal balance wheel, striking with all-or-none safety; case and face new and appropriate, case 34 mm diameter.

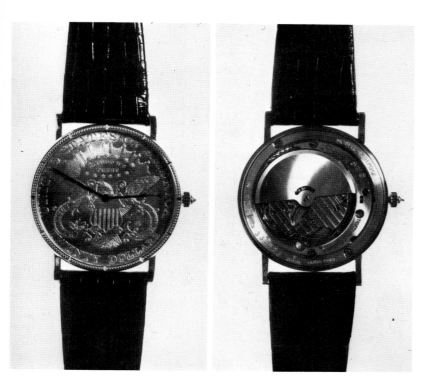

678a, b *Man's wristwatch with automatic winding by Corum, made since 1974; the American "Double Eagle" $20 gold coin serves as a case; anchor movement with eccentrically located rotor, which powers the watch in one direction, height of the movement 2.40 mm, 35 jewels, "Kif" shock resistance and combined "Duofix" mounting of anchor wheel pivot bearings (the watch was made with hand winding since about 1968).*

679a, b *Man's wristwatch by Corum, made since about 1975; the movement is built into a 15-gram gold bar; 18-jewel anchor movement, "Kif" shock resistance, "Duofix" mounting of anchor wheel pivot bearings.*

680a, b *"Golden Bridge" man's wristwatch by Corum, this model circa 1981, currently in production, rectangular gold case with in-line movement, with all wheels and pinions are arranged in a straight line; Incabloc shock resistance.*

681a, b *Man's wristwatch "Squelette", by Vacheron & Constantin, present production; 18-karat white gold case, hand-wound skeletal anchor movement of 14-karat white gold, 17 jewels, movement height 1.64 mm.*

681c *Front view of the "Squelette" automatic movement, 2.45 mm high, with 21-karat gold rotor and "Kif-Elastor" shock resistant.*

682 *Man's wristwatch "Structura", by Vacheron & Constantin, present production; 18-karat gold case, chased anchor movement which was built into the case turned 180 degrees, so the back, with the balance wheel, is visible through the dial.*

Wristwatches with alarms, varieties and curiosities

683a, b *Early alarm wristwatch by Zenith, presumably circa 1920, in 800 silver case. White enamel dial with secondary dials for seconds and alarm setting. Blue steel pear-shaped hands. Two barrels, for the works and the alarm. Bimetallic balance and Breguet hairspring. The two mainsprings are wound by one stem; the crown wheel meshes with the lower*

ratchet when turned to the left, with the upper when turned to the right. The upper lever sets the hands, the lower lever sets the alarm time; one moves the lever toward the stem when setting. The alarm is made by a hammer striking a small sound spring.

684, 685 *Vulcain "Cricket" men's alarm wristwatches, made from 1947 on; the "Cricket" existed with central and eccentric second, with and without calendar; 12-line anchor movement, basic caliber 120, movement 5.6 mm high, 17 jewels; the alarm hammer strikes a membrane, as in the "Golden Voice", over which a perforated back lid is pressed.*

686a, b *Vulcain "Golden Voice" woman's alarm wristwatch, produced from 1958 on; 8.75-line alarm movement with 17 jewels, 2 mainsprings, "Exactomatic" balance arbor bearings (the cap jewel does not, as usual, have a flat surface at a right angle to the balance arbor, rather a lightly angled one; the pivot ends of the balance arbor are completely flat; with horizontal bearings, the balance pivot lies right against the cap jewel and the wall of the hole jewel, so as to prevent isochronism faults), the alarm membrane is made of gold, hence the name "Golden Voice".*

687a, b *Junghans "Minivox" man's alarm wristwatch, circa 1952 (patented 1949); steel case, 34 mm diameter, 12.5-line anchor movement with indirect central second, caliber 89, one mainspring for clockwork and alarm (a drive mechanism prevents the mainspring from winding down completely when the alarm rings), Junghans shock resistance; the knob by the 2 sets the alarm time, that by the 4 turns the alarm on and off.*

688a, b *Man's alarm wristwatch, marked "Berna", circa 1960; steel case, 34 mm diameter; anchor movement, caliber Venus 230, 11.5 lines, 17 jewels, Incabloc shock resistance, direct central second, monometallic screw balance, flat hairspring; in the window at right near the 9 a green or red dot shows whether the alarm is turned on or off.*

689a, b *Man's alarm wristwatch by Camy Watch, circa 1958; AS alarm movement with 21 jewels, 11.5 lines, two mainsprings, monometallic screw balance, flat hairspring, Incabloc shock resistance, direct central second.*

690a, b *Pierce "Duofon" man's alarm wristwatch, circa 1960; doublé case, 35 mm diameter; 13-line alarm movement, 21 jewels, Incabloc shock resistance; an unusual feature of this alarm is that the alarm can be set to either loud or soft volume.*

691 *Man's wristwatch with alarm, signed "Leonidas", circa 1960 (see also #688a, b).*

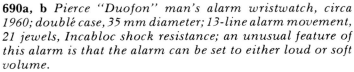

692 *Man's alarm wristwatch, marked "Lanco", Langendorf Watch, circa 1960; doublé case, 33 mm diameter, 12.5-line anchor movement, "Lanco-Fon" caliber 1241, 17 jewels, 2 mainsprings, direct central second; hand and alarm setting, and running and alarm winding, by one stem; a red or white dot shows in a window under the 12 to tell whether alarm or clockwork is being wound.*

693a, b *Man's wristwatch with automatic winding and alarm, Jaeger-LeCoultre "Memovox", circa 1960; steel case, 36 mm diameter; 14-line anchor movement, caliber 825, 17 jewels, automatic winding of the clockwork by a swinging pendulum in one direction, "Kif Flector" shock resistance, calendar; the "Memovox" automatic alarm watch was the first alarm watch that offered automatic winding, alarm and calendar; also available without calendar as caliber 815.*

695 *Man's wristwatch with alarm and calendar by Omega, "Memomatic"; automatic winding for just one mainspring, which powers clockwork and alarm; apparatus to prevent mainspring from unwinding fully on alarm; unlike all other alarm wristwatches, this allows exact to-the-minute alarm setting with an hour-and-minute marker; 19-jewel anchor movement, caliber SL 980, 13.5 lines, fine tuning for the regulator by an eccentric screw, 21,600 half-swings per hour, Incabloc shock resistance, steel case, 40 mm diameter.*

694 *Man's alarm wristwatch by Dugena, circa 1963; steel case, 34 mm diameter; 17-jewel anchor movement, 11.5 lines, AS caliber with two mainsprings, direct central second, shock resistance.*

696a, b *Man's alarm wristwatch "Poljot", USSR, circa 1966; 11½-line alarm movement, Poljot caliber 2612/= caliber AS 1475, 18 jewels, "Kirowskie-Poljot" shock resistance.*

697a, b *Man's wristwatch with automatic winding, calendar and alarm by Certina, Kurth Frères, circa 1975; steel case, 39 mm diameter; 25-jewel anchor movement, 13.75 lines, Certina caliber 681S/= AS 5008, Incabloc shock resistance, balance-stopping mechanism for setting the watch; two separate mainspring barrels for clockwork and alarm, the rotor winds the clockwork mainspring when it turns right, the alarm mainspring when it turns left.*

698 *Wristwatch for the blind with hand winding, "STOWA" brand, made by Walter Storz, circa 1960; nickel case, 33 mm diameter, the rim of the glass opens when the button in the stem knob is pushed; 10.25-line anchor movement, 15 jewels, shock resistance.*

699 *Wristwatch for the blind with automatic winding, marked "Lignal", made by Prorubis, circa 1970; nickel-plated case with raising glass rim, 34 mm diameter; anchor movement, caliber Eta 2784, 25 jewels, Incabloc shock resistance, monometallic ring balance, flat hairspring, 21,600 half-swings per hour, automatic winding by an unlimited rotor in both directions.*

700, 701a, b *Man's wristwatch by Mauthe, circa 1965, given by the Volkswagen firm in recognition of the attainment of 100,000 kilometers; 10.5-line caliber 612, 19 jewels, direct centralsecond, Contrachoc shock resistance.*

702 *Man's wristwatch with lighted dial, "Tourist Everlight", circa 1958; 11.5-line anchor movement, FHF caliber 72, 17 jewels, Incabloc shock resistance; screwed steel case, 35 mm dial; battery fastened to the rear lid can be charged with a 1.5 V cell. Pushing the button by the 2 makes a bulb light the dial.*

703 *Man's wristwatch with lighted dial, "Flash", by Ernest Borel, made since 1958; patented construction including a chargeable battery in the watertight case. A bulb lights the dial when the button by the 2 is pushed.*

704 *Man's wristwatch with lighted dial, marked "Dogma prima Rayolux", by Aubry Frères, circa 1960; 15-jewel anchor movement; steel case, 37 mm diameter, with built-in battery and bulb to light the dial when the button by the 2 is pushed.*

705 *Man's wristwatch, "Solunar", by Heuer, circa 1955; steel case, 36 mm diameter, anchor movement, which uses a cross on a turning disc over the 6, plus an hour scale around it on the dial, to show the "Solunar" periods of a geographical place of the owner's choice. The four colored sectors indicate ebb and flood tides at that place: yellow + ebb, blue + flood. The button by the 4 sets the turning disc, which then operates automatically to show the changing tide times.*

706 *Woman's wristwatch "Lunastar" by Consul, circa 1965; the central second hand of this watch is shaped like a comet, the rear end of the minute hand like the moon.*

707 *Man's wristwatch with automatic winding, date, moon phase and tide indication, anonymous, Swiss, presumably post-1975; doublé case, 37 mm diameter; 17-jewel AS automatic movement.*

708 *Man's wristwatch with automatic winding, day and date indication as well as high and low tide, "Solunar" by Heuer, circa 1975; unlike the "Solunar in #705, this watch does not switch the indications automatically, but must be set manually every two weeks.*

709 *Man's wristwatch with springing second by Doxa, circa 1960; doublé case, 34 mm diameter, Ebauches Chézard anchor movement, caliber 116, central minute and second hands, hour shown by a panel and a window in which the sun or moon appears to indicate day or night; the watch in the photo shows ten minutes after 9:00 P.M.*

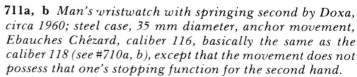

710a, b *Man's wristwatch with independent springing second by Doxa, circa 1960; barrel-shaped doublé case, 34 mm diameter; 11.5-line anchor movement, Ebauches Chézard, caliber 118, 21 jewels, Incabloc shock resistance, monometallic screw balance, self-compensating flat hairspring; the movement includes a secondary drive, constantly wound by the movement, that lets the central second hand move one second farther with every five swings of the balance; the stem knob allows two functions to be changed: when the stem is pulled, the watch is stopped and the hands can be set exactly; when it is pushed in, the watch runs, but the second hand remains stopped; thus the watch can be used as a simple chronograph.*

711a, b *Man's wristwatch with springing second by Doxa, circa 1960; steel case, 35 mm diameter, anchor movement, Ebauches Chézard, caliber 116, basically the same as the caliber 118 (see #710a, b), except that the movement does not possess that one's stopping function for the second hand.*

712a, b *Man's wristwatch with springing second by Werba, circa 1960; doublé case, diameter 34 mm; Ebauches Chézard anchor movement, caliber 7400, 11.5 lines, 17 jewels, Incabloc shock resistance, monometallic screw balance, self-compensating flat hairspring; the "mechanism for stepwise forward movement of the second hand by clock-work drive" was patented in Germany on June 3, 1949, and includes in its second-hand drive two wheels of different sizes but with the same number of teeth, "elastically flexibly" linked by a spring; the movement also includes a balance-stopping mechanism for exact setting of the watch.*

713a, b *Man's wristwatch marked "P.W.C. Giro-Lunette", by Perfecta S.A., circa 1960; doublé case, 34 mm diameter; hand-wound movement, Felsa caliber, 15 jewels, Incabloc shock resistance, Geneva stripes; winding and setting by turning the glass.*

714 *Man's wristwatch with visible balance, seller's name "Beyer Zürich" on the dial, circa 1965 (watch presumably made by Luxor); 17-jewel anchor movement with mono-metallic screw balance, self-compensating flat hairspring, Incabloc shock resistance.*

715a, b *Man's wristwatch with automatic winding and time for 24 world cities, by Tissot, circa 1952; 18-karat gold case, 37 mm diameter; 12.5 -ine automatic movement, caliber 28.5 N 21, made since 1944, 17 jewels, Incabloc shock resistance, winding in one direction of a swinging pendulum limited by screw springs; the hour hand turns once in 12 hours; time is read on the outer glass. The inner disc with the names of 24 cities turns once every 24 hours, with the 24-hour dial showing local times. The marking between Auckland and Midway indicates the Date Line. The hands can be set independently of the city disc by using the button near the 2.*

716 *Man's wristwatch with world time indication, by Jaeger-Le Coultre, circa 1950.*

717 *Man's wristwatch with automatic winding, "Edox Geoscope", of 1970. The inner world map turns once in 24 hours, showing local times on the 24-hour dial. The winding, setting and world time setting knobs are on the left side of the watch.*

718a, b *Man's wristwatch showing the time in two time zones, "Long Distance", by Ardath, 1963; nickel-plated case, 38 mm diameter, the watch includes two different women's watch calibers, Eta 2551, 7.75 lines, 17 jewels, Incabloc shock resistance, 21,600 half-swings per hour, automatic winding in both rotor directions, direct central second and calendar; FEF (Fabrique d'ebauches de Fleurier) caliber 430 with hand winding, 5 x 7 lines, 17 jewels, Incabloc shock resistance, 18,000 half-swings per hour; the left automatic movement shows the time at home, the right movement shows the time wherever one is (another Ardath model had the movements one above the other in a rectangular case).*

719 *Man's wristwatch with world time indication by Patek Philippe, made since 1955; 18-karat gold case; anchor movement, caliber 12-400; this watch allows simultaneous reading of times in various cities of the world.*

720 *Man's wristwatch with additional and independently settable hour hand by Patek Philippe, made since 1962; 18-karat gold case, 12-line anchor movement, caliber 12-400, 18 jewels, self-compensating Breguet hairspring, monometallic screw balance, gooseneck fine regulation; the button in the case rim allows the blue hour hand to be set, making possible the use of the watch as a two-zone watch.*

722 *Man's wristwatch with automatic winding, calendar, 12- and 24-hour indication, "Unitime" by Breitling, circa 1965; 11.5-line anchor movement, Felsa caliber 711; 17 jewels, direct central second, winding in both rotor directions.*

721a, b *Man's wristwatch with springing 24-hour indication (1 to 12 and 13 to 24 o'clock) by Gruen, circa 1960; the hour digits spring automatically at 12 and 24 o'clock.*

723 *One-hand wristwatch, "Philosophic" by Audemars Piguet, present productional 18-karat gold case; the entire movement and dial turn inside a gold ring with 12 stopping points. One can thus use it as a world time watch: one turns the watch the number of hours' difference from the point of departure and has the new local time. The time can, to be sure, be read only to the nearest quarter of an hour. When the hand points to the "gold nugget", the time at home is either noon or midnight. Winding by a knob on the back of the watch.*

724 *Man's wristwatch marked "Stowa", with 12-and 24-hour indication, circa 1968; doublé case, 36 mm diameter, 11.5-line anchor movement, Durowe caliber 471-1, 17 jewels, shock resistance, 21,600 half-swings of the balance per hour; these watches were consigned to, among others, people working by the day.*

725 *Man's wristwatch with automatic winding and 24-hour indication by Juvenia, circa 1965.*

726 *Man's wristwatch with automatic winding, calendar and 24-hour indication by Tissot, "Navigator", circa 1975; doublé case, 36 mm diameter; 21-jewel anchor movement, caliber 788, Incabloc shock resistance, fine tuning for the regulator by eccentric screw, automatic winding in both rotor directions.*

727 *Man's wristwatch with automatic winding, date and 12 and 24-hour indication in watertight steel case, "Sherpa' Jet" by Enicar, circa 1965; the 24-hour lunette inside the case can be turned to a second time zone with the help of the upper crown.*

728a-d *Man's wristwatch with built-in altimeter, "bivouac", by Favre-Leuba, built since 1963; steel case, 40 mm diameter, anchor movement, caliber Peseux 320, 10.5 lines, 17 jewels, Incabloc shock resistance; the barometer mechanism is built onto the movement, the membrane box is screwed into the case, the arbor for the barometer hand goes through the*

bored-out minute wheel arbor; the dial has an outer scale to indicate air pressure in mm of mercury, the turning glass has a height scale ranging from 0 to 3000 meters and marked every 25 meters; when starting on a mountain trip, the glass is adjusted to the altitude there; the meters of height covered on the trip can then be read from the glass.

729a, b *Man's wristwatch with calculator and Windrose "Easy Math" by Dugena, sold from 1965 on; steel case, 37 mm diameter; watch made by Fortis, Grenchen; Swiss anchor movement, F.H.F. Standard, caliber 96, 11.5 lines, 17 jewels, monometallic ring balance, flat hairspring, Incabloc shock resistance; the upper knob operates the calculator and the Windrose; in sunny weather the watch can be used as a compass: one holds the hour hand toward the sun; south is half the angle between the hour hand and the 12; the south marking of the Windrose can be turned to that point to give all four directions.*

730 *Man's wristwatch with 24-hour indication and calculator, "Computer", by Ollech & Wajs, circa 1968; steel case, 39 mm diameter; 11.5-line anchor movement, 17 jewels, Incabloc shock resistance; the upper knob makes the outer dial ring turn and act as a calculator.*

731 *Freemason wristwatch, marked "Waltham" on the dial, made in Switzerland; doublé case in equilateral triangle form with upper attachment ring encircling a lodge emblem; dial with varicolored Freemason emblems and motto "Love your fellow man, lend him a helping hand"; 17-jewel anchor movement, manual winding by the knob in the lower right corner of the case.*

732 *Freemason wristwatch in square doublé case with dial cut out as equilateral triangle, no maker's name, Swiss, presumably 1960; 17-jewel anchor movement, Cyma caliber 120.*

733a, b *Etui watch in 900 silver case, outer dimensions 30 x 40mm, finely machine-patterned, circa 1940; small second; signed Eszeha (now Chopard); round anchor movement without shock resistance, 15 jewels, size 8¾ lines, monometallic screw balance, movement with Geneva stripes.*

734a, b *Ring watch, 14-karat gold case with gold topaz inset; metal dial with inlaid markings, signed Lotos, Switzerland, circa 1955; rectangular formed movement, 4½ lines, 17 jewels, Nivarox hairspring and monometallic balance with screws.*

735a-c *Ornamental watch, circa 1935; by opening the outer wall, decorated with meanders, it can also be used as a miniature table watch; lunette and rear in blue-green enamel; sterling silver case, gilded; case dimensions (without bows) 35 x 29mm, signed Juvenia in several places, two-tone (white & black) enamel dial with gold numerals and hands; rectangular Swiss formed movement, 6¾ x 11 lines, with bimetallic balance, 15 jewels, no shock resistance, with two fine regulations; winding and hand setting from above.*

736 Gold 18-karat ring watch, outer dimensions 24 x 14mm; signed Emka Geneve on the dial; raised line markings, gilded stave hands; circa 1965; unsigned 17-jewel formed anchor movement, 6 x 7¼ lines, monometallic balance, Incabloc shock resistance.

737a, b Moire evening handbag with silver clasp and imitation jewel ornamentation, with a wristwatch movement built in; metal dial with red 12, additional numerals 13 to 24 in an inner ring; burnished metal hands; circa 1915; unsigned round cylinder movement, gilded, 10 jewels; size 8¾ lines; winding and hand setting from below.

738a, b Man's wristwatch by Universal, marked "Railrouter Chronomètre", circa 1955; 17-jewel anchor movement, Incabloc shock resistance, balance-stopping mechanism (by pulling the stem, the watch is stopped for exact setting of the second hand); this watch, with certificate, was especially protected against magnetic influences.

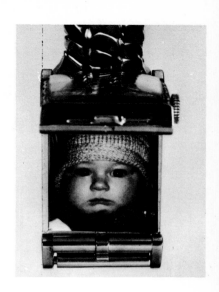

739a, b *Man's wristwatch "Amagnetic" by Patek Philippe & Co., 1961, 18-karat gold case with special movement protection against magnetic influences; magnetic fields up to 800 Gauss do not lead to running irregularities, watch stops in fields from 1500 Gauss (power lines parallel to movement surface); caliber 27 AM movement, 18 jewels, Gyromax balance, free-swinging self-compensating hair-spring, 19,800 half-swings per hour, "Kif-Flector" shock resistance.*

740a, b *Plated wristwatch "Photo-Watch" by Bulova, circa 1955, made chiefly for the American market; a small button on the case wall below the 6 makes the upper part of the case with the movement spring upward, giving a view of the picture underneath; 17-jewel anchor movement.*

741a, b *Man's wristwatch in nickel-plated brass case, marked on the dial "Players", 38 mm diameter, made circa 1950; 12-line movement by FHF (Fabrique d'horlogerie Fontaine-melon), caliber 27, 17 jewels, without shock resistance, monometallic screw balance, flat hairspring, Geneva stripes; the watch has four counters with which, by using the buttons, the goals (but) and corners of two soccer teams can be counted.*

744 *Man's wristwatch with automatic winding and digital time indication, "Directime" by Itraco, circa 1958; 11.5-line AS caliber 1902, 17 jewels, Incabloc shock resistance, winding by unlimited rotor; the top window in the dial shows the springing hour, the middle one the monute and the lower one the second.*

742 *Man's rectangular wristwatch with retrograde hour and minute, plus digital date indication through a window in the the lower right corner, by Le Phare, circa 1965; 17-jewel anchor movement, Peseux caliber 7046, 10½ lines, with raised retrograde time-indicating mechanism, monometallic ring balance, self-compensating flat hairspring, Incabloc shock resistance.*

743 *Man's wristwatch with automatic winding, dial in retrograde arrangement, and calendar, by Wittnauer, circa 1970, in steel case; anchor movement with automatic winding in both directions by unlimited rotor, Eta-caliber, 11.5 lines, 17 jewels; the red hour and white minute hands move downward and spring back to the top at the end of 12 hours and 60 minutes respectively.*

745 *Man's wristwatch with digital time and calendar, marked "Sheffield Instantime", Swiss, circa 1960; 21-jewel anchor movement, Incabloc shock resistance; the dial windows, from top to bottom, show the date, minutes and hours, the watch has a centrally mounted second hand.*

747 *Man's wristwatch marked "Carsic", circa 1965; hand-wound anchor movement with 17 jewels; the upper hand indicates the hours, the central one the seconds, and the lower one the minutes.*

746a, b *Man's digital wristwatch with automatic winding by Lip, circa 1970; chromed case, 32 x 35 mm, 11.5-line anchor movement, AS caliber 1902, 17 jewels, Incabloc shock resistance, 21,600 half-swings per hour; the windows, from left to right, show the springing hour, the minutes and the seconds.*

748 *Man's wristwatch with automatic winding and calendar, marked "Spaceman", made by Choisi S.A., circa 1970; fiber-glass case with integrated plastic band, 42 mm diameter, 11.5-line automatic movement, AS caliber 1913, 25 jewels, Incabloc shock resistance, monometallic ring balance, self-compensating flat hairspring, date indicator changes at midnight; dial must be looked at from an angle because of the glass covering.*

749 *Man's wristwatch with digital hour, minute and date indication by Sicura, circa 1965; hook anchor movement.*

750a, b *Man's wristwatch in chromed case, portrait of Hitler on the dial with inscription "Deutschland erwache" (Germany, awaken!); circa 1933; Swiss Roskopf movement without jewels.*

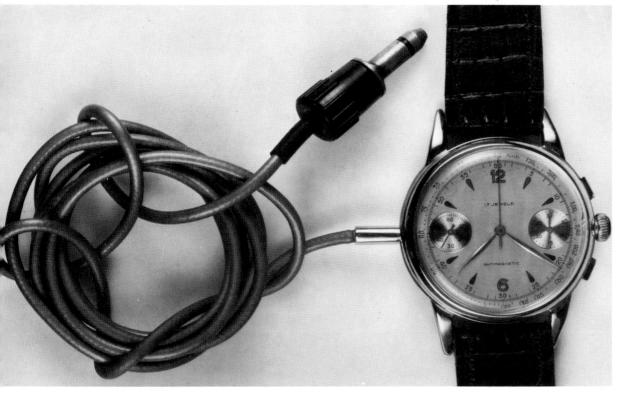

751 *Wristwatch case with built-in listening microphone, disguised as chronograph with 30-minute counter; there is no movement in the case; circa 1940.*

752a, b *Child's watch with Mickey Mouse picture on the dial, Swiss, current production; Roskopf movement with hook anchor escapement, Ebauches Bettlach, 1 jewel, no shock resistance, central second; Mickey Mouse's arms are the hands of the watch.*

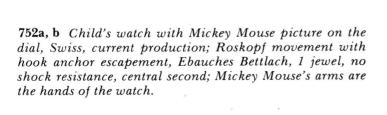

753 *Wristwatch for motorists by Bifora, circa 1970; plastic case and band, case diameter 37 mm; the watch is fastened to the wrist so it can be read while holding the steering wheel; 9.75-line anchor movement, caliber 91/1, 17 jewels, shock resistance.*

754 *Promotional wristwatch with dial inscribed "Curaçao Hilton Casino"; made in Switzerland with Roskopf movement, sunken numerals, a loose ball (now at the 7) can be set in motion by turning the watch.*

755a, b *Man's wristwatch with erotic picture on the dial, made by the Hafner Watch Co., circa 1975; 1-jewel hook anchor movement, Ebauches Bettlach, caliber 8810, 13 lines, shock resistance; instead of a second hand the watch has a polarizing panel that turns once a minute and makes the erotic picture visible every 30 seconds.*

756 *Wristwatch for the 200th anniversary of the U.S. Declaration of Independence, 1976; plastic case, dial represents the American flag; made by Gisa AG (Gisiger-Greder Sohn in Selzach); 17-jewel movement; the circle of stars turns as a second indicator.*

757 *"Research" man's wristwatch by Tissot, circa 1972, made, except for a few parts, fully of fiberglass; because of its faulty performance, it did not establish itself on the market.*

758a, b *Electromechanical wristwatch by Lip, circa 1960; the Lip movement, caliber R 27, is based on a construction patented in France in 1952; 17 jewels, electrodynamically driven balance, 18,000 half-swings per hour, 2 batteries, each of 1.45 V, are the energy source; this watch is also found with the "Porta-Lip" name on the dial.*

759a, b *Man's wristwatch with electrically driven balance by Hamilton, patented in the USA in 1954 and in England in 1955, produced since 1957; 18-karat gold case; movement caliber 500, 12.5 lines, 12 jewels, 18,000 half-swings of the electrodynamically driven balance per hour; energy source is a 1.5 V 110mAh battery. Hamilton was the first firm to put an electric wristwatch into series production.*

760 *Man's wristwatch, "Accutron", by Bulova, announced 1959 and put on the market 1965; this watch was revolutionary in its time, as it used the tuning fork as a swinging element. The frequency of 360 Hz can be heard clearly when one puts the watch to one's ear. Shown is the "Spaceview" model, in which the movement with the tuning fork is visible from the front. Bulova guaranteed its "Accutron" (the name combines "accuracy" and "Electronic") as having a maximal deviation of 60 seconds per month. The "Spaceview" has hand setting from behind. When the bow is lifted for setting, the second hand stops. So as not to damage the highly sensitive ratchet system, the Accutron may be set only by turning the hands forward.*

761a, b *Man's wristwatch with electrodynamically driven balance, "elechron", by Porta, circa 1963; 12.5-line movement, caliber PUW 1001, 7 jewels, Incabloc shock resistance, "Triovis" fine regulation, 28,800 half-swings per hour, 1.5 V battery with 160 mAh is energy source.*

762a, b *Woman's wristwatch with electrodynamically driven balance, "Ladychron" by Porta, circa 1965; 7-jewel movement, "Rufa-Anti-Shock" shock resistance; 28,800 half-swings of the balance per hour.*

763a, b *Man's wristwatch, "Dato-Chron", by Junghans, circa 1968; doublé case, 36 mm diameter; 13½-line movement, caliber 600-12, 17 jewels, the watch has a contactless transistor-controlled swing system with a frequency of 3 Hz (/ = 21,600 half-swings of the balance per hour), "Star Shock" shock resistance, fine tuning of the regulator by eccentric screw; the watch was tested in the state commerce department's watch testing center in Stuttgart and certified as officially having passed the chronometer test.*

764a, b *Timex Lady Electric, circa 1965; plated case, rectangular with diagonal corners, size 30 x 15 mm, height 10 mm; metal dial with raised marking stripes, central second; very early electric movement for women's wristwatches, Timex caliber 900, 6¾ x 8 lines; shock resistance, 8 jewels, 21,600 swings per hour, switching anchor with double stopping function via magnets, electrodynamic drive by both half-swings.*

765 Man's wristwatch, "Constellation Chronometer", by Omega, circa 1969; the movement is powered by a tuning fork with a frequency of 300 Hz.

766a, b Wristwatch with quartz movement by Girard Perregaux, post-1970.

767a, b Man's wristwatch with electronic balance drive by Porta, circa 1970; this movement was a further development of the already described caliber 1001, the balance likewise has a frequency of 4 Hz (= 28,800 half-swings per hour), instead of mechanical contracts, though, this movement has an electronic switch which completes the circuit to the battery via two isolated leading springs and the main hairspring. In the PUW caliber 2002 this switch worked via 3 transistors, 3 resistors and a condenser, in the traditional way, the movement shown at right has an integrated switching circle (IC).

768 *Man's wristwatch with quartz movement "Megaquartz" by Omega, 1972; caliber 1510, frequency 2.4 mHz, case of 18-karat gold, aventurin dial representing the starry sky.*

769a, b *Man's wristwatch with chronograph, 30-minute and 12-hour counters, weekday and date calendar, Longines "Ultronic"; tuning-fork movement, Longines caliber 249.2; steel case.*

770 *Man's wristwatch with calendar date, moon phase and moon's meridian position indication, marked "Eberhard Planetario", present production; quartz movement "Eta Flatline", 7 jewels, available in various cases, diameter 32 mm.*

771 *Man's wristwatch with date and moon phase indication by Comor. The watch could be had until about 1980 with an Automatik-Uhrwerk AS caliber 5206, 17-jewel, with automatic winding in one rotor direction. Since then it has had a quartz movement. Doublé case, 35 mm diameter.*

Index